# Theology
## *The Basics*

Also by Alister E. McGrath from Wiley-Blackwell

*Theology: The Basic Readings* (2012)
*Darwinism and the Divine* (2011)
*The Christian Theology Reader*, 4th edn (2011)
*Christian Theology: An Introduction*, 5th edn (2011)
*Science and Religion: A New Introduction*, 2nd edn (2009)
*Christianity: An Introduction,* 2nd edn (2006)
*The Blackwell Companion to Protestantism* (edited with
  Darren C. Marks, 2003)
*The Intellectual Origins of the European Reformation,* 2nd edn (2003)
*A Brief History of Heaven* (2003)
*The Future of Christianity* (2002)
*Christian Literature: An Anthopology* (edited, 2000)
*Reformation Thought: An Introduction*, 3rd edn (1999)
*Christian Spirituality: An Introduction* (1999)
*Historical Theology: An Introduction* (1998)
*The Blackwell Encyclopedia of Modern Christian Thought* (1995)

For a complete list of Alister E. McGrath's publications from
Wiley-Blackwell, visit http://www.wiley.com/go/religion.

# Theology
## *The Basics*
### Third Edition

Alister E. McGrath

A John Wiley & Sons, Ltd., Publication

*Library of Congress Cataloging-in-Publication Data*

McGrath, Alister E., 1953–Theology : the basics / Alister E. McGrath. – 3rd ed.
  p. cm.
  Includes bibliographical references and index.
  ISBN 978-0-470-65675-4 (pbk. : alk. paper)
1. Theology, Doctrinal–Popular works.   I. Title.
BT77.M382 2012
230—dc22

                                                              2011010579

A catalogue record for this book is available from the British Library.

This book is published in the following electronic formats: ePDFs 9781444343847; ePub 9781444343854; Mobi 9781444343861

Set in 10.5/13pt Bembo by SPi Publisher Services, Pondicherry, India
Printed and bound in Singapore by Ho Printing Singapore Pte Ltd

5   2014

# Brief Contents

# Contents

# Illustrations

# Preface

What is theology? The word has been used by Christians since the third century to mean "talking about God." "Christian theology" thus means something like "talking about God in a Christian way," recognizing that the word "god" means quite different things to different religious traditions. Christians think about their faith; "theology" is the term used for both this process of reflection and its outcome. To study theology is to thus think systematically about the fundamental ideas of Christianity. It is intellectual reflection on the act, content, and implications of the Christian faith.

Sometimes this means deciding what is the best way of understanding some aspect of the Christian faith. A good example is provided by the doctrine of the church. For some, the church is a "mixed body," consisting of believers and unbelievers; for others, it is a "pure body," consisting only of believers. Other examples can easily be given. So where do these different approaches come from? And what are their merits? And their implications? What difference do they make to the business of Christian living?

At other times, it means trying to understand why the Christian churches committed themselves to ideas which, at least on first sight, seem complicated and even a little implausible. Why should Christians believe that Jesus Christ is "truly divine and truly human," when this seems much more difficult than a simpler statement such as "Jesus Christ is truly human." Or, to take another familiar example, why should anyone want to believe that God is a Trinity – "one God, three persons" – when this seems so much more complicated than simply believing in God? Doesn't this just make faith unnecessarily complicated?

There are many reasons for wanting to think about the Christian faith in more detail. Those who are not Christians will be interested in learning what Christians believe, and why. Theology offers an explanation of the Christian faith, and helps us to understand why Christians differ on certain points of importance. As the eleventh-century theologian Anselm of Canterbury (ca. 1033–1109) once remarked, theology is basically "faith seeking understanding." Part of the inner dynamic of the life of faith is a desire to understand what is believed. Theology can be thought of as the Christian's discipleship of the mind.

For Christians, theological reflection can lead to personal enrichment, and a deepened appreciation of their faith. For the great Christian theologian Augustine of Hippo (354–430), there is a genuine intellectual excitement to wrestling with God. He spoke of an *"eros of the mind"* – a sense of longing to understand more about God's nature and ways – and the transformative impact that this could have on people's lives. Other Christian writers have stressed the practical importance of theology, noting how it is essential for the ministry of the church. Preaching, spirituality, and pastoral care, many argue, are ultimately grounded in theology. This business of "thinking about God" takes place at many levels – in church study groups, in Bible studies, through preaching, and in academic seminars. Yet the study of theology has relevance beyond the Christian church. At least a basic understanding of Christian theology will be invaluable to anyone studying western cultural history, literature, or art.

This short, basic introduction to Christian theology is aimed specifically at those who are approaching it for the first time, and who feel intimidated by the thought of studying theology. It sets out to introduce you to some of its basic themes, problems, and personalities, and to whet your appetite to know more. There are severe limits to what can be dealt with in such a short book, and many readers will find themselves frustrated by the brevity of some discussions, and the omission of much material that is so clearly relevant to its topics. Happily, there are plenty of other works that will be able to take your studies further. This book, which is perhaps best seen as a "taster" in Christian theology, will make specific suggestions about what you can do next, once you have finished this introduction.

This book sets out to explore some of the basic ideas of Christianity, engaging with some of its leading representatives. It *aims* to introduce you to the basics of Christian theology. It *assumes* that you know nothing about the subject. It *introduces and explains* the following aspects of Christian theology:

- some of its leading ideas, as they are found in the Apostles' Creed – about which more presently;
- how those ideas were developed and justified;
- the basic vocabulary, especially technical terms, used in discussion of those ideas;
- some of the key debates that have influenced Christian thinking during the last two thousand years;
- some of the leading thinkers who have shaped Christian theology down the centuries.

It also encourages you to *interact* with these ideas, by helping you to engage with some texts setting out some approaches to these questions. By the time you have finished this book, you will be able to go on to deal with more advanced works in the field, including the two standard theological primers written by the present author.

The book does not set out to advocate any one specific form of Christian theology, but to introduce its readers to a wide variety of ideas. The work is generous, both in terms of the range of Christian opinions noted, and the positive attitude adopted towards them. No attempt is made to settle the longstanding disputes of Christian theology. Instead, the reader is introduced to them, and helped to understand the points at issue. Catholicism, Orthodoxy, and Protestantism are all represented in this work.

This book builds on the success of two earlier textbooks from the present author and publisher: *Christian Theology: An Introduction* and *The Christian Theology Reader*. The former, now in its fifth edition, provides a thorough university-level introduction to Christian theology, including comprehensive coverage of the history of theology, the basics of theological method, and detailed engagement with ten major areas of theology. The latter, now in its fourth edition, provides more than 375 primary texts of relevance to the study of theology, along with individual introductions, commentary, and study questions. Although the present book is intended to be a brief introduction to the themes of Christian theology, it can also be used to lay the groundwork for a more detailed engagement with these two textbooks. The work tries to avoid any form of denominational bias, and aims to treat all positions examined respectfully and fairly. The approach adopted in this book has been tested on student audiences in Oxford over several years, and I am grateful to those who have helped me evaluate it.

The scale of the success of this shorter work took both the publisher and author by surprise. When it became clear that the book was being so widely used, we decided as a matter of some urgency to commission detailed evaluation of the work by its end users. This has produced many helpful suggestions for improvements, some of which were incorporated into the second edition. As the numbers of users grew, additional evaluation was commissioned, leading to the production of the third edition, which includes further significant improvements – most notably, a chapter dedicated to the theology of the Holy Spirit. It is our hope that this new edition will prove to be an asset to those teaching and studying theology. We look forward to receiving feedback which will help us when the time comes to produce a fourth edition in due course.

Users of this work may like to use it alongside a short collection of readings, designed to complement this textbook. *Theology: The Basic Readings*, now in its second edition, provides 62 readings, arranged in ten chapters paralleling those of this work. This makes it an ideal resource to help you take your reflections further. The first edition of this work was very well received, and it has been developed and expanded in the light of comments from its users. It is hoped that this additional work will be helpful in developing your grasp of Christian theology.

Alister McGrath
London

# The Apostles' Creed

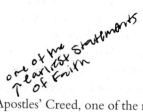

one of the earliest statements of Faith

This book is loosely modeled on the Apostles' Creed, one of the most familiar and widely cited summaries of the Christian faith. It is regularly included in public worship, and is often the subject of sermons, textbooks, and study guides. Its simple structure creates an ideal framework for exploring some of the central themes of Christian theology. Although many earlier versions are known, this creed reached its final form in the eighth century.

> I believe in God, the Father Almighty,
> creator of heaven and earth.
>
> I believe in Jesus Christ, God's only Son, our Lord,
> who was conceived by the Holy Spirit,
> born of the Virgin Mary,
> suffered under Pontius Pilate,
> was crucified, died, and was buried;
> he descended to the dead.
> On the third day he rose again;
> he ascended into heaven,
> he is seated at the right hand of the Father,
> and he will come to judge the living and the dead.
>
> I believe in the Holy Spirit,
> the holy catholic Church,
> the communion of saints,
> the forgiveness of sins,
> the resurrection of the body,
> and the life everlasting. Amen.

# Getting Started

Theology is "talk about God"; Christian theology is "talk about God" from a Christian perspective. It begins by recognizing that Christians have quite distinct ideas about who God is and what God is like. We find these expressed in the Bible, which all Christians regard as being of immense importance to matters of faith. Christian theology can be seen both as the *process* of reflecting on the Bible and weaving together its ideas and themes, and as the *result* of this process of reflection in certain ideas – ideas that are often referred to as "doctrines" (from the Latin word *doctrina*, meaning "teaching").

There are also other documents which Christians regard with great respect, such as the "creeds." The word "creed" comes from the Latin word *credo*, meaning "I believe." A creed is basically a brief statement of the main points of the Christian faith. The best known of these are the Apostles' Creed and the Nicene Creed. These ancient creeds set out some of the basics of the faith, and are often used widely for teaching purposes. Many theologians would argue that Christian theology is the exploration of the basic ideas of these creeds, investigating their basis in the Bible, and their impact on Christian thinking and living.

So how do we go about studying theology? One way of studying theology is to read some theologians, and see what kind of approach they adopt. How do they develop their ideas? How do they assess arguments? How do they use the Bible and other theologians in their approach? Two theologians from the classic era of Christian theology might be mentioned here:

- Thomas Aquinas (ca. 1225–74), a great theologian of the Middle Ages, whose *Summa Theologiae* (Latin: The "Totality of Theology") is one of the most admired works of systematic theology.
- John Calvin (1509–64), whose *Institutes of the Christian Religion* is a landmark in Protestant theology.

In the twentieth century, two theologians are often singled out as being of especial interest:

- The Protestant writer Karl Barth (1886–1968), whose *Church Dogmatics* are often regarded as the most important theological publication of this period.
- The Catholic theologian Karl Rahner (1904–84), whose *Theological Investigations* reestablished the short theological essay as a major way of conducting theological debate and exploration.

This approach has many merits. It does, however, make considerable demands on students. For a start, the writings of these theologians are often rather long. In addition, you need to know a lot of background material before you can really make sense of them. Anyway, why limit the study of theology to such a limited number of figures?

For this reason, some writers suggest that a *historical* approach is better. This means looking at the history of Christian theology, and seeing how it developed down the ages. Instead of focusing on a single individual, this approach allows students to see how Christian thinking has evolved. Again, it is a good way of doing theology. Yet it makes huge demands on students. Two thousand years of history takes a long time to master!

That history is often broken down into sections, to make it more manageable.

**Figure 1**  Karl Rahner (1904–84). © Bettmann/Corbis.

While every theologian will have views on how best to divide two thousand years of Christian history, many use a framework which looks something like this.

The first hundred years is often referred to as the *apostolic* period. The fundamental sense of this term is "originating with the apostles" or "having a direct link with the apostles." This is the period during which the works now included in the New Testament were written, usually considered to be limited to the first century. During this time, Christianity was spreading throughout the Mediterranean region and beyond. The missionary journeys of St. Paul, described in the Acts of the Apostles, are an excellent example of this activity.

This is followed by the *patristic* period, which is usually held to begin about the year 100, and end with the Council of Chalcedon in 451. The term "patristic" derives from the Greek term *patres*, meaning "fathers," a term used to refer to the writers of this formative era. (Sadly, there were very few women among them.) The Council of Chalcedon marked a landmark in Christian thinking, especially over the identity of Jesus Christ, and is seen by many writers as bringing this important period of theological development to a close. The patristic period witnessed important theological explorations of the doctrine of the church, the identity of Jesus Christ, the doctrine of the Trinity, and the relation of grace and free will.

This is followed by the *medieval* period, which is widely regarded as extending from the Council of Chalcedon until about the year 1500. The term "medieval" means "a middle age" or "an intervening period." It was invented by humanist writers in the sixteenth century to refer to the (to them, uninteresting) period between the classical era and the Renaissance. However, the term is now widely used without this polemical or critical sense. The medieval period was immensely productive theologically, and produced some theological giants. We have already noted Thomas Aquinas' great thirteenth-century work, the *Summa Theologiae*. Many other examples could be set alongside this, such as the writings of Duns Scotus (1266–1308) and William of Ockham (1280–1349). Among the many issues to be explored in detail during this period were the relation between faith and reason, and the theology of the sacraments. Alongside this, of course, there was continuing exploration of issues debated during the patristic period, including the identity of Christ and the relation of grace and free will.

The sixteenth century marked a period of radical change in the western church. This period of *reformation* witnessed the birth of the Protestant reformation, associated with writers such as Martin Luther (1483–1546) and John Calvin, which opened up a period of new theological debate. Certain theological topics became especially hot around this time, particularly the place of the Bible in theological debate, the doctrine of the church, and the question of what it is necessary to do in order to be saved.

The Catholic church also went through a period of reformation around this time, with the Council of Trent (1544–63) setting out the definitive Catholic position on issues of importance at this time. Many scholars also include the seventeenth century in this period, arguing that this represents the Protestant and Catholic consolidation of the developments that began in the previous century. It was during this century that Christians emigrated to North America, and began to establish that region as a major player in theological debates.

Finally, the *modern* period is generally understood to mean the period since the eighteenth century. This was a period of considerable instability in western Europe, especially following the French Revolution of 1789, and later through the rise of Marxism in eastern Europe in the twentieth century. Despite these anxieties, it was a period of remarkable theological creativity throughout western Europe and North America. In addition, a growing Christian presence in Africa and Asia during the twentieth century led to an increasing interest in developing "local theologies" in these new regions. These local theologies would be grounded in the Christian tradition, but sensitive to their local situations.

To survey these developments, which have been sketched with extreme brevity in these paragraphs, would be an impossible task. The end result would be very superficial and unsatisfactory. For this reason, a historical approach has not been adopted in this work. While studying the history of theology is a fascinating thing to do, it needs to be done in much greater depth than this brief work allows. Happily, there is another way of introducing theology, which avoids this problem: the *topical* approach, which considers individual subject areas.

The topical approach adopted in this work involves looking at a number of areas of Christian thought, and exploring what Christian theologians have said about them and how they developed those ideas. This allows us to begin to wrestle with some of the great questions of Christian theology in a manageable way. It allows you to develop tools to think about theological issues, rather than just learning what certain great theologians have thought about them.

Any serious engagement with theology is going to involve examining specific theological topics and individual theologians, as well as the general history of the discipline. It is impossible to do theology properly without being aware of what theologians have thought about things in the past, and how this might be relevant today. However, a short book like this cannot hope to do justice to the complexities of individual thinkers or history. Yet the topical approach being used will allow us to look at the history of a debate, where this is relevant to the topic being discussed – and also at individual theologians, when they have a particular contribution to make to the discussion. This volume provides two useful additional resources to help with this process of interaction: a brief glossary of theological terms, and the biographical details of the major theologians mentioned in the text.

Throughout its long history, Christian theology has made an appeal to three fundamental resources: the Bible, tradition, and reason. The topical approach allows us to explore the place of each of these resources in theological debate. In view of their importance, we shall examine each of them in a little detail, before moving on to our first topic.

## Introducing the Bible

The word "Bible" comes from the Greek word *biblia* ("books"). It refers to a collection of books which Christians regard as having authority in matters of thought and life. The Bible is divided into two major sections, known as the *Old Testament* and *New Testament*.

The term "Old Testament" is used by Christian writers to refer to those books of the Christian Bible which were (and still are) regarded as sacred by Judaism. For Christians, the Old Testament is seen as setting the scene for the coming of Jesus of Nazareth, who brings its

leading themes and institutions to fulfillment. These texts are sometimes also referred to as "the Hebrew Bible."

The word "testament" needs explanation. In this theological context, the word really means "covenant" or "dispensation." The basic
idea is that the same God who once entered into a covenant with the
people of Israel (the "old covenant") has now entered into a "new
covenant" with all of humanity, leading to the emergence of the
Christian church. The basic points being made here are:

1. The same God who called the people of Israel also called the
   Christian church. Both are "chosen peoples," to use the biblical
   language.
2. That a new phase in God's dealings with humanity came about in
   Jesus Christ. This is usually referred to as a "new covenant" or
   "new dispensation."

This has important implications for the way in which Christians
read the Old Testament. For Christians, the Old Testament antici-
pates the coming of Christ. This idea is regularly developed in
the New Testament. If you would like to explore this briefly,
read the first two chapters of the gospel according to Matthew, the
first book of the New Testament, and try answering these two
questions:

1. How many times does a phrase like "this took place to fulfill the
   prophecy of ..." occur in these two chapters?
2. Why do you think that Matthew regards it as so important that
   Jesus Christ fulfills Old Testament prophecy?

There is widespread agreement within Christianity that the Bible
has a place of especial importance in theological debate and personal
devotion. All the Protestant confessions of faith stress the centrality of
the Bible in relation to Christian thought and life. More recently,
the Second Vatican Council (1962–5) reaffirmed its importance for
Catholic theology and preaching. The authority of the Bible is seen
as linked with the idea of "inspiration" – in other words, that in
some way, the words of the Bible convey the words of God. This is
stated clearly by most Protestant confessions of faith, such as the

"Gallic Confession of Faith" (1559), which includes the following declaration:

> We believe that the Word contained in these books has proceeded from God, and receives its authority from him alone, and not from human beings.

The *Catechism of the Catholic Church* (1992) sets out a similar position:

> God is the author of Sacred Scripture. The divine revealed realities, which are contained and presented in the text of Sacred Scripture, have been written down under the inspiration of the Holy Spirit. For Holy Mother Church, relying on the faith of the apostolic age, accepts as sacred and canonical the books of the Old and the New Testaments, whole and entire, with all their parts, on the grounds that, written under the inspiration of the Holy Spirit, they have God as their author and have been handed on as such to the Church herself. God inspired the human authors of the sacred books.

There are some disagreements within Christianity over exactly what is included in the Bible. The most important of these concerns a group of works usually referred to as "the Apocrypha" (from the Greek word for "hidden") or as "Deuterocanonical works." This includes books such as the Wisdom of Solomon and the book of Judith. These books, though dating from the period of the Old Testament, were not originally written in the Hebrew language, and are thus not included in Jewish or Hebrew Bibles. These are sometimes referred to as the "Tanakh" – an acronym of the Hebrew words for "law, prophets, and writings (*torah, nevi'im, ketuvim*)."

Protestants tend to regard these "apocryphal" books as interesting and informative, but not as being of doctrinal importance. Catholics and Orthodox Christians, on the other hand, regard them as part of the text of the Bible. This difference is reflected in the way in which Protestant and Catholic Bibles are laid out. Protestant Bibles – such as the famous King James Bible of 1611 or the New International Version – include these texts as a third section of the Bible, known as the "Apocrypha." Catholic Bibles – such as the Jerusalem Bible – include them within the Old Testament section of the Bible.

## Tradition

A series of controversies in the early church brought home the importance of the concept of "tradition." The word "tradition" comes from the Latin term *traditio* which means "handing over," "handing down," or "handing on." It is a thoroughly biblical idea; we find St. Paul reminded his readers that he was handing on to them core teachings of the Christian faith which he had himself received from other people (1 Corinthians 15:1–4).

The term "tradition" can refer to both the action of passing teachings on to others – something which Paul insists that must be done within the church – and to the body of teachings which are passed on in this manner. Tradition can thus be understood as a *process* as well as a *body of teaching*. The Pastoral Epistles (three New Testament letters that are particularly concerned with questions of church structure, and the passing on of Christian teaching: 1 Timothy, 2 Timothy, and Titus) in particular stress the importance of "guarding the good deposit which was entrusted to you" (2 Timothy 1:14). The New Testament also uses the notion of "tradition" in a negative sense, meaning something like "human ideas and practices which are not divinely authorized." Thus Jesus Christ was openly critical of certain human traditions within Judaism (e.g., see Matthew 15:1–6; Mark 7:13).

The importance of the idea of tradition first became obvious in a controversy which broke out during the second century. The "Gnostic controversy" centered on a number of questions, including how salvation was to be achieved. (The word "Gnostic" derives from the Greek word *gnosis*, "knowledge," and refers to the movement's belief in certain secret ideas that had to be known in order to secure salvation.) Christian writers found themselves having to deal with some highly unusual and creative interpretations of the Bible. How were they to deal with these? If the Bible was to be regarded as authoritative, was every interpretation of the Bible to be regarded as of equal value?

Irenaeus of Lyons (ca. 130–ca. 200), one of the church's greatest theologians, did not think so. The question of how the Bible was to be interpreted was of the greatest importance. Heretics, he argued, interpreted the Bible according to their own taste. Orthodox believers, in contrast, interpreted the Bible in ways that their apostolic authors would have approved. What had been handed down from the apostles through the church was not merely the biblical texts themselves, but a certain way of reading and understanding those texts.

> Everyone who wishes to perceive the truth should consider the apostolic tradition, which has been made known in every church in the entire world. We are able to number those who are bishops appointed by the apostles, and their successors in the churches to the present day, who taught and knew nothing of such things as these people imagine.

Irenaeus' point is that a continuous stream of Christian teaching, life, and interpretation can be traced from the time of the apostles to his own period. The church is able to point to those who have maintained the teaching of the church, and to certain public standard creeds which set out the main lines of Christian belief. Tradition is thus the guarantor of faithfulness to the original apostolic teaching, a safeguard against the innovations and misrepresentations of biblical texts on the part of the Gnostics.

This development is of major importance, as it underlies the emergence of "creeds" – public, authoritative statements of the basic points of the Christian faith, which are based upon the Bible, but avoid maverick interpretations of biblical material. This point was further developed in the early fifth century by Vincent of Lérins (died before 450), who was concerned that certain doctrinal innovations were being introduced without good reason. There was a need to have public standards by which such doctrines could be judged. So what standard was available, by which the church could be safeguarded from such errors? For Vincent, the answer was clear – tradition. For Vincent, tradition was "a rule for the interpretation of the prophets and the apostles in such a way that is directed by the rule of the universal church."

## Creeds

Having noted the importance of creeds, we may explore how they came about in their present forms. Their emergence was stimulated by two factors of especial importance.

1. The need for public statements of faith which could be used in teaching, and defense of the Christian faith against misrepresentations.
2. The need for personal "confessions of faith" at the time of baptism.

We have already touched on the first point; the second needs further exploration. It is known that the early church attached especial importance to the baptism of new members. In the third and fourth centuries, a definite pattern of instruction and baptism developed: new members of the church were instructed in the basics of the Christian faith during the period of Lent, and baptized on Easter Day. These new members of the church were asked to confirm their faith by assenting to key statements of Christian belief.

According to the *Apostolic Tradition*, a work written by Hippolytus of Rome (died ca. 236) in the early years of the third century, three questions were put to each baptismal candidate: "Do you believe in God, the Father Almighty? Do you believe in Jesus Christ, our Savior? Do you believe in the Holy Spirit, the holy church, and the forgiveness of sins?" As time went on, the answers to these questions were gradually enlarged into a statement of faith, which each candidate was asked to affirm.

The most important creed to emerge from these "baptismal creeds" is the "Apostles' Creed," which is widely used in Christian worship today. Traditionally, this creed is set out as twelve statements, each of which is attributed to one of the twelve apostles. Although it is now widely agreed that this creed was not actually written by the apostles themselves, it is nevertheless "apostolic" in the sense that it contains the main ideas of the Christian faith that the church received from those apostles. The present form of the creed can be traced to the eighth century. In its present form (see p. xvi), it consists of three parts, corresponding to the three questions that Hippolytus reports as being asked of baptismal candidates back in the third century. Although each of the questions has been expanded, the same basic structure can still be identified.

The Apostles' Creed offers a very convenient summary of some of the main topics of the Christian faith, and we shall regularly use it as a basis for discussion throughout this book.

# Reason

Finally, we need to note the importance of reason in Christian theology. Traditionally, Christian theology has seen reason as operating in a subservient role to revelation. Thomas Aquinas argued that supernatural truths needed to be revealed to us. Human reason, on its own, could not hope to gain access to divine mysteries. It could, however, reflect on them, once they had been revealed. This has been the position adopted by most Christian theologians. Reason allows us to reflect on revelation – but it must be used critically.

This critical yet positive attitude towards human reason can be found throughout the writings of Augustine of Hippo, perhaps the most important and influential writer of the Latin west. Augustine's argument is that human reason, and philosophies based upon it, have much to offer theology – provided they are not used uncritically. He uses an interesting biblical analogy to make this point. When Israel left Egypt at the time of the exodus, they took with them many "treasures of the Egyptians." Using the exodus as a model, Augustine argues that there is no reason why Christians should not extract all that is good in philosophy, and put it to the service of preaching the gospel. Just as Israel left behind the burdens of Egypt, while carrying off its treasures, so theology can discard what is useless in philosophy, and exploit what is good and useful.

> If those who are called philosophers, particularly the Platonists, have said anything which is true and consistent with our faith, we must not reject it, but claim it for our own use . . . The Egyptians possessed idols and heavy burdens, which the children of Israel hated and from which they fled; however, they also possessed vessels of gold and silver and clothes which our forebears, in leaving Egypt, took for themselves in secret, intending to use them in a better manner (Exodus 3:21–2; 12:35–6) . . . In the same way, pagan learning is not entirely made up of false teachings and superstitions . . . It contains also some excellent teachings, well suited to be used by truth, and excellent moral values.

Augustine's attitude shaped much of the Christian discussion of the place of reason until the early modern period.

All this changed during the great "Age of Reason" in western culture, which most historians suggest is to be dated to the two hundred years between 1750 and 1950. This era saw a new confidence in the capacy of unaided human reason to explain and master the world. Reason, it was argued, was capable of deducing anything that needed to be known about God. There was no need to propose divine revelation. Instead, we could rely totally upon reason. This position is generally known as "rationalism," and is still encountered today in some quarters. However, its credibility has been severely shaken on account of the growing realization that different cultures have different understandings of rationality. Reason, it turned out, was not the universal quality that many rationalists believed it to be. As the great Florentine poet Dante Alighieri (ca. 1265–1321) noted, reason has "short wings".

There is, of course, continued interest today in the role of reason in theology. The most obvious sign of this is the ongoing debate over "arguments for the existence of God." Although it is very much open to question whether these arguments prove very much, let alone the existence of the Christian god, the fact that there is so much interest in them demonstrates that there is a continuing role for reason in theological debate. We shall consider some of these arguments briefly at a later point in this volume.

We now turn to consider one of the most interesting aspects of the relation of faith and reason – the use of "helpmates" or "dialogue partners" in theology, often referred to using the Latin term *ancilla theologiae*, which literally means "a handmaid of theology."

## The "handmaid": dialogue between theology and culture

There is a long tradition within Christian theology of drawing on intellectual resources outside the Christian tradition as a means of developing a theological vision. This approach (which, as we noted, is usually referred to using the Latin phrase *ancilla theologiae*), is grounded in the basic idea that philosophical systems can be a very helpful way of stimulating theological development, and enabling a dialogue to be opened up between Christian thinkers and their

**Figure 2**   Detail from *The School of Athens* by Raphael (1483–1520), showing the great ancient Greek philosophers Plato and Aristotle. Stanza della Segnatura, Vatican. Photo Scala, Florence.

cultural environment. The two most important historical examples of this approach to theology are the dialogues with Platonism and Aristotelianism.

The dialogue with Platonism was of immense importance during the first five centuries of the Christian church, especially in the Greek-speaking world of the eastern Mediterranean. As Christianity expanded in that region, it encountered rival worldviews, of which Platonism was the most important. Such worldviews could be seen positively or negatively: they were both an opportunity for dialogue and intellectual development, and also a threat to the existence of Christianity. The task faced by writers such as Justin Martyr (ca. 100–ca. 165) or Clement of Alexandria (ca. 150–ca. 215) was how to make use of the obvious intellectual merits of Platonism in constructing a Christian worldview, without compromising the integrity of Christianity itself. After all, despite their occasional similarities, Christianity is *not* Platonism.

A new debate opened up in the thirteenth century, during the golden age of scholastic theology. The rediscovery of Aristotle by medieval writers seemed to offer new resources to help in every aspect of intellectual life, including physics, philosophy, and ethics. It was inevitable that theologians should also want to see what use they could make of Aristotelian ideas and methods in constructing a systematic theology – such as Thomas Aquinas' massive *Summa Theologiae*, widely regarded as one of the greatest works of theology ever written.

In both these cases, using another intellectual discipline as the *ancilla theologiae* offers opportunities and risks in about equal measure. It is clearly important to appreciate what these opportunities and risks are. The two major *opportunities* offered to theology by the critical appropriation of another discipline can be summarized as follows.

1. It allows for a much more rigorous exploration of ideas than would otherwise be possible. Problems that Christian theology encounters in trying to develop its ideas often have their parallels in other disciplines. Thomas Aquinas, for example, found Aristotle's notion of an "unmoved mover" helpful in setting out some reasons for defending the existence of God.

2. It allows Christian theology to engage in a dialogue with another worldview – a major element of the church's witness to its secular context. In the second century, Justin Martyr clearly believed that many Platonists would be so impressed by the parallels between Platonism and Christianity that they might consider conversion. Similarly, in his "Areopagus address" (Acts 17:22–31), Paul draws on some themes from Stoic philosophy in attempting to communicate the Christian message to Athenian culture.

Yet alongside these positive aspects of such an engagement, an obvious risk must also be noted – that ideas which are not distinctively Christian come to play a significant (perhaps even decisive) role in Christian theology. For example, Aristotelian ideas about the proper manner of logical reasoning, or Cartesian ideas about the proper starting point for any intellectual discipline, might find their way into Christian theology. On some occasions, this might turn out to be a neutral development; on others, it may eventually be recognized to have negative implications, undermining the integrity of Christian theology, and ultimately causing it to be distorted. Martin Luther, the great German reformer, argued that medieval theology had allowed a number of such distortions to arise through an excessive, and partially uncritical, use of Aristotelian ideas in the Middle Ages.

Despite these concerns, the approach continues to be widely used. Many German theologians of the nineteenth century found G. W. F. Hegel (1770–1831) and Immanuel Kant (1724–1804) to be helpful dialogue partners. In the twentieth century, Rudolf Bultmann (1884–1976) and Paul Tillich (1886–1965) both found a dialogue with existentialism to be theologically productive. More recently, I myself have argued that the working methods and assumptions of the natural sciences can be theologically significant (see my three-volume work *A Scientific Theology*).

## Moving on . . .

This chapter has sketched something of the background to Christian theology. Yet it has left huge areas completely untouched. The best way of filling in these many gaps is to begin to explore some specific theological topics, and use these as ways of reflecting on some of the issues, ideas, personalities, and debates of Christian theology. To do this, we shall use a framework. Rather than just explore issues at random, I will allow the structure of the Apostles' Creed to set the parameters of our reflections.

In making this decision, I have been influenced by two particular considerations. Many users of this book will be taking part in church or college study groups, where the Apostles' Creed is an obvious reference point for discussion. Many colleges teach courses in basic Christian doctrine using the Apostles' Creed to frame the lectures, which will allow this book to be helpful background reading. However, the basic approach of the book does not tie it down in any particular way. The topics identified for further exploration are of wide theological interest, irrespective of the context in which you are studying them.

So where shall we begin? The obvious place is to consider what it means to say that we have faith in God. The Apostles' Creed opens with the words "I believe." So what does this mean? And what issues does it raise? We may turn immediately to explore these questions.

CHAPTER 1

# Faith

"I believe in God." This terse opening phrase of the Apostles' Creed leads us directly into our first theological topic. What does it mean to talk about "believing in God"? What are we to understand by words such as "belief" and "faith"?

## What is faith?

*[handwritten: — trusting in God]*

The biblical sense of the word "faith" has a number of aspects. One biblical theme is of particular importance – the idea of trusting in God, related in the famous Old Testament account of the calling of Abraham (Genesis 15:1–6). This tells of how God promised to give Abraham countless descendants, as numerous as the stars of the night sky. Abraham believed God – that is, trusted the promise that was made to him. Similarly, the crowds around Jesus are often described as having "faith" – meaning that they believed that he had some special status, identity, or authority, and would be able to heal them from their illnesses, or deal with their concerns (e.g., Luke 5:20; 17:19). Here again the basic idea is trust, in this case mingled with discernment that there is something about Jesus which merits such an attitude of trust.

*[handwritten margin:  Belief = trust]*

*[handwritten margin:  faith = belief]*

In everyday language, words like "faith" and "belief" have come to mean something like "a weak form of knowledge." I know that the chemical formula for water is $H_2O$, or that the earth rotates around the sun. When I say "I know" that "the capital of the United States of America is Washington, DC," I mean that this statement can be

*Theology: The Basics*, Third Edition. Alister E. McGrath.
© 2012 Alister E. McGrath. Published 2012 by Blackwell Publishing Ltd.

verified. But when I say "I believe in God," this is widely understood to mean something like "I think that there is a God, but I cannot demonstrate this with any degree of certainty."

This everyday use of the terms "faith" and "belief" is misleading, however, as it does not do justice to the complexity of the theological notion of "faith." In the eighteenth and nineteenth centuries, western philosophy widely believed that anything worth believing could be *proved* – whether by logical reasoning or by scientific experimentation. As the great nineteenth-century mathematician W. K. Clifford (1845–79) argued, "it is wrong always, everywhere, and for anyone, to believe anything upon insufficient evidence." This "positivism" had a deep impact on western culture, and its influence still lingers. The idea of "faith in God" was ridiculed by some rationalist writers, who argued that unless God's existence could be proved, it was an utterly irrelevant notion.

Yet with the passing of time, the credibility of this position has been severely weakened. It has become increasingly clear that many of the fundamental beliefs of western culture lie beyond proof. The philosopher of science Michael Polanyi (1886–1964) argued that certain unprovable beliefs lay behind the working methods of the natural sciences. As Alfred, Lord Tennyson (1809–92) pointed out in his poem *The Ancient Sage*, nothing that was actually worth believing could be proved in the way that people like Clifford demanded:

> For nothing worthy proving can be proven,
> Nor yet disproven: wherefore thou be wise,
> Cleave ever to the sunnier side of doubt.

Since then, philosophers have become much more realistic about things. Some things can indeed be proved; but some, by their very nature, lie beyond proof. God is one of these.

## Can God's existence be proved?

The basic Christian attitude to proofs for the existence of God can be set out as follows.

3 attitudes

1. The existence of God is something that reason cannot prove conclusively. Yet the fact that the existence of God lies _beyond_ reason does not for one moment mean that the existence of God is *contrary* to reason.

2. Certain excellent reasons may be put forward for suggesting that God exists; these do not, however, count as "proofs" in the sense of "rigorous logical demonstrations" or "conclusive scientific experiments."

3. Faith is about trust in God, rather than just agreeing that God exists.

In what follows, we shall explore this aspect of Christian theology in a little more detail, focusing on Thomas Aquinas, probably the most famous and influential theologian of the Middle Ages. Born in Italy, he achieved his fame through his teaching and writing at the university of Paris and other northern universities. His fame rests chiefly on his *Summa Theologiae*, composed towards the end of his life and not totally finished at the time of his death. However, he also wrote many other significant works, particularly the *Summa contra Gentiles*, which represents a major statement of the rationality of the Christian faith, and especially the existence of God.

Aquinas believed that it was entirely proper to identify pointers towards the existence of God, drawn from general human experience of the world. His "Five Ways" represent five lines of argument in support of the existence of God, each of which draws on some aspect of the world which "points" to the existence of its creator.

So what kind of pointers does Aquinas identify? The basic line of thought guiding Aquinas is that the world mirrors God, as its creator – an idea which is given more formal expression in his doctrine of the "analogy of being." Just as an artist might sign a painting to identify it as his handiwork, so God has stamped a divine "signature" upon the creation. What we observe in the world – for example, its signs of ordering – can be explained if God was its creator. If God both brought the world into existence, and impressed the divine image and likeness upon it, then something of God's nature can be known from the creation.

So where might we look in creation to find evidence for the existence of God? Aquinas argues that the ordering of the world is the most convincing evidence of God's existence and wisdom.

agreed !

This basic assumption underlies each of the "Five Ways," although it is of particular importance in the case of the argument often referred to as the "argument from design" or the "teleological argument." We shall consider the first and last of these two "ways" to illustrate the issues.

The first way begins from the observation that things in the world are in motion or change. The world is not static, but is dynamic. Examples of this are easy to list. Rain falls from the sky. Stones roll down valleys. The earth revolves around the sun (a fact, incidentally, unknown to Aquinas). This, the first of Aquinas' arguments, is normally referred to as the "argument from motion"; however, it is clear that the "movement" in question is actually understood in more general terms, so that the term "change" is more appropriate as a translation at points.

So how did nature come to be in motion? Why is it changing? Why isn't it static? Aquinas argues that everything which moves is moved by something else. For every motion, there is a cause. Things don't just move; they are moved by something else. Now each cause of motion must itself have a cause. And that cause must have a cause as well. And so Aquinas argues that there is a whole series of causes of motion lying behind the world as we know it. Now unless there is an infinite number of these causes, Aquinas argues, there must be a single cause right at the origin of the series. From this original cause of motion, all other motion is ultimately derived. This is the origin of the great chain of causality which we see reflected in the way the world behaves. From the fact that things are in motion, Aquinas thus argues for the existence of a single original cause of all this motion. This, Aquinas insists, is none other than God.

In more recent times, this argument has been restated in terms of God as the one who brought the universe into existence. For this reason, it is often referred to as the "cosmological" argument (from the Greek word *kosmos*, meaning "universe"). The most commonly encountered statement of the argument runs along the following lines:

1. Everything within the universe depends on something else for its existence;
2. What is true of its individual parts is also true of the universe itself;

3. The universe thus depends on something else for its existence for as long as it has existed or will exist;

4. The universe thus depends on God for its existence.

The argument basically assumes that the existence of the universe is something that requires explanation. It will be clear that this type of argument relates directly to modern cosmological research, particularly the "big bang" theory of the origins of the cosmos.

5) The fifth and final way is known as the teleological argument, which derives its name from the Greek word *telos*, meaning "purpose" or "goal." Aquinas notes that the world shows obvious traces of intelligent design. Natural processes and objects seem to be adapted with certain definite objectives in mind. They seem to have a purpose. They seem to have been designed. But things don't design themselves: they are caused and designed by someone or something else. Arguing from this observation, Aquinas concludes that the source of this natural ordering must be conceded to be God.

This argument was developed by William Paley (1743–1805). According to Paley, the world was like a watch. It showed evidence of intelligent design, and having been created for a purpose. If there was a watch, there must also be a watchmaker. Paley was particularly impressed by the construction of the human eye, which he argued to be so complex and highly developed that it could only be the result of intelligent design and construction.

Paley's argument was highly influential in nineteenth-century England. However, its plausibility was eroded by the theory of evolution proposed by Charles Darwin (1809–82), which offered an alternative explanation of how such complex structures arose. In his *Origin of Species* (1859), Darwin insisted that these could be explained on a purely natural basis, without need for an intelligent divine designer. Nevertheless, the "argument from design" remains an intriguing idea, which continues to fascinate people.

It will be obvious that Aquinas' arguments are similar in terms of their structure. Each depends on tracing a causal sequence back to its single origin, and identifying this with God. These are thus not "proofs" in the strict sense of the word, as they actually presuppose God's existence! Aquinas' approach is actually rather different.

His argument is that, if we presuppose that God made the world, we end up with a way of making sense of the world that makes a lot of sense of things. In other words, Aquinas is arguing that, seen from the Christian perspective, the existence of God resonates well with what can be observed of the world. It is thus a confirmation, but not a proof, of God's existence.

## Are these proofs of any use?

But other theologians have viewed such "proofs" with skepticism. The great French mathematician and philosopher Blaise Pascal (1623–62) had two major concerns about the kind of approach adopted by Aquinas. First, he found it difficult to accept that the rather abstract philosophical "god" which resulted from such arguments was anything like the living God of the Old and New Testaments. In his *Pensées*, Pascal put it like this: "The metaphysical proofs for the existence of God are so remote from human reasoning, and so complex, that they have little impact."

But second, Pascal argued that these "proofs" assumed that God was known primarily through reason. For Pascal, the human heart also had its reasons for believing (or not believing!) in God. "We know the truth, not only through our reason, but also through our heart." The appeal of God to the human condition went far beyond any resonance between the world as we know it and the ideas of the Christian faith. It extends to include a deep-seated longing for God, which Pascal held to be of major importance in the long, unended human quest for God and final meaning.

In the end, according to Pascal, you cannot argue someone into the Kingdom of God. The existence of God is not something that can be proved. Equally, it is not something that can be *disproved*. It is easy to overlook the fact that atheism is also a faith. An atheist believes that there is no God. This belief, however, is just as difficult to prove as the Christian belief that there is indeed a God.

One of the most severe and perceptive critics of such rational proofs for God's existence is the Austrian philosopher Ludwig Wittgenstein (1889–1951). His point is simple: the so-called "proofs of God's existence" are generally provided by people who already believe in

God for other reasons, but hold that it is important to provide a reasoned defense of their faith.

> A proof of God's existence ought really to be something by means of which one could convince oneself that God exists. But I think that what *believers* who have furnished such proofs have wanted to do is to give their "belief" an intellectual analysis and foundation, although they themselves would never have come to believe as a result of such proofs.

*a true believer shouldn't have to find proof*

## Faith is beyond reason but not contrary to reason

One of the most important recent discussions of the relation of faith and reason is found in Pope John Paul II's 1998 encyclical letter *Fides et Ratio* ("Faith and Reason"). In this letter, John Paul II (Karol Josef Wojtyla, 1920–2005) set out the classic Christian approach to the relation of faith and reason in a very accessible way.

The letter opens with a declaration that faith and reason can work together. "Faith and reason are like two wings on which the human spirit rises to the contemplation of truth; and God has placed in the human heart a desire to know the truth – in a word, to know himself – so that, by knowing and loving God, men and women may also come to the fullness of truth about themselves." This is a rich and powerful statement, which deserves close attention. The basic idea is that human beings long to know the truth, and are constantly searching for it. "In the far reaches of the human heart there is a seed of desire and nostalgia for God."

So can reason alone lead humanity to this truth? The letter pays a handsome tribute to philosophy, as the legitimate human quest for truth. Philosophy is "one of the noblest of human tasks," which is "driven by the desire

**Figure 3** John Paul II celebrates Mass in Bellahouston Park, Glasgow, during his visit to Scotland in 1982. © Bettmann/ Corbis.

to discover the ultimate truth of existence." Yet unaided human reason cannot fully penetrate to the mystery of life. It cannot answer questions such as "why are we here?" For this reason, God graciously chose to make these things known through revelation which would otherwise remain unknown. "The truth made known to us by Revelation is neither the product nor the consummation of an argument devised by human reason."

The letter stresses that faith is not blind trust, opposed to the evidence of the world. Rather, it points out that the world – which Christians see as God's creation – is studded with hints of God's existence and nature. It appeals to Paul's sermon preached at the Areopagus in Athens (Acts 17) in arguing that it is entirely reasonable to infer the existence of God from the wonders of nature and a human sense of divinity within us. These do not count as "proofs"; they are, however, confirmation or corroboration of the basic themes of faith. In the eleventh century, Anselm of Canterbury argued that "faith seeks understanding." Having believed, we long to understand the inner dynamics and structures of our faith.

Similar lines of argument are developed by John Polkinghorne (born 1930), one of Britain's leading theoretical physicists with a strong interest in Christian theology. Throughout his many books, Polkinghorne stresses that Christianity, like the natural sciences, is concerned about making sense of the world on the basis of the evidence that is available. "Faith is not a question of shutting one's eyes, gritting one's teeth, and believing the impossible. It involves a leap, but a leap into the light rather than the dark." Faith is to be understood as "motivated belief, based on evidence." It is rigorously based on reflection on the world – on the various "clues" it offers to its origins and nature.

For example, Polkinghorne argues that science shows us a universe that is deeply intelligible, rationally beautiful, finely tuned for fruitfulness, intrinsically rational, partly veiled in character, open in its process, and information-generating in its nature. These remarkable properties, he argues, are not just happy accidents. They are something that needs to be explained. For Polkinghorne, the best explanation of these observations is that the world is the orderly creation of God. The approach is evidence-based, asking how what we observe may best be explained. It is not conclusive; it is, however, highly suggestive.

Polkinghorne also stresses the importance of the figure of Jesus of Nazareth for Christian faith. Jesus is part of the evidence that has to be assessed.

> The center of my faith lies in my encounter with the figure of Jesus Christ, as I meet him in the gospels, in the witness of the church and in the sacraments. Here is the heart of my Christian faith and hope. Yet, at a subsidiary but supportive level, there are also hints of God's presence which arise from our scientific knowledge. The actual way we answer the question "How?," turns out to point us on to pressing also the question "Why?," so that science by itself is found not to be sufficiently intellectually satisfying.

Although some atheist writers persist in portraying Christian faith as a blind leap in the dark, it is clear that this is not the case. Faith, as Thomas Aquinas points out, has its reasons.

Up to this point, we have considered faith primarily in terms of intellectual assent. For Thomas Aquinas, faith could be defined as "assent to divine revelation." Yet there is more to the idea than this. During the sixteenth century, particular emphasis came to be placed on the relational aspects of faith. To "believe in God" is about more than accepting that God exists; it is about *trusting* that God. In what follows, we shall consider this important aspect of faith.

## Faith and God's promises

Martin Luther is one of a number of writers who stressed that faith, as the Christian church understands the term, is far more than intellectual assent. Certainly, faith believes that certain things are true. There is unquestionably an element of understanding to faith. But there is more to it than that. For Luther, faith is fundamentally trust. He often uses the Latin word *fiducia*, which could be translated as "confidence," to denote the aspect of faith he wants to emphasize. Faith is about trusting a God who makes promises, and whose promises may be relied upon. In his major 1520 essay *The Babylonian Captivity of the Church*, Luther stressed this aspect of faith.

Where there is the Word of the God who makes promises, there must necessarily be the faith of the person who accepts those promises. It is clear that the beginning of our salvation is a faith which clings to the Word of a promising God who, without any effort on our part, in free and unmerited mercy goes before us and offers us a word of promise.

Three points relating to Luther's idea of faith may be singled out for discussion:

*personal*
*trust*
*unification*

1. Faith has a personal, rather than a purely historical, reference.
2. Faith concerns trust in the promises of God.
3. Faith unites the believer to Christ.

We shall consider each of these points individually.

First, faith is not simply historical knowledge. Luther argues that a faith which is content to believe in the historical reliability of the gospels is not a faith which changes our relationship with God. Sinners are perfectly capable of trusting in the historical details of the gospels; but these facts of themselves are not adequate for true Christian faith. Saving faith has to do primarily with believing and trusting that Christ was born for us personally, and has accomplished for us the work of salvation. As Luther puts this point:

*faith in Christ*

> I have often spoken about two different kinds of faith. The first of them is like this: you believe that it is true that Christ is the person who is described and proclaimed in the gospels, but you do not believe that he is such a person for you. You doubt if you can receive that from him, and you think: "Yes, I'm sure he is that person for someone else (like Peter and Paul, and for religious and holy people). But is he that person for me? Can I confidently expect to receive everything from him that the saints expect?" You see, this faith is nothing. It receives nothing of Christ, and tastes nothing of him either. It cannot feel joy, nor love of him or for him. This is a faith related to Christ, but not a faith in Christ ... The only faith which deserves to be called Christian is this: you believe unreservedly that it is not only for Peter and the saints that Christ is such a person, but also for you yourself – in fact, for you more than anyone else.

*2 faiths*

The second point concerns faith as "trust" (Latin: *fiducia*). This notion of faith is prominent in the sixteenth-century conception of faith, and occurs frequently in the writings of both Luther and Calvin. Luther uses a nautical analogy to bring out the importance of trust and commitment in the life of faith. "Everything depends upon faith. The person who does not have faith is like someone who has to cross the sea, but is so frightened that he does not trust the ship. And so he stays where he is, and is never saved, because he will not get on board and cross over." Faith is not merely believing that something is true; it is being prepared to act upon that belief, and rely upon it. To use Luther's analogy: faith is not simply about believing that a ship exists; it is about stepping into it, and entrusting ourselves to it.

But what are we being asked to trust? Are we being asked simply to have faith in faith? The question could perhaps be phrased more accurately: who are we being asked to trust? For Luther, the answer was unequivocal: faith is about being prepared to put one's trust in the promises of God, and the integrity and faithfulness of the God who made those promises. Believers "must be certain that the one who has promised forgiveness to whoever confesses their sins will most faithfully fulfill this promise." For Luther, faith is only as strong as the one in whom we believe and trust. The efficacy of faith does not rest upon the intensity with which we believe, but in the reliability of the one in whom we believe. It is not the greatness of our faith, but the greatness of God, which counts. As Luther puts it:

> Even if my faith is weak, I still have exactly the same treasure and the same Christ as others. There is no difference ... It is like two people, each of whom owns a hundred gold coins. One may carry them around in a paper sack, the other in an iron chest. But despite these differences, they both own the same treasure. Thus the Christ who you and I own is one and the same, irrespective of the strength or weakness of your faith or mine.

The foundation of one's faith thus matters far more than its intensity. It is pointless to trust passionately in someone who is not worthy of trust; even a weak faith in someone who is totally reliable is vastly to be preferred to a strong faith in a scoundrel or trickster. Trust is not, however, an occasional attitude. For Luther, it is an undeviating trusting outlook upon life, a constant stance of conviction in the trustworthiness of the promises of God. As Karl Barth put this in the twentieth century: "In God alone is there faithfulness, and faith is the trust that we may hold to Him, to His promise and to His guidance. To hold to God is to rely on the fact that God is there for me, and to live in this certainty."

In the third place, faith unites the believer with Christ. Luther states this principle clearly in his 1520 writing, *The Liberty of a Christian*:

> Faith unites the soul with Christ as a bride is united with her bridegroom. As Paul teaches us, Christ and the soul become one flesh by this mystery (Ephesians 5:31–2). And if they are one flesh, and if the marriage is for real – indeed, it is the most perfect of all marriages, and human marriages are poor examples of this one true marriage – then it follows that everything that they have is held in common, whether good or evil. So the believer can boast of and glory in whatever Christ possesses, as though it were his or her own; and whatever the believer has, Christ claims as his own. Let us see how this works out, and see how it benefits us. Christ is full of grace, life, and salvation. The human soul is full of sin, death, and damnation. Now let faith come between them. Sin, death, and damnation will be Christ's. And grace, life, and salvation will be the believer's.

Faith, then, is not assent to an abstract set of doctrines – perhaps a possible weakness of Aquinas' approach. Rather, it is a "wedding ring" (Luther), pointing to mutual commitment and union between Christ and the believer. It is the response of the whole person of the believer to God, which leads in turn to the real and personal presence of Christ in the believer.

"To know Christ is to know his benefits," wrote Philip Melanchthon (1497–1560), Luther's colleague at Wittenberg. Faith makes both Christ and his benefits – such as forgiveness, justification, and hope – available to the believer. Calvin makes this point with characteristic clarity. "Having ingrafted us into his body, [Christ] makes us partakers, not only of all his benefits, but also of himself." Christ, Calvin insists, is not "received merely in the understanding and imagination. For the promises offer him, not so that we end up with the mere sight and knowledge of him, but that we enjoy a true communication of him."

# Faith and doubt: the problem of suffering

Faith can never fully prove its claims. This is not, however, a problem that is unique to Christianity. Any belief-system finds itself in the same position – including, incidentally, atheism. Belief in God can neither be proved nor disproved with total certainty. In this section, we shall explore one area of theology which confronts a difficulty that many Christians encounter. If God is good, why is there suffering and pain in the world? How can the presence of evil or suffering be reconciled with the Christian affirmation of the goodness of the God who created the world? In what follows, we shall explore some of the ways in which this has been explored within the Christian tradition.

The approach developed by the second-century writer Irenaeus of Lyons has been particularly influential. For Irenaeus, human nature is a potentiality – something that emerges. Humans are created with certain capacities for growth toward maturity. That capacity for spiritual maturing cannot develop in an abstract situation. It needs to be in contact with and have experience of good and evil, if truly informed decisions are to be made. This tradition tends to view the world as a "vale of soul-making" (to use a term taken from the English poet John Keats, 1795–1821), in which encounter with evil is seen as a necessary prerequisite for spiritual growth and development.

In the modern period, this approach has been developed by the philosopher John Hick (born 1922), now widely regarded as its most influential and persuasive recent exponent. In his *Evil and the God of Love*, Hick emphasizes that human beings are created incomplete. In order for them to become what God intends them to be, they must participate in the world. God did not create human beings as automatons, but as individuals who are capable of responding freely to God. Unless a real choice is available between good and evil, the biblical injunctions to "choose good" are meaningless. Good and evil are thus necessary presences within the world, in order that informed and meaningful human development may take place.

A quite different approach is found in the writings of the philosopher Alvin Plantinga (born 1932), who offers a "free will defense" that is deeply rooted in the Christian tradition. Plantinga's approach picks up on some themes developed by Augustine of Hippo, especially his argument that evil arises from an abuse of human free will. Plantinga's basic approach can be summarized as follows:

1. Free will is morally important. That means that a world in which human beings possess free will is superior to a hypothetical world in which they do not.
2. If human beings were forced to do nothing but good, that would represent a denial of human free will.
3. God must bring into being the best possible world that he is able to do.
4. It must therefore follow that God must create a world with free will.
5. This means that God is not responsible if human beings choose to do evil. God is operating under self-imposed constraints that mean he will not compel human beings to do good.

Hick and Plantinga both offer philosophical solutions to the problem of evil. Others have tried to adopt a more rigorously theological approach, based on the specific ideas of the Christian faith. One of the most influential of these has been the argument that God suffers – in other words, that God shares in the sufferings of the world. In *The Crucified God* (1974), Jürgen Moltmann (born 1926) argued that the suffering of Christ on the cross is both the foundation and the criterion of an authentically *Christian* theology. Precisely because Jesus is God incarnate (an idea we shall explore later in this work), the suffering of Christ is also the suffering of *God*.

Moltmann argues that a God who cannot suffer is a *deficient*, not a perfect, God. Stressing that God cannot be *forced* to change or undergo suffering, Moltmann declares that God willed to undergo suffering. The suffering of God is the direct consequence of the divine *decision* to suffer, and the divine *willingness* to suffer. "In the passion of the Son, the Father himself suffers the pains of abandonment. In the death of the Son, death comes upon God himself, and the Father suffers the death of his Son in his love for forsaken man."

Moltmann's approach has opened up a new way of thinking about the problem of suffering. Traditionally, one of the major concerns here has been the feeling that God is somehow immune from the sufferings of the world, standing over and above it as a detached, uninvolved

*but he suffers when we suffer*

spectator. How, many asked, could anyone believe in such a God, who, having created the world, then abandons it to pain and suffering? Annie Besant's influential book *Why I Do Not Believe in God* (1887) expresses this concern particularly well: "I do not believe in God. My mind finds no grounds on which to build up a reasonable faith. My heart revolts against the specter of an Almighty Indifference to the pain of sentient beings." Moltmann's response is that God chooses to share the suffering of that world. Far from being "indifferent," he shows his commitment and compassion by entering into this vale of soul-making, bearing its sorrow and pain.

**Figure 4**   Jürgen Moltmann (born 1926). Courtesy of the Episcopal Church.

Does this approach help reduce the intellectual difficulties created for faith by the existence of suffering? It is a moot point. Yet it points to another aspect of the issue, which is of no small importance to an understanding of the nature of faith. One can address the problem of suffering in two quite different ways. One tries to make sense of it; the other tries to help people cope with it – to live meaningfully and courageously in the face of suffering and pain.

This is seen well in the writings of Dietrich Bonhoeffer (1906–44). For Bonhoeffer, "our God is a suffering God" – one who bears our sin, pain, and anguish. The deepest meaning of the cross of Christ is that there is no suffering on earth that is not also borne by God. The church, for Bonhoeffer, is the continuing presence of the suffering Christ in history, a body of persons called to share in the messianic suffering of God by being there for others, carrying their burdens and thus fulfilling the duty laid on them by Christ himself. It is through suffering that Christians learn to turn the final outcome of their actions over to God, who alone can perfect them in glory. And it is in dying that they find true freedom as they meet God face to face. A suffering God, according to Bonhoeffer, has not abandoned his people. Far from it; he stands by them as a fellow-sufferer, and will bring them home to a place from which suffering and pain have been removed.

The twentieth century witnessed much ink being spilled over the question of what the existence of suffering has to say about the existence of God. The results have been inconclusive, not least because there has been a growing realization that the debate is going precisely nowhere. As philosopher William Alston (born 1921) has pointed out, any *logical* argument which attempts to show that evil is logically incompatible with the existence of God "is now acknowledged on (almost) all sides" to be completely bankrupt. Yet it remains an important debate, even if its final resolution may be indefinitely postponed!

## Engaging with a text

In this opening chapter, we have explored some aspects of faith. We have seen how faith can be understood in a number of ways. To believe in God is both about accepting that a God exists, and also that this God can be known and trusted. We have already looked at some ideas in the writings of Thomas Aquinas and Martin Luther to illustrate these points. Now we are going to try to take things further, and interact with a theological text.

Why is this so important? Because at some point, you are going to need to begin reading works of theology for yourself. It is therefore important to begin interacting with these in a manageable way as soon as possible. Some chapters of this book have a section which will help you to engage with a short extract from a leading theologian or theological document. These will be drawn from a variety of Christian traditions, offering you experience of a number of different approaches. You will be guided through this process. To begin with, the texts will be short – but gradually, they will become longer. Initially, you will be given a lot of help – but as you gain in confidence, there will be less need for this assistance. We are going to begin this process of engagement with a short but fascinating extract from a leading Protestant writer on the theme of "faith."

The text in question is John Calvin's *Institutes of the Christian Religion*, which was first published in 1536 and went through many editions until the final, definitive edition of 1559. Calvin is a very precise and logical theologian, who is generally very easy to read and understand. In what follows, we are going to interact with the definition of faith which he sets out in this major work. Here is the definition:

> Now we shall have a right definition of faith if we say that it is a steady and certain knowledge of the divine benevolence towards us, which is founded upon the truth of the gracious promise of God in Christ, and is both revealed to our minds and sealed in our hearts by the Holy Spirit.

Take a few moments to read this through, and take in what Calvin is saying. Then use these questions as a way of engaging with his ideas.

1. Note how Calvin's definition of faith is *Trinitarian*. We shall be exploring this aspect of the Christian faith in more detail later (chapter 6). For the moment, note how Calvin ascribes different aspects of faith to each of the three persons of the Trinity – Father, Son, and Spirit. Try to identify each of these aspects. If you are studying this book in a discussion group, spend some time talking about this, making sure that you are happy about the threefold structure of this definition.

2. Now note that the first part of this definition declares that faith is a "steady and certain knowledge of the divine benevolence towards us." Notice first how Calvin uses language that expresses confidence in God, and stresses God's reliability. Notice also how faith is defined as "knowledge" – but a certain very specific kind of knowledge. It is not just "knowledge"; in fact, it is not even "knowledge of God." It is specifically "knowledge of *God's benevolence towards us*." Calvin's language is very specific and intentional. Faith is grounded and based in God's *goodness*. It is not simply about accepting that God exists, but about encountering God's kindness to us. Do you agree with Calvin at this point? Yes

3. The definition now goes on to declare that faith is "founded upon the truth of the gracious promise of God in Christ." Once more, notice how faith is again affirmed to be about knowledge – the use of the word "truth" is very important here. Calvin wants to make it absolutely clear that faith is not a human invention or delusion, but something that is grounded in

the bedrock of truth. But notice how Calvin then proceeds to link this with a "gracious promise of God." For Calvin, we are dealing with a God who makes promises to us – promises which can be trusted and relied upon. You might like to compare this idea with Luther's views on the matter, which we considered earlier in this chapter, and notice their similarity at this point. It is important to see how Calvin identifies Christ as the confirmation or means of disclosure of these promises. You might like to look up 2 Corinthians 1:20, and see how Calvin's approach relates to that text.

4. Calvin clearly holds that faith involves both mind and heart. If you are in a discussion group, you might like to explore how he approaches each of these. Note how, once more, Calvin affirms that faith is indeed about knowledge – something that affects the way in which we think, affecting our minds. Yet it is more than this: it is something that transforms us internally. Notice how Calvin's language about the "heart" points to a deeper change within us than just mental acceptance of an idea. Calvin sees God as active throughout the process of coming to faith. Faith is not human insight; it is personal knowledge of God made possible by the Holy Spirit.

Having explored the meaning of "faith," we may now turn to explore its content – beginning with God.

# CHAPTER 2

# *God*

*who He truly is*

The reality of God lies at the heart of Christian theology. Many of the most fundamental theological questions have to do with how this God can be represented and described. Yet there is perhaps an even more important question that needs to be asked: *which* God are we talking about? It is clear that the little word "God" needs extensive amplification. Israel's reflections on the identity of its God – which they styled using phrases such as "the Lord God of Israel" – took place against a background of polytheism (belief in many gods).

Each nation in the Ancient Near East had its own god; many had highly developed pantheons, recognizing many different gods, each with its own special name, distinctive function, or sphere of influence. The Old Testament refers to some of these by name – such as "Baal," the Canaanite fertility god. Simply talking about "God" was thus not particularly informative. It begged the obvious (and perfectly legitimate) question: which of these gods do you mean? Part of the task of Christian theology is to identify the God in which Christians believe.

This process of identification can be seen in both the Old and New Testaments. For the Old Testament prophets, Israel knew and worshipped the God who had delivered them from exile in Egypt, and led them into the promised land of Canaan. In the New Testament, we find this idea picked up and developed further. Christians believe in the same God as the great Old Testament figures of faith – such as Abraham, Isaac, Jacob, and Moses; this God is, however, finally and fully disclosed in Jesus Christ. Thus Paul speaks of "the God and Father of our Lord Jesus Christ" (2 Corinthians 1:3).

*Theology: The Basics*, Third Edition. Alister E. McGrath.
© 2012 Alister E. McGrath. Published 2012 by Blackwell Publishing Ltd.

The basic idea we find throughout the New Testament is that Christians worship and know the same God as Israel. Nevertheless, Christians hold that this God is revealed supremely and finally in Christ. Thus the letter to the Hebrews opens by declaring that the same God who spoke to Israel "in many times and in various ways" through the prophets has now "spoken to us through a Son," who is to be recognized as the "exact representation" of God (Hebrews 1:1–3). This point is of great importance, as it demonstrates how the Christian understanding of God is linked with the person of Christ. To know Christ is to know God. Or, as a second-century Christian writer put it, "we must learn to think of Jesus as of God" (1 Clement 1:1).

So what do Christians believe about this God? The opening words of the Apostles' Creed get us off to a good start: Christians believe in a God who is "the Father Almighty, Creator of heaven and earth." We shall turn to explore the very rich and powerful theme of creation in the following chapter. To begin with, we shall look at the idea of God as "Father Almighty." We can break this down into two segments, each of which really deserves a chapter to itself. However, limits on space mean that we will have to consider them both briefly, beginning with the question of what it means to speak of God as "Father."

## Analogies in theology

One of the most noticeable things about the way in which the Christian Bible refers to God is its extensive use of imagery. God is depicted as a shepherd, a king, a rock – and a father. Before we begin to explore what it means to talk about God as "father," it will be helpful to look at the general question of the use of analogies in theology.

The Bible uses many analogies to speak about God. To explore some of the issues that arise from using analogies in theology, we may turn to consider one of the most familiar biblical verses: Psalm 23:1, "The Lord is my shepherd." This image of God as a shepherd is encountered frequently in the Old Testament (e.g., Psalm 80:1; Isaiah 40:11; Ezekiel 34:12), and is taken up in the New Testament to refer to Jesus, who is the "good shepherd" (John 10:11). But what does this analogy tell us about God? How can we develop this image theologically? The easiest way of answering this question is to wrestle with the image and see what happens. If you are in a discussion group, close this book and talk about the question which follows. If you're working on your own, write down what comes into your mind in response to the following question.

What ideas come to mind when we talk of a "shepherd"? For most people, four ideas come to mind, as follows.

First, there is the idea of the loving care of the shepherd for the sheep. The shepherd was committed to his flock of sheep on a full-time basis. Indeed, the shepherd tended to be regarded as a social outcast in Israel, precisely on account of the enormous amount of time he was obliged to spend with his flock, which prevented him from taking part in normal social activities. To speak of God as a shepherd thus conveys the idea of the total commitment of God to Israel and the church. The idea is developed very powerfully in the New Testament, especially in the parable of the lost sheep (Luke 15:3–7). Here the shepherd actively seeks out the lost sheep, in order to bring it home. The final intensification of the image is found in John's gospel, where it is emphasized that the good shepherd – who is immediately identified as Jesus – will willingly go so far as to lay down his life for the safety of his sheep (John 10:11–16).

Second, thinking of God as a shepherd affirms God's guidance. The shepherd knows where food and water are to be found, and guides the sheep to them. To liken God to a shepherd is to emphasize God's constant presence with Israel and the church. It is to affirm God's ability to protect from the dangers which life offers and to bring people to a place of plenty and safety. God "tends his flock like a shepherd. He gathers the lambs in his arms and carries them close to his heart; he gently leads those that have young" (Isaiah 40:11).

Third, the image of God as shepherd tells us something about ourselves, from a Christian perspective. We are the sheep of God's pasture (Psalm 79:13; 95:7; 100:3). We are like sheep, incapable of looking after ourselves, and continually going astray. We are not self-sufficient: just as the sheep rely upon the shepherd for their existence, so we have to learn to rely upon God. We may like to think that we are capable of looking after ourselves, but a Christian understanding of human nature demands that we recognize our total dependence upon God. Thus human sinfulness is often compared with running away from God, like a stray sheep. "We all, like sheep, have gone astray; each of us has turned to his own way" (Isaiah 53:6; cf. Psalm 119:176; 1 Peter 2:25).

And just as the shepherd goes to look for his lost sheep, so God came to find us in our lostness and bring us home. The parallels with the parable of the prodigal son (Luke 15:11–32) will be obvious. In that gospel chapter, we find three stories of "lostness" being turned to "being found" and "rejoicing." The shepherd finds his lost sheep (Luke 15:3–8); the woman finds her lost coin (Luke 15:8–10); the father finds his lost son (Luke 15:11–32). And in all these analogies we find the same constant emphasis of the Christian faith: that we are lost, and that God has come into the world in Jesus Christ in order to find us and bring us home.

To speak of "God as a shepherd" is thus to affirm that "God is *like* a shepherd." In other words, the image of a shepherd helps us think about the nature of God, and allows us to gain insights into his nature. It does not mean that God is *identical* to a human shepherd. Rather, it means that some aspects of a human shepherd help us think about God more effectively.

But is *every* aspect of the human analogy valid in thinking about God? Every analogy breaks down at some point. How far can we press this analogy before it ceases to be reliable? To explore this issue, we could draw up a brief list of things that are true about shepherds.

1. Shepherds look after sheep.
2. Shepherds protect their sheep against danger.
3. Shepherds lead their sheep to food and water.
4. Shepherds are human beings.

It is immediately clear that the first three aspects of the analogy can be incorporated into our thinking about God. God cares, protects, and leads. In all these respects, the analogy of the shepherd works well, and illuminates the character of God.

Yet shepherds are ultimately human beings. Is *this* aspect of the analogy also to be incorporated into our idea of God? It is quite clear we are not meant to think of God as a human being. While God is *not* a human being, it is still true that the behavior of one particular group of human beings is seen as helping us to get a better understanding of the nature of God. So it would seem that this is one aspect of the analogy which we are not meant to press too far.

Now these are very simple points to make, and you might feel that they are out of place in any serious discussion of Christian theology. In fact, this is far from the case. What we have been doing is exploring the important theological issue of how far an analogy of God is to be pressed, and how these analogies can offer powerful visual stimulus to theological reflection. It also raises the question of why we should use images of God in this way. Why not use more conceptual or abstract ways of speaking or thinking about God? The answer within the Christian theological tradition could be summarized as follows.

There is no way in which a created human mind would be capable of beholding God directly. As a result, we need to think of God in a scaled-down manner, appropriate to our ability to cope. Some early Christian writers used to compare understanding God with looking directly into the sun. The human eye is simply not capable of withstanding the full brilliance of the sun. In the same way, the human mind cannot cope with the full glory of God.

The story is told of the Roman emperor Hadrian engaging the Jewish rabbi Joshua ben Hananiah in conversation in the early second century. The emperor asked to be allowed to see Joshua's god. The rabbi replied that this was impossible, an answer which failed to satisfy the emperor. So the rabbi took the emperor outside, and asked him to stare at the midday summer sun. "Impossible!" replied the emperor. "If you cannot look at the sun, which God created," replied the rabbi, "how much less can you behold the glory of God himself!"

Even though the human eye cannot cope with the full brightness of the sun, however, it is nevertheless possible to look at the sun through a piece of dark glass. This greatly reduces the brilliance of the sun, so that the human eye can cope with it. Otherwise, looking at the sun would be completely beyond its capacities. In much the same way, it is helpful to think of the scriptural models or pictures of God as revealing God in manageable proportions, so that the human mind can cope with him.

John Calvin argued that God knows our limited ability to cope with ideas, and thus reveals himself in ways that we can handle. According to Calvin, God's revelation is adapted or "accommodated" to our capacity for reflection. Calvin insists that God simply cannot be comprehended by the human mind. What is known of God is known by revelation; and that revelation is adapted to our capacity as finite, fallen human creatures. This does not reflect any weakness or inadequacy on God's part. It is simply a reflection of God's generous and kindly nature, by which God takes our weakness into account. Calvin comments that "God accommodates himself to our ability" – meaning that God uses words, ideas, and images that we can relate to.

So having explored the use of analogies in theology, we may now turn to the specific analogy that we encounter in the creed – the analogy of God as a *father*.

## God as father

The image of God as father is deeply embedded within the Christian faith, not least because of the prayer that Christ taught his disciples, now known as the "Lord's Prayer." Its opening words will be familiar to every reader: "Our Father ..." If Jesus Christ referred to God in this way, it is clearly of major importance to Christian faith. But how are we to interpret this image?

Once more, we are dealing with an analogy. So what sort of ideas does the analogy convey? You might like to spend a few moments jotting down some of the ideas that the image conveys, much as we did earlier in the case of the shepherd analogy. The following ideas might come to mind, and we shall explore each of them briefly.

1. Fathers are human beings.
2. Fathers bring their children into existence.
3. Fathers care for their children.
4. Fathers are male.

The first of these characteristics is clearly not meant to be transferred to our thinking about God. As we saw in the case of the shepherd analogy, this is the inevitable consequence of using language drawn from the created order to refer to the creator.

The second is clearly important. God is our *originator*, the one who brought us into existence. Without God, we would not be here. Both the Old and New Testaments stress our complete dependence upon God from beginning to end. The analogy of God as father conveys the idea of care. The Old Testament in particular often compares God's relation with his people to a father's relationship with his young son. When the son is very young, he is totally dependent upon his father for everything, and their relationship is very close. But as the son grows older, he gradually comes to exercise his independence and break away from his father, so that the relationship becomes more distant. The prophet Hosea uses this illustration to bring out how Israel has become a virtual stranger to the God who called her into existence:

> When Israel was a child, I loved him, and out of Egypt I called my son. But the more I called Israel, the further they went away from me. They sacrificed to the Baals, and they burned incense to images. It was I who taught Ephraim to walk, taking them by the arms, but they did not realize it was I who healed them. I led them with the cords of human kindness, with ties of love. (Hosea 11:1–4)

As Jesus Christ pointed out in the Sermon on the Mount (Matthew 7:9–11), even human fathers want to give their children good things. So how much more will God, as our heavenly father, want to give good things to those who ask for them in prayer.

It is the fourth aspect of this analogy which has generated most debate, and which needs further discussion. Both Old and New Testaments use male language about God. The Greek word for "god" (*theos*) is unquestionably masculine, and most of the analogies used for God throughout Scripture – such as father, king, and shepherd – are also male. Does this mean that God *is* male?

Before answering this question properly, it is important to note that the Bible also uses female imagery to refer to the love of God for humanity. Just as a mother can never forget or turn against her child, so God will not forget or turn against his people (Isaiah 49:15). There is a natural bond of affection and sympathy between God and his children, simply because he has brought them into being. Thus God loved us long before we loved God (1 John 4:10, 19). Psalm 51:1 refers to God's "great compassion." It is interesting to note that the Hebrew word for "compassion" (*rachmin*) is derived from the word for "womb" (*rechmen*). God's compassion towards his people is that of a mother towards her child (cf. Isaiah 66:12–13). Compassion stems from the womb.

So is God male? Does speaking of God as "father" mean that Christianity believes in a male deity? Earlier, we noted the analogical nature of theological language. Individual persons or social roles, largely drawn from the rural world of the Ancient Near East, are identified as models for the divine activity or personality. One such analogy is that of a shepherd; another is that of a father. Yet the statement that "a father in ancient Israelite society is a suitable analogy for God" is not equivalent to saying that "God is male." To speak of God as father is to say that the role of the father in ancient Israel allows us insights into the nature of God. It is not to say that God *is* a male human being. Yet the Old Testament is clear that mothers were also analogies for aspects of God's love for Israel. Although there are many more references to paternal role models than to maternal, there is no doubt that both fathers and mothers function as analogies for God in the Bible.

The important point to appreciate here is that *neither* male nor female sexuality is to be attributed to God. For sexuality is an attribute of the created order, which cannot be assumed to correspond directly to any such polarity within the creator God. Indeed, the Old Testament completely avoids attributing sexual functions to God, on account of the strongly pagan overtones of such associations. The Canaanite fertility cults emphasized the sexual functions of both gods and goddesses; the Old Testament refuses to endorse the idea that the gender or the sexuality of God is a significant matter.

The important German Lutheran theologian Wolfhart Pannenberg (born 1928) develops this point in his *Systematic Theology* (1990):

> The aspect of fatherly care in particular is taken over in what the Old Testament has to say about God's fatherly care for Israel. The sexual definition of the father's role plays no part . . . To bring sexual differentiation into the understanding of God would mean polytheism; it was thus ruled out for the God of Israel . . . The fact that God's care for Israel can also be expressed in terms of a mother's love shows clearly enough how little there is any sense of sexual distinction in the understanding of God as Father.

In an attempt to bring out the fact that God is not male, a number of recent writers have explored the idea of God as "mother" (which brings out the female aspects of God), or as "friend" (which brings out the more gender-neutral aspects of God). An excellent example of this is provided by the American theologian Sallie McFague (born 1933), in her *Models of God*. Recognizing that speaking of "God as father" does not mean that God is male, she writes:

> God as mother does not mean that God is mother (or father). We imagine God as both mother and father, but we realize how inadequate these and any other metaphors are to express the creative love of God ... Nevertheless, we speak of this love in language that is familiar and dear to us, the language of mothers and fathers who give us life, from whose bodies we come, and upon whose care we depend.

The new interest in the issues raised by the maleness of most of the biblical images of God has led to a careful reading of the spiritual literature of early periods in Christian history, resulting in an increased appreciation of the use of female imagery during these times. An excellent example of this is provided by the *Revelations of Divine Love*, an account of sixteen visions which appeared to the English writer Julian of Norwich (1342–ca. 1416) in May 1373. The visions are notable for their distinctive tendency to refer to both God and Jesus Christ in strongly maternal terms.

> I saw that God rejoices to be our Father, and also that he rejoices to be our Mother; and yet again, that he rejoices to be our true Husband, with our soul as his beloved bride ... He is the foundation, substance and the thing itself, what it is by nature. He is the true Father and Mother of what things are by nature.

Talking about God as "shepherd" or "father" leads us on to another important theme of Christian thinking about God – namely, the concept of a *personal* God, to which we now turn.

**Figure 5** Julian of Norwich, statue by David Holgate at Norwich Cathedral. © Jason Bye/Alamy.

## A personal God

Down the ages, theologians and ordinary Christian believers alike have had no hesitation in speaking about God in personal terms. For example, Christianity has ascribed to God a whole series of attributes, such as love, trustworthiness, and purpose, which are generally thought to have strongly personal associations. Many writers have pointed out that the Christian practice of prayer seems to be modeled on the relationship between a child and a parent. Prayer expresses a gracious relationship of personal trust in God. Similarly, one of Paul's leading soteriological images – reconciliation – is clearly modeled on human personal relationships. It implies that the transformation through faith of the relationship between God and sinful human beings is like the reconciliation of two persons, such as an alienated husband and wife.

For early Christian writers, the word "person" is an expression of the individuality of a human being, as seen in his or her words and actions. Above all, there is an emphasis upon the idea of social relationships. A person is someone who plays a role in a social drama, who relates to others. A person has a part to play within a network of social relationships. "Individuality" does not imply social relationships, whereas "personality" relates to the part played by an individual in a web of relationships, by which that person is perceived to be distinctive by others. The basic idea expressed by the idea of "a personal God" is thus a God with whom we can exist in a relationship which is analogous to that which we could have with another human person.

It is helpful to consider what overtones the phrase "an impersonal God" would convey. The phrase suggests a God who is distant or aloof, who deals with humanity (if God deals with us at all) in general terms which take no account of human individuality. The idea of a personal relationship, such as love, suggests a reciprocal character to God's dealings with us. This idea is incorporated into the notion of a personal God, but not into impersonal conceptions of the nature of God. There are strongly negative overtones to the idea of "impersonal," which have passed into Christian thinking about the nature of God.

It is also important to appreciate that personal relationships establish the framework within which such key biblical themes as "love," "trust," and "faithfulness" have their meaning. Both the Old and New Testaments are full of statements concerning the "love of God," the "trustworthiness of God," and the "faithfulness of God." "Love" is a word which is used primarily of personal relationships. Furthermore, the great biblical theme of promise and fulfillment is ultimately based upon a personal relationship, in that God promises certain quite definite things (such as eternal life and forgiveness) to certain individuals. One of the great themes which dominates the Old Testament in particular is that of the covenant between God and people, by which they mutually bind themselves to each other. "I will be their

**Figure 6** Martin Buber (1878–1965). David Rubinger/Time & Life Pictures/Getty Images.

God, and they will be my people" (Jeremiah 31:33). The basic idea underlying this is that of personal commitment of God to God's people, and of God's people to their God.

A twentieth-century philosophical analysis of what it means to speak of a "person" is also helpful in clarifying what it means to speak of a personal God. In his major work *I and Thou* (1927), the Jewish writer Martin Buber (1878–1965) drew a fundamental distinction between two categories of relations: *I–Thou* relations, which are "personal," and *I–It* relations, which are impersonal. We shall explore these basic distinctions further, before considering their theological importance.

1. *I–It relations:* Buber uses this category to refer to the relation between subjects and objects; for example, between a human being and a pencil. The human being is active, whereas the pencil is passive. This distinction is often referred to in more philosophical language as a *subject–object relation*, in which an active subject (in this case, the human being) relates to an inactive object (in this case, the pencil). According to Buber, the subject acts as an *I*, and the object as an *It*. The relation between the human being and pencil could thus be described as an *I–It* relation.

2. *I–Thou relations:* At this point, we come to the heart of Buber's philosophy. An I–Thou relation exists between two active subjects, between two _persons_. It is something which is *mutual* and *reciprocal*. "The I of the primary word I–Thou makes its appearance as a person, and becomes conscious of itself." In other words, Buber is suggesting that human personal relationships exemplify the essential features of an I–You relation. It is the relationship itself, that intangible and invisible bond which links two persons, which is the heart of Buber's idea of an I–Thou relation.

What, then, are the theological implications of this approach to personhood? How does Buber's philosophy help us to understand and explore the idea of God as a person? A number of key ideas emerge, all of which have important and helpful theological applications. Furthermore, Buber anticipated some of these himself. In the final sections of *I and Thou* he explores the implications of his approach to thinking and speaking about God – or, to use his preferred term, "the Absolute Thou."

1. Buber's approach means that God cannot be reduced to a concept, or to some neat conceptual formulation. According to Buber, only an "It" can be treated in this way. For Buber, God is the "Thou who can, by its nature, never become an It. That is, God is a being who escapes all attempts at objectification and transcends all description." Theology must learn to acknowledge and wrestle with the presence of God, realizing that this presence cannot be reduced to a neat package of contents.

2. Buber's approach allows valuable insights into the idea of revelation. For Christian theology, God's revelation is not simply a making known of facts about God, but a *self-revelation* of God. Revelation of information about God is to be supplemented by revelation of God as a person – a presence as much as a content. We could make sense of this by saying that revelation includes knowledge of God as both an "It" and as a "Thou." We come to know things about God; yet we also come to know God. Similarly, "knowledge of God" includes knowledge of God as both "It" and "Thou." "Knowing God" is not simply a collection of data about God, but a personal relationship.

3. Buber's "dialogical personalism" also allows Christian theology to steer clear of the discredited idea of God as an object, perhaps

the weakest and most heavily criticized aspect of some nineteenth-century liberal Protestant theology. The characteristic non-inclusive nineteenth-century phrase "man's quest for God" summed up the basic premise of this approach: God is an "It," a passive object, waiting to be discovered by (male) theologians, who are viewed as active subjects. In his 1938 work *Truth as Encounter*, Emil Brunner (1889–1966) argued that God had to be viewed as a "Thou," an active subject. As such, God could take the initiative away from humans, through self-revelation and a willingness to be known in a historical and personal form – namely, Jesus Christ. Theology would thus become the human response to God's self-disclosure, rather than the human quest for God.

The idea of God as a person is, however, of importance in other areas of theology. In addition to helping us think about the idea of revelation, it is also illuminating as we consider the idea of salvation. Paul talks about God "reconciling" us to himself through Jesus Christ (2 Corinthians 5:18–19). This idea of "reconciliation" is one of a number of ideas that is used in the New Testament to represent the consequences of the death of Christ on the cross. What is particularly interesting is that in this passage Paul uses exactly the same Greek word to refer to the restoration of the relationship between God and humanity that he had used earlier to refer to the restoration of the relationship between a man and his wife who had fallen out with each other (1 Corinthians 7:10–11).

Paul seems to be suggesting that Christ is mediator or go-between, restoring the relationship between God and humanity to what it once was. A notion taken from the world of personal relationships thus helps clarify the nature of salvation, and the difference that the death and resurrection of Christ makes to things.

## God as almighty

The Creed, however, goes on to speak of God as "almighty." So what do we mean when we say that God is "almighty" in this way? At first sight, the everyday meaning of the word "almighty" seems perfectly obvious. It means "all-powerful," and thus "capable of doing anything." And as we believe that God is indeed almighty, we are simply saying that God can do anything. This would appear to bring discussion of the matter to an end. What more is there to say?

Yet one of the tasks of theology is to encourage us to use language critically – to make us think about what we really mean when we talk about God. Is it really quite as simple as this? Might not the word "almighty" have a subtle difference when applied to God than when applied to a human? To explore this, let's consider a simple statement, as follows:

"To say that God is almighty means that God can do anything."

If you are part of a study group, you might like to discuss this statement. If you are working on your own, pause at this point, and think about it. Is it right? What issues does it raise? At first, it seems fairly straightforward. Yet it runs into some difficulties at an early stage. Consider the following question: "Can God draw a triangle with four sides?" It does not take much thought to see that this question has to be answered in the negative. Triangles have three sides; to draw something with four sides is to draw a quadrilateral, not a triangle.

Now we may turn to another question. "Can God create a stone which is too heavy for God to lift?" This question involves a nice logical puzzle. If God cannot create such a stone, there is something that God cannot do. Yet if God can create such a stone, then God will not be able to lift it – and so there is something else God cannot do. Whatever way the question is answered, God's ability to do anything is called into question. In other words, God's omnipotence is called into question in each situation.

However, on further reflection, it is not clear that these questions cause problems for the Christian understanding of God. Four-sided triangles do not and cannot exist. The fact that God cannot make such a triangle is not a serious issue. It just forces us to restate our simple statement in a more complicated way. "To say that God is almighty means that God can do anything that does not involve logical contradiction." Or we can follow Thomas Aquinas, who remarked that it was not that God could not do such things; it was simply that such things cannot be done.

Yet theology is about rather more than such logical riddles. The real issue concerns the divine nature itself. We can begin to engage with this important matter by considering a question beloved of medieval philosophers:

"Can God force someone who loves him to hate him?"

Again, you might like to pause at this point, and think about this, perhaps discussing it in a group. At first sight, the question seems a little strange. Why should God want to turn someone's love for him into hatred? The question appears unreal and pointless. On closer examination, however, the question begins to make sense. At one level, there is no problem. "To say that God is almighty means that God can do anything that does not involve logical contradiction." There is clearly no such contradiction here. God must have the ability to turn someone's love into hatred. Yet there is obviously a deeper issue here, concerning the *character* of God. Can we ever imagine God *wanting* to do this?

To make this important point clearer, let us ask another question. "Can God break promises?" There is no logical contradiction involved in breaking promises. It happens all the time. It may be regrettable, but there is no intellectual difficulty here. If God can do anything that does not involve a logical contradiction, God can certainly break a promise.

Yet, for Christians, this suggestion is outrageous. The God who we know and love is one who remains faithful to what has been promised. If we cannot trust God, whom can we trust? The suggestion that God might break a promise contradicts a vital aspect of God's character – namely, God's faithfulness and truthfulness. One of the great themes of both Old and New Testaments is the total trustworthiness and reliability of God. Humans may fail; God remains faithful. Consider these biblical verses:

> Know therefore that the LORD your God is God. He is the faithful God, keeping his covenant of love to a thousand generations. (Deuteronomy 7.9)

> The LORD is faithful to all his promises. (Psalm 145:13)

The point here is that there is a tension between power and trust. An all-powerful cheater can make promises which cannot be relied upon. Yet one of the greatest insights of the Christian faith is that we know a God who *could* do anything – but who *chose* to redeem us. God did not need to enter into a covenant with Israel – but God chose

*2 God
characteristics*

to do so, and having done so, remains faithful to this promise. We see here the important idea of divine self-limitation – the notion that God freely chooses to behave in certain ways, and in doing so, places limits on divine action. God cannot be accused of acting arbitrarily or whimsically; rather, God acts reliably and faithfully.

If God is indeed revealed in Christ, we must realize that God's power is not symbolized by the sword or the chariot – common symbols of military and political might in the world of his day – but by the cross, a symbol associated with shame, defeat, and *powerlessness*. Perhaps the most dramatic statement of this notion of divine self-limitation can be found in Dietrich Bonhoeffer's *Letters and Papers from Prison*, dating from the closing years of World War II:

> God lets himself be pushed out of the world on to the cross. He is weak and powerless in the world, and that is precisely the way, the only way, in which he is with us and helps us . . . The Bible directs us to God's powerlessness and suffering; only the suffering God can help.

In an age which has become increasingly suspicious of the idea of "power," it is important to be reminded that talk about "an almighty God" does not imply that God is a tyrant. For Bonhoeffer, it means that God chooses to stand alongside people in their powerlessness – a major theme in interpretations of the cross of Christ, to which we shall return shortly.

But let us return to the question with which we began. Can God do anything? The commonsense answer would be simple and straightforward. If God is almighty, God must be capable of doing anything. Yet Christian theology insists that God's omnipotence is to be set within the context of God's nature – that of a righteous and faithful God, whose promises are to be trusted. As proves so often to be the case, we must be very careful in transferring concepts from their human contexts and using them when referring to God.

## Engaging with a text

The *Catechism of the Catholic Church* (1992) is one of the most important theological documents of the twentieth century, and has won much admiration for its clarity of presentation. In its discussion of what it means to refer to God as "father," the *Catechism* brings together a number of important points, all of which are worth careful consideration. Here is the text.

> By calling God "Father," the language of faith indicates two main things: that God is the first origin of everything and transcendent authority; and that he is at the same time goodness and loving care for all his children. God's parental tenderness can also be expressed by the image of motherhood, which emphasizes God's immanence, the intimacy between Creator and creature. The language of faith thus draws on the human experience of parents, who are in a way the first representatives of God for man. But this experience also tells us that human parents are fallible and can disfigure the face of fatherhood and motherhood. We ought therefore to recall that God transcends the human distinction between the sexes. He is neither man nor woman: he is God. He also transcends human fatherhood and motherhood, although he is their origin and standard: no one is father as God is Father.

You may find the following framework helpful as you interact with this text, on your own or within a discussion group.

1. What are the two main points that the *Catechism* believes are made through using the image of God as father? You might like to try and identify some biblical passages which underlie these.
2. The *Catechism* also stresses the importance of maternal imagery. In what ways does this supplement the paternal imagery? And how are these themes held together by an appeal to the "parental" love of God?
3. What do you think the *Catechism* means when it says that "no one is father as God is Father"? No one can compare b/c He is not human — He is perfection & not all human fathers are.

# CHAPTER 3

# Creation

All Christian creeds emphasize that God is the creator of the world. This theme is found throughout the Christian Bible, and is the first theme that the reader of the Bible encounters when reading that work in its canonical order – in other words, when beginning with the book of Genesis (a Greek word, which literally means "beginning" or "origin"). It is therefore appropriate to begin this chapter by exploring the Old Testament understanding of creation.

## Creation in the Old Testament

The theme of "God as creator" is of major importance within the Old Testament. Attention has often focused on the creation narratives found in the first two chapters of the book of Genesis, with which the Old Testament canon opens. However, it must be appreciated that the theme is deeply embedded throughout the Old Testament. It is found in all three of the major types of Old Testament writings – the historical, wisdom, and prophetic literature. For example, Job 38:1–42:6 (a form of wisdom literature) sets out what is unquestionably the most comprehensive understanding of God as creator to be found in the Old Testament, stressing the role of God as creator and sustainer of the world.

It is possible to discern two distinct, though related, contexts in which the notion of "God as creator" is encountered in the Old

*Theology: The Basics*, Third Edition. Alister E. McGrath.
© 2012 Alister E. McGrath. Published 2012 by Blackwell Publishing Ltd.

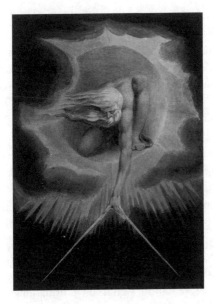

**Figure 7**   William Blake's *Ancient of Days*, 1794, relief etching with watercolor, 23.3 × 16.8 cm. British Museum, London. Blake here depicts God speaking out of the whirlwind, described in Job 38–42. AKG Images/Erich Lessing.

Testament: first, in contexts which reflect the praise of God within Israel's worship, both individual and corporate; and secondly, in contexts which stress that the God who created the world is also the God who liberated Israel from bondage, and continues to sustain her in the present.

Of particular interest for our purposes is the Old Testament theme of "creation as ordering," and the manner in which the critically important theme of "order" is established on and justified with reference to cosmological foundations. It has often been pointed out how the Old Testament portrays creation in terms of an engagement with and victory over forces of chaos. This "establishment of order" is generally represented in two different ways:

1. Creation can be thought of as the imposition of order on a formless chaos. This model is especially associated with the image of

a potter working clay into a recognizably ordered structure (e.g., Isaiah 29:16; 44:8; Jeremiah 18:1–6).

2. Creation can be thought of as God's victorious conflict with a series of chaotic forces, often depicted as a dragon or another monster (variously named "Behemoth," "Leviathan," "Nahar," "Rahab," "Tannim," or "Yam") who must be subdued (Job 3:8; 7:12; 9:13; 40:15–32; Psalm 74:13–15; 139:10–11; Isaiah 27:1; 41:9–10; Zechariah 10:11).

It is clear that there are parallels between the Old Testament account of God engaging with the forces of chaos and similar accounts found in other religious texts of the Ancient Near East – for example, Ugaritic and Canaanite mythology. Nevertheless, there are significant differences at points of importance, not least in the Old Testament's insistence that the forces of chaos are not to be seen as divine. Creation is not to be understood simply as the forming or shaping of the universe, but in terms of God's mastery of chaos and ordering of the world.

Perhaps one of the most significant affirmations which the Old Testament concept of creation makes is that *nature is not divine*. The Genesis creation account stresses that God created the moon, sun, and stars. The significance of this point is too easily overlooked. Each of these celestial entities was worshipped as divine in the ancient world. Many of these were worshipped as gods by Israel's neighbors. By asserting that they were created by God, the Old Testament is insisting that they are subordinate to God, and have no intrinsic divine nature.

## The concept of creation "out of nothing"

Having briefly introduced some aspects of the concept of creation, we may now pass on to consider some of its aspects in a more theological manner. One of the most important developments of the doctrine of creation arose in response to the Gnostic controversy of the second century. For Gnosticism, in most of its significant forms, a sharp distinction was to be drawn between the God who redeemed humanity from the world, and a somewhat inferior deity (often termed "the demiurge") who created that world in the first place.

The Gnostics thus regarded the Old Testament as dealing with this lesser deity, whereas the New Testament was concerned with the redeemer God. Christians, however, saw both Testaments as referring to one and the same God – a God who both creates and redeems. (This idea of the continuity of divine action is often referred to as the "economy of salvation.") As such, belief in God as creator and in the authority of the Old Testament came to be interlinked at an early stage in Christian theology. Of the early writers to deal with this theme, Irenaeus of Lyons is of particular importance.

A distinct, though related, debate centered on the question of creation "out of nothing" (Latin: *ex nihilo*). It must be remembered that Christianity initially took root and then expanded in the eastern Mediterranean world of the first and second centuries, which was dominated by various Greek pagan philosophies. The general Greek pagan understanding of the origins of the world could be summarized as follows. God is not to be thought of as having *created* the world. Rather, God is to be thought of as an architect, who ordered preexistent matter. Matter was already present within the universe, and did not require to be created; it needed to be given a definite shape and structure. God was therefore thought of as the one who fashioned the world from this already existing matter. Thus in one of his dialogues (*Timaeus*), Plato developed the idea that the world was made out of preexistent matter, which was fashioned into the present form of the world.

This idea was taken up by most Gnostic writers, who were here followed by individual Christian theologians such as Theophilus of Antioch (died ca. 184) and Justin Martyr. They professed a belief in preexistent matter, which was shaped into the world in the act of creation. In other words, creation was not *ex nihilo*; rather, it was to be seen as an act of construction, on the basis of material which was already to hand, as one might construct an igloo out of snow, or a house from bricks. The existence of evil in the world was thus to be explained on the basis of the intractability of this preexistent matter. God's options in creating the world were limited by the poor quality of the material available. The presence of evil or defects within the world are thus not to be ascribed to God, but to deficiencies in the material from which the world was constructed.

However, the conflict with Gnosticism forced reconsideration of this issue. In part, the idea of creation from preexistent matter was discredited by its Gnostic associations; in part, it was called into question by an increasingly sophisticated reading of the Old Testament creation narratives. Reacting against this Platonist world-view, several major Christian writers of the second and third centuries argued that *everything* had to be created by God. There was no preexistent matter; everything required to be created out of nothing. Irenaeus argued that the Christian doctrine of creation affirmed the inherent goodness of creation, which contrasted sharply with the Gnostic idea that the material world was evil.

Tertullian (ca. 155–230) emphasized the divine decision to create the world. The existence of the world is itself due to God's freedom and goodness, not to any inherent necessity arising from the nature of matter. The world depends on God for its existence. This contrasted sharply with the Aristotelian view that the world depended on nothing for its existence, and that the particular structure of the world was intrinsically necessary. Yet not all Christian theologians adopted this position at this early stage in the emergence of the Christian tradition. Origen, perhaps one of the most Platonist of early Christian writers, clearly regarded the doctrine of creation from preexistent matter to have more going for it than its critics allowed.

## Creation and dualism

The central issue relating to the doctrine of creation which had to be debated in the first period of Christian theology was thus that of *dualism* – a view of the world which holds that there are two ultim-ately distinct principles, or spheres, such as good and evil, or matter and spirit. The classic example of this is found in some of the forms of Gnosticism, so forcefully opposed by Irenaeus, which argued for the existence of two gods – a supreme god, who was the source of the invisible spiritual world, and a lesser deity who created the world of material things. This approach is strongly dualist, in that it sets up a fundamental tension between the spiritual realm (which is seen as being good) and the material realm (which is seen as being evil). The doctrine of creation affirmed that the material world was created good by God, despite its subsequent contamination by sin. A similar outlook is associated with Manichaeism, a Gnostic worldview which Augustine found attractive as a young man.

By the end of the fourth century, most Christian theologians had rejected the Platonist approach, even in the form associated with Origen, and argued for God being the creator of both the spiritual and material worlds. The Nicene Creed opens with a declaration of faith in God as "maker of heaven and earth," thus affirming the divine creation of both the spiritual and material realms. During the Middle Ages, forms of dualism once more made their appearance, particularly in the views of some heretical sects. The Cathars and Albigenses, for example, taught that matter is evil, and was created *ex nihilo* by the devil. Against such views, the Fourth Lateran Council (1215) taught explicitly that God created a good creation out of nothing.

> We firmly believe and openly confess that there is only one true God...the one principle of the universe, Creator of all things invisible and visible, spiritual and physical, who from the beginning of time and by his omnipotent power made everything from nothing (*ex nihilo*).

## Implications of the doctrine of creation

The doctrine of God as creator has several major implications, of which four may be noted here.

First, a distinction must be drawn between God and the creation. A major theme of Christian theology from the earliest of times has been to resist the temptation to merge the creator and the creation. The theme is clearly stated in Paul's letter to the Romans, the opening chapter of which criticizes the tendency to reduce God to the level of the world. According to Paul, there is a natural human tendency, as a result of sin, to serve "created things rather than the creator" (Romans 1:25). A central task of a Christian theology of creation is to distinguish God from the creation, while at the same time to affirm that it is *God's* creation.

This process may be seen at work in the writings of Augustine; it is of considerable importance in the writings of reformers such as Calvin, who were concerned to forge a world-affirming spirituality in response to the general monastic tendency to renounce the world, evident in writings such as Thomas à Kempis' (1380–1471) *Imitation of Christ*, with its characteristic emphasis upon the "contempt of the world." There is a dialectic in Calvin's thought between the world as the creation of God himself, and the world as the fallen creation. In that it is God's creation, it is to be honored, respected, and affirmed; in that it is a fallen creation, it is to be criticized with the object of redeeming it. These two insights could be described as the twin foci of the ellipse of Calvin's world-affirming spirituality. A similar pattern can be discerned in Calvin's doctrine of human nature, where – despite his stress upon the sinful nature of fallen humanity – he never loses sight of the fact that it remains God's creation. Though stained by sin, it remains the creation and possession of God, and is to be valued for that reason. The doctrine of creation thus leads to a critical world-affirming spirituality, in which the world is affirmed, without falling into the snare of treating it as if it were God.

In the second place, creation implies God's authority over the world. A characteristic biblical emphasis is that the creator has authority over the creation. Humans are thus regarded as part of that creation, with special functions within it. The doctrine of creation leads to the idea of *human stewardship of the creation*, which is to be contrasted with a secular notion of *human ownership of the world*. The creation is not ours; we hold it in trust for God. We are meant to be the stewards of God's creation, and are responsible for the manner in which we exercise that stewardship. This insight is of major importance in relation to ecological and environmental concerns, in that it provides a theoretical foundation for the exercise of human responsibility toward the planet.

In the third place, the doctrine of God as creator implies the goodness of creation. Throughout the first biblical account of creation, we encounter the affirmation: "And God saw that it was good" (Genesis 1:10, 18, 21, 25, 31). (The only thing, incidentally, that is "not good" is that Adam is alone. Humanity is created as a social being, and is meant to exist in relation with others.) There is no place in Christian theology for the Gnostic or dualist idea of the world as an inherently evil place. As we shall explore elsewhere, even though the world is fallen through sin, it remains God's good creation, and capable of being redeemed.

This is not to say that the creation is presently perfect. An essential component of the Christian doctrine of sin is the recognition that the world has departed from the trajectory upon which God placed it in the work of creation. It has become deflected from its intended course. It has fallen from the glory in which it was created. The world as we see it is not the world as it was intended to be. The existence of human sin, evil, and death is itself a token of the extent of the departure of the created order from its intended pattern.

For this reason, most Christian reflections on redemption include the idea of some kind of restoration of creation to its original integrity, in order that God's intentions for his creation might find fulfillment. Affirming the goodness of creation also avoids the suggestion, unacceptable to most theologians, that God is responsible for evil. The constant biblical emphasis upon the goodness of creation is a reminder that the destructive force of sin is not present in the world by God's design or permission.

In the fourth place, the doctrine of creation affirms that human beings are created in the image of God (Genesis 1:26–7). This insight, central to any Christian doctrine of human nature, is of major importance as an aspect of the doctrine of creation itself. "You made us for yourself, and our hearts are restless until they find their rest in you" (Augustine of Hippo). With these words, the importance of the doctrine of creation for a proper understanding of human experience, nature, and destiny is established. We shall return to this theme shortly.

## Models of God as creator

The manner in which God acts as creator has been the subject of intense discussion within the Christian tradition. A number of models of, or ways of picturing, the manner in which God is to be thought of as creating the world have been developed, each of which casts some light on the complex and rich Christian understanding of the notion of "creation."

1. *Emanation.* This term was widely used by early Christian writers to clarify the relation between God and the world. Although the term is not used by either Plato or Plotinus, many patristic writers sympathetic to the various forms of Platonism saw it as a convenient and appropriate way of articulating Platonic insights. The image that

dominates this approach is that of light or heat radiating from the sun, or a human source such as a fire. This image of creation (hinted at in the Nicene Creed's phrase "light from light") suggests that the creation of the world can be regarded as an overflowing of the creative energy of God. God is to the universe as the sun is to light. The sun is the source of light, but does not itself require illumination. Just as light derives from the sun and reflects its nature, so the created order derives from God, and expresses the divine nature. There is, on the basis of this model, a *natural* or *organic* connection between God and the creation.

However, the model has weaknesses, of which two may be noted. First, the image of a sun radiating light, or a fire radiating heat, implies an involuntary emanation, rather than a conscious decision to create. The Christian tradition has consistently emphasized that the act of creation rests upon a prior decision on the part of God to create, which this model cannot adequately express.

This naturally leads on to the second weakness, which relates to the impersonal nature of the model in question. The idea of a personal God, expressing a personality both in the very act of creation and the subsequent creation itself, is difficult to convey by this image. Nevertheless, the model clearly articulates a close connection between creator and creation, leading us to expect that something of the identity and nature of the creator is to be found in the creation. Thus the beauty of God – a theme which was of particular importance in early medieval theology, and has emerged as significant again in the later writings of Hans Urs von Balthasar (1905–88) – would be expected to be reflected in the nature of the creation.

2. *Construction.* Many biblical passages portray God as a master builder, deliberately constructing the world (for example, Psalm 127:1). The imagery is powerful, conveying the ideas of purpose, planning, and a deliberate intention to create. The image is important, in that it draws attention to both the creator and the creation. In addition to bringing out the skill of the creator, it also allows the beauty and ordering of the resulting creation to be appreciated, both for what it is in itself, and for its testimony to the creativity and care of its creator.

However, the image has a deficiency, which relates to a point we noted made in connection with Plato's dialogue *Timaeus*.

This portrays creation as involving preexistent matter. Here, creation is understood as giving shape and form to something which is already there – an idea which, we have seen, causes at least a degree of tension with the doctrine of creation *ex nihilo*. The image of God as a builder would seem to imply the assembly of the world from material which is already to hand, which is clearly deficient.

Nevertheless, despite this difficulty, it can be seen that the model expresses the insight that the character of the creator is, in some manner, expressed in the natural world, just as that of an artist is communicated or embodied in her work. In particular, the notion of "ordering" – that is, the imparting or imposing of a coherence or structure to the material in question – is clearly affirmed by this model. Whatever else the complex notion of "creation" may mean within a Christian context, it certainly includes the fundamental theme of ordering – a notion which is especially significant in the creation narratives of the Old Testament.

3. *Artistic expression.* Many Christian writers, from various periods in the history of the church, speak of creation as the "handiwork of God," comparing it to a work of art which is both beautiful in itself, as well as expressing the personality of its creator. This model of creation as the "artistic expression" of God as creator is particularly well expressed in the writings of the eighteenth-century North American theologian Jonathan Edwards (1703–58), as we shall see presently.

The image is profoundly helpful, in that it supplements a deficiency of both the two models noted above – namely, their impersonal character. The image of God as artist conveys the idea of personal expression in the creation of something beautiful. Once more, the potential weaknesses need to be noted; for example, the model could easily lead to the idea of creation from preexistent matter, as in the case of a sculptor with a statue carved from an already existing block of stone. However, the model offers us at least the possibility of thinking about creation from nothing, as with the author who writes a novel, or the composer who creates a melody and harmony. It also encourages us to seek for the self-expression of God in the creation, and gives added theological credibility to a natural theology. There is also a natural link between the concept of creation as "artistic expression" and the highly significant concept of "beauty."

## Humanity and creation: the "image of God"

"What are human beings, that you are mindful of them?" (Psalm 8:4). From the beginning of history, people have wondered about their place in the greater scheme of things. Why are we here? What is our destiny? What is the meaning of human existence? The doctrine of creation offers a framework for understanding and appreciating these questions.

One of the most fundamental themes of a Christian doctrine of creation is that humanity has been created "in the image of God" (Genesis 1:27). This brief yet deeply significant phrase opens the way to a right understanding of human nature, and our overall place within the created order. Although humanity is not divine, it possesses a relationship with God which is different from that of other creatures. *Humanity bears the image of God.* For some, this is a statement of the privileged position of humanity within creation. Yet, for most Christian theologians, it is above all an affirmation of *responsibility* and *accountability* towards the world in which we live.

So how are we to understand this relationship to God? How can we visualize it? A number of models have been developed within Christian theology, of which we may note three. Each is worth close scrutiny in its own right.

1. *The sovereignty of God.* The "image of God" can be seen as a reminder of the authority of God over humanity. In the Ancient Near East, monarchs would often display images of themselves as an assertion of their power in a region (see, for example, the golden statue of Nebuchadnezzar, described in Daniel 3:1–7). To be created in the "image of God" could therefore be understood as being *accountable to God*. This important point underlies an incident in the ministry of Jesus Christ (Luke 20:22–5). Challenged as to whether it was right for Jews to pay taxes to the Roman authorities, Jesus requested that a coin be brought to him. He asked, "Whose image and title does it bear?" Those standing around replied that it was Caesar's. Christ then tells the crowd to give to Caesar what is Caesar's, and to God what is God's. While some might take this to be an evasion of the question, it is nothing of the sort. It is a reminder that those who bear God's image – that is, humanity – must dedicate themselves to him.

2. *Human correspondence to God.* The idea of the "image of God" can be taken to refer to some kind of correspondence between human reason and the rationality of God as creator. On this understanding of things, there is an intrinsic resonance between the structures of the world and human reasoning. This approach is set out with particular clarity in Augustine's major theological writing *On the Trinity*:

> The image of the creator is to be found in the rational or intellectual soul of humanity ... [The human soul] has been created according to the image of God in order that it may use reason and intellect in order to apprehend and behold God.

For Augustine, we have been created with the intellectual resources which can set us on the way to finding God by reflecting on the creation.

In more recent years, the importance of this point has been explored by the physicist turned theologian John Polkinghorne, formerly professor of theoretical physics at Cambridge University. Polkinghorne points out that some of the most beautiful patterns thought up by the mathematicians are found actually to occur in the structure of the physical world around us. There seems to be some deep-seated relationship between the reason within (the rationality of our minds – in this case mathematics) and the reason without (the rational order and structure of the physical world around us). The two fit together like a glove. So why are our minds so perfectly shaped to understand the deep patterns of the world around us?

Polkinghorne argues that there seems to be some kind of "resonance" or "harmonization" between the ordering of the world and the capacity of the human mind to discern and represent it. "If the deep-seated congruence of the rationality present in our minds with the rationality present in the world is to find a true explanation, it must surely lie in some more profound reason which is the ground of both. Such a reason would be provided by the Rationality of the Creator."

3. *Image and relationality.* A third approach holds that the "image of God" is about the capacity to relate to God. To be created in the "image of God" is to possess the potential to enter into a relationship with God. The term "image" here expresses the idea that God has created humanity with a specific goal – namely, to relate to God.

This theme has played a major role in Christian spirituality. We are meant to exist in a relationship with our creator and redeemer.

This has been an important theme in the writings of C. S. Lewis (1898–1963). For Lewis, there is a God-shaped gap within us, which only God can fill. And in his absence, we experience a deep sense of longing – a longing which is really for God, but which fallen and sinful humanity misreads, accidentally or deliberately, as a longing for things within the world. And these things never satisfy. If we are made for God, and God alone, then there is nothing else that will satisfy. And, as Lewis constantly pointed out, this God-given sense of longing proves a key to answering the great questions of life with which humanity has wrestled.

## Creation and natural theology

So if God created the world, what may be known of God from the world? This question has been debated within Christian theology for centuries. "The heavens declare the glory of God; the heavens proclaim the work of God's hands" (Psalm 19:1). This well-known text can be seen as representing a general theme within the Christian Bible – that something of the wisdom of the God who made the world can be known through the world that was created. The exploration of this theme has proved to be one of the most fruitful areas of theology. We begin our discussion by considering what is widely regarded as a landmark in this matter – the contribution of Thomas Aquinas.

Thomas Aquinas' *Summa contra Gentiles* was written during the period 1259–61, initially at Paris and subsequently at Naples. One of its most significant discussions concerns the manner in which God may be understood to be related to the creation – a relationship which Aquinas analyzes in terms of causality, as follows.

For Aquinas, there exists a fundamental "likeness [*similitudo*] to God" within the created order as a consequence of God being the cause, in some sense of the word, of all created things. In that no created thing can be said to come into existence spontaneously, the existence of all things can be considered to be a consequence of a relationship of causal dependence between the creation and its creator.

**Figure 8** *The Triumph of Saint Thomas Aquinas*, painting by Benozzo de Gozzoli, ca. 1420–97, tempera. Musée du Louvre, Paris. The Art Archive/Musée du Louvre, Paris/Gianni Dagli Orti.

Using what are essentially Aristotelian categories of causality, Aquinas sets out a position which we may summarize as follows:

1. Suppose that A causes B;
2. Suppose also that A possesses a quality Q;
3. Then B will also possess that quality Q as a result of its being caused by A.

The full argument set out by Aquinas is complex, and not without its difficulties; nevertheless, its conclusion is clear. There are, so to speak, physical or metaphysical fingerprints within creation, which provide the basis for an inductive argument to the existence of its cause and origins.

If God made the world, God's "signature" (so to speak) may be found within the created order. Thomas Aquinas puts this point as follows:

> Meditation on [God's] works enables us, at least to some extent, to admire and reflect on God's wisdom... We are thus able to infer God's wisdom from reflection upon God's works... This consideration of God's works leads to an admiration of God's sublime power, and consequently inspires reverence for God in human hearts... This consideration also incites human souls to the love of God's goodness... If the goodness, beauty, and wonder of creatures are so delightful to the human mind, the fountainhead of God's own goodness (compared with the trickles of goodness found in creatures) will draw excited human minds entirely to itself.

Something of the torrent of God's beauty can thus be known in the rivulets of the beauty of the creation.

Another theologian to explore this issue is John Calvin. The first book of Calvin's *Institutes* opens with discussion of this fundamental problem of Christian theology: how do we know anything about God? Calvin affirms that a general knowledge of God may be discerned throughout the creation – in humanity, in the natural order, and in the historical process itself. Two main grounds of such knowledge are identified, one subjective, the other objective.

The first ground is a "sense of divinity" (*sensus divinitatis*) or a "seed of religion" (*semen religionis*), which has been planted within every human being by God. God has endowed human beings with some inbuilt sense or presentiment of the divine existence. It is as if something about God has been engraved in the heart of every human being. Calvin identifies three consequences of this inbuilt awareness of divinity: the universality of religion (which, if uninformed by the Christian revelation, degenerates into idolatry), a troubled conscience, and a servile fear of God. All of these, Calvin suggests, may serve as points of contact for the Christian proclamation.

The second ground of knowledge of God as creator lies in experience of and reflection upon the ordering of the world. The fact that God is creator, together with an appreciation of the divine wisdom and justice, may be gained from an inspection of the created order, culminating in humanity itself.

It is important to stress that Calvin makes no suggestion whatsoever that this knowledge of God from the created order is peculiar to, or even restricted to, Christian believers. Calvin is arguing that *anyone*, by intelligent and rational reflection upon the created order, should be able to arrive at the idea of God. The created order is a "theater" or a "mirror" for the displaying of the divine presence, nature, and attribute. Although invisible and incomprehensible, God wills to be known under the form of created and visible things within creation. The creator God can be known, although to a limited extent, through the creation itself.

Calvin then introduces the notion of revelation. Scripture reiterates what may be known of God through nature, while simultaneously clarifying this general revelation and enhancing it. "The knowledge of God, which is clearly shown in the ordering of the world and in all creatures, is still more clearly and familiarly explained in the Word." It is only through scripture that the believer has access to knowledge of the redeeming actions of God in history, culminating in the life, death, and resurrection of Jesus Christ. For Calvin, revelation is focused upon the person of Jesus Christ; our knowledge of God is mediated through him. God may thus be fully known only through Jesus Christ, who may in turn be known only through scripture. However, the created order provides important points of contact for this revelation.

The basic idea is that a knowledge of God the creator may be had both through nature and through revelation, with the latter clarifying, confirming, and extending what may be known through the former. Knowledge of God the redeemer – which for Calvin is a distinctively *Christian* knowledge of God – may only be had by the Christian revelation, in Christ and through scripture.

Yet not all theologians are persuaded of the merits and legitimacy of natural theology. Perhaps the most negative attitude to have been adopted in recent Christian theology is that of Karl Barth, whose 1934 controversy with Emil Brunner over this issue has become a landmark in theological debate. In 1934, Brunner published a work entitled *Nature and Grace*. In this work, he argued that "the task of our theological generation is to find a way back to a legitimate natural theology." Brunner located this approach in the doctrine of creation, specifically the idea that human beings are created in the *imago Dei*, the "image of God." Human nature is constituted in such a way that there is an analogue with the being of God. Despite the sinfulness of human nature, the ability to discern God in nature remains. Sinful human beings remain able to recognize God in nature and in the events of history, and to be aware of their guilt before God. There is thus a "point of contact" for divine revelation within human nature as a consequence of the doctrine of creation.

Brunner argued that human nature is constituted in such a way that there is a ready-made point of contact for divine revelation. Revelation thus addresses itself to a human nature which already has some idea of what that revelation is about. For example, take the gospel demand to "repent of sin." Brunner argues that this makes little sense, unless human beings already have some idea of what "sin" is. The gospel demand to repent is thus addressed to an audience which already has at least something of an idea of what "sin" and "repentance" might mean. Revelation brings with it a fuller understanding of what sin means – but in doing so, it builds upon an existing human awareness of sin.

Barth reacted with anger to this suggestion. His published reply to Brunner – which brought their longstanding friendship to an abrupt end – has one of the shortest titles in the history of religious publishing: *Nein!* ("No!"). Barth was determined to say "no!" to Brunner's positive evaluation of natural theology. It seemed to imply that God needed help to become known, or that human beings somehow cooperated with God in the act of revelation. For Barth, this subverted God's freedom and sovereignty in revelation. "The Holy Spirit . . . needs no point of contact other than that which that same Spirit establishes," was his angry retort. For Barth, there was no "point of contact" inherent within human nature. Any such "point of contact" was itself the result of divine revelation. It is something that is evoked by the Word of God, rather than something which is a permanent feature of human nature.

Underlying this exchange is another matter, which is too easily overlooked. Beneath Brunner's appeal to nature is an idea, which can be traced back to Luther, known as "the orders of creation." According to Luther, God providentially established certain "orders" within creation, in order to prevent it collapsing into chaos. Those orders included the family, the church, and the state. (The close alliance between the church and the state in German Lutheran thought can be seen as reflecting this idea.) Nineteenth-century German liberal

Protestantism had absorbed this idea, and developed a theology which allowed German culture, including a positive assessment of the state, to become of major importance theologically.

The Barth–Brunner debate took place in 1934, the year in which Adolf Hitler gained power in Germany. This raised a series of difficulties for the idea of the "orders" of creation, as it appeared to create conceptual space for governments to be seen as divinely authorized, or reflecting the nature of God. Part of Barth's concern was that Brunner, perhaps unwittingly, has laid a theological foundation for allowing the state to become a model for God. And who, Barth wondered, really wanted to model God on Adolf Hitler's Nazi Germany and its institutions?

Others, however, have wondered about the accuracy of this criticism. Does the belief that God can be known to some limited extent really imply that we construct God in the image of Hitler? Critics of Barth, such as the Old Testament scholar James Barr (1924–2006), argued that this was a remote possibility, which had been given undue credibility in Barth's writings on account of the political situation of his day. Yet it seemed to Barr to be a remote possibility. Rightly understood, natural theology had little, if anything, to do with the political situation in Nazi Germany. Yet Barth's critique of natural theology remains significant, despite this cautionary comment.

## Creation and creationism

In recent years, especially in North America, controversy has emerged over how the opening chapters of the book of Genesis are to be interpreted, and how these relate to the scientific discussion of the biological evolution of humanity. The term "creationism" has come to be used to refer to writers who hold that humanity was brought into existence in its present form by a direct creative act of God. This stands in contrast to the standard evolutionary model, based on Charles Darwin's *Descent of Man*, which holds that humanity evolved into its present form over an extended period of time. At least four positions on this matter can be identified in contemporary North American Protestantism.

One approach is known as "young earth creationism." This position represents the continuation of interpretations of the book of Genesis that were widely encountered in popular and at least some academic writing before 1800. On this view, the earth was created in its basic form between 6,000 and 10,000 years ago. Young earth creationists generally read the first two chapters of the book of Genesis very literally, in a way that allows for no living creatures of any kind before Eden, and no death before the Fall. Most young earth creationists hold that all living things were created simultaneously, within the timeframe proposed by the Genesis creation accounts, with the Hebrew word *yom* ("day") meaning a period of 24 hours. This view, of course, encounters considerable scientific difficulties, not least from fossil records, which point to a much greater timescale and to the existence of extinct species.

An alternative version is known as "old earth creationism." This is probably the majority viewpoint within conservative Protestant circles. It has no particular difficulty with the vast age of the world, and argues that the "young earth" approach requires modification in at least two respects. First, that the term "day" in the Genesis creation accounts is to be interpreted as a long period of time, not a specific period of 24 hours. Second, that there may be a large chronological gap between Genesis 1.1 and Genesis 1.2. In other words, there may be a substantial period of time intervening between the primordial act of creation of the universe, and the emergence of life on earth. This viewpoint is advocated by the famous *Schofield Reference Bible*, first published in 1909, although the ideas can be traced back to writers such as the earlier nineteenth-century Scottish divine Thomas Chalmers (1780–1847).

A third possibility has gained much attention in recent years, and is generally known as "Intelligent Design." This approach argues that biological life shows an "irreducible complexity" which makes it impossible to explain its origins and development in any other way than by intelligent design by a creator God. Intelligent design does not deny biological evolution as such; its most fundamental criticism of Darwinism is directed against its core belief that evolution has no goal. The Intelligent Design movement argues that standard Darwinism runs into significant explanatory difficulties, which can only be adequately resolved through the intentional creation of individual species. Its critics argue that these difficulties are overstated, or that they will in due course be resolved by future theoretical advances.

A fourth option, which goes back to the appearance of Darwin's pioneering work, is to see creation as referring to an ongoing process, not a one-off event. God initiates a process which leads eventually to the emergence of humanity. This position is often referred to as "theistic evolution." Its representatives include the Victorian novelist and theologian Charles Kingsley (1819–75), who insisted that the most distinctive aspect of the Christian doctrine of creation was that God made things to make themselves. In 1884, Frederick Temple (1820–1902), who later became archbishop of Canterbury, argued that God did something rather more splendid than just make the world; he makes the world *make itself.*

This debate has become particularly important in North America in recent years, due to pressure from conservative Christian pastors and organizations who believe that creationist accounts of the origins of humanity ought to be taught alongside Darwinian accounts in American public schools. This represents an important example of a theological debate with political consequences. Yet whatever the outcome of this particular controversy might be, the debate reminds us that the seemingly simple verb "create" may be more complex than at first meets the eye.

## Engaging with a text

We have already noted John Calvin's strong affirmation of a natural knowledge of God. This gave a significant stimulus to the development of the concept of natural theology on the part of his followers within the Reformed tradition. A good example of this is found in the Gallic Confession (1559), a Calvinist statement of faith which declared that God was revealed to humanity in two quite distinct manners:

> First, in [God's] works, both in their creation and their preservation and control. Second, and more clearly, in his Word, which was revealed through oracles in the beginning, and which was subse-quently committed to writing in the books which we call the Holy Scriptures.

A related idea was set out in the Belgic Confession – or, to use its rather more fulsome title, "The Confession of Faith of the Reformed Walloon and Flemish Churches" – which was drawn up by Guido des Brès in 1561. This expanded the brief statement on natural theology found in the Gallic Confession. Once more, knowledge of God is affirmed to come about by two means: through nature and through scripture. The two basic themes found in these confessional statements can be summarized as follows:

1. There are two ways of knowing God, one through the natural order, and the second through scripture.
2. The second way is clearer and fuller than the first.

In what follows, we shall examine the teaching on this issue set out in the second article of the Belgic Confession. The document is clearly dependent upon the earlier Gallic Confession at times, and can be seen as an expansion of its ideas at certain points.

> We know [God] in two manners. First, by the creation, preservation, and government of the universe, which is before our eyes as a most beautiful book, in which all creatures, great and small, are like so many characters leading us to contemplate the invisible things of God, namely, his eternal power and Godhead, as the Apostle Paul declares (Romans 1:20). All of these things are sufficient to convince humanity, and leave them without excuse. Second, he makes himself known more clearly and fully to us by his holy and divine Word; that is to say, as far as is necessary for us to know in this life, to his glory and our salvation.

This brief statement proved to be of considerable importance to the development of both the biological and physical sciences in the Lowlands. The development of the microscope at the end of the seventeenth century by Anton van Leeuwenhoek (1632–1723), a Dutch clockmaker, can be seen as an attempt to inspect the "little book" of nature in more detail, and hence to appreciate to a greater extent the wisdom of God in creation.

To help you interact with this text, either on your own or in group discussion, you might like to use the following framework.

1. Look up Romans 1:20, the text that plays such an important role in this document. Read it in its original context, beginning at verse 18. What point does Paul make here? How is this developed within the Belgic Confession?
2. What understanding of the relation of natural and revealed knowledge of God is set out in the document itself?
3. Might this encourage its readers to want to study nature in greater depth? And if so, for what reasons? And how might this relate to the historical observation that the natural sciences seem to have flourished in this region of Europe?

# CHAPTER 4

# *Jesus*

One of the most basic tasks of Christian theology is to clarify the identity and significance of Jesus Christ, the central figure of Christian faith. Christians have always insisted that there was something special, something qualitatively different about Jesus, which sets him apart from other religious teachers or thinkers. But what exactly is it that is special about him? This question is addressed in the area of Christian theology traditionally known as *Christology*. If theology can be understood as "trying to make sense of God," then Christology is about "trying to make sense of Jesus Christ." A related term of importance should be noted here: "soteriology" (from the Greek word *soteria*, "salvation"), meaning "making sense of salvation."

Part of the task of Christian theology is to weave together the various elements of the biblical witness to the identity and significance of Jesus. The various biblical motifs that need to be integrated in this way include:

1. The terms that the New Testament uses to refer to Jesus.
2. What Jesus is understood to have achieved, which is understood to be directly related to his identity. There is a close link between the Christian understanding of the *person* of Christ and the *work* of Christ. In other words, discussion of the *identity* of Christ is interlocked with discussion of the *achievement* of Christ. We shall explore this issue further when reflecting on salvation in the following chapter.
3. The impact that Jesus made upon people during his ministry – for example, through his healing.

*Theology: The Basics*, Third Edition. Alister E. McGrath.
© 2012 Alister E. McGrath. Published 2012 by Blackwell Publishing Ltd.

4. The resurrection, which New Testament writers interpret as an endorsement and validation of Jesus' exalted status in regard to God. Thus for Paul, the resurrection demonstrates that Jesus is the Son of God (Romans 1:3–4).

The limited space available for our discussion means that we cannot hope to explore all of these properly. However, we can at least begin to open up this fascinating area of Christian theology.

To start with, we shall reflect on some titles used to refer to Jesus by New Testament writers, and their implications for his identity.

## Messiah
*- NT*

The title "Christ" or "Messiah" is widely used to designate Jesus in the New Testament. These two words refer to the same idea, the former being the Greek version, the latter the Hebrew. (Both the Greek and Hebrew words are mentioned together in John 1:41.) When Peter recognized Jesus as "the Christ, the Son of the living God" (Matthew 16:16), he was identifying Jesus with the long-awaited Messiah. It is very easy for a modern western reader to assume that "Christ" was simply Jesus' surname, and to fail to appreciate that it is actually a title — "Jesus the Christ."

The term "Messiah" literally means "the anointed one" – someone who has been anointed with oil. This Old Testament practice indicated that the person anointed in this way was regarded as having been singled out by God as having special powers and functions. Thus a king was often referred to as "the Lord's anointed" (1 Samuel 24:6). The basic sense of the word could be said to be "the divinely appointed King of Israel." As time passed, the term gradually came to refer to a deliverer, himself a descendant of David, who would restore Israel to the golden age she enjoyed under the rule of David.

During the period of Jesus' ministry, Palestine was occupied and administered by Rome. There was fierce nationalist feeling at the time, fueled by intense resentment at the presence of a foreign occupying power, and this appears to have given a new force to the traditional expectation of the coming of the Messiah. For many,

*The Christ = the long anointed Messiah*

the Messiah would be the deliverer who expelled the Romans from Israel, and restored the royal line of David. It is clear that Jesus refused to see himself as Messiah in this sense of the term. At no point in his ministry do we find any violence against Rome suggested or condoned, nor even an explicit attack on the Roman administration. Jesus' attacks are directed primarily against his own people. Thus after his triumphal entry into Jerusalem (Matthew 21:8–11), which gives every indication of being a deliberate Messianic demonstration or gesture, Jesus immediately evicts the merchants from the temple (Matthew 21:12–13).

Jesus does not appear to have been prepared to accept the title "Messiah" in the course of his ministry. Mark's gospel should be read carefully to note this point. When Peter acclaims Jesus as Messiah – "You are the Christ!" – Jesus immediately tells him to keep quiet about it (Mark 8:29–30). It is not clear what the full significance of the "Messianic secret" is. Why should Mark emphasize that Jesus did not make an explicit claim to be the Messiah, when he was so clearly regarded as such by so many?

Perhaps the answer may be found later in Mark's gospel, when he recounts the only point at which Jesus explicitly acknowledges his identity as the Messiah. When Jesus is led, as a prisoner, before the High Priest, he admits to being the Messiah (Mark 14:61–62). Once violent or political action of any sort is no longer possible, Jesus reveals his identity. He was indeed the deliverer of the people of God – but not, it would seem, in any political sense of the term. The misunderstandings associated with the term, particularly in radical Jewish nationalist circles, appear to have caused Jesus to play down the Messianic side of his mission.

Jews did not expect their Messiah to be executed as a common criminal. It is worth noting that, immediately after Peter acknowledges Jesus as the Messiah, Jesus begins to explain to his disciples that he must suffer, be rejected by his own people, and be killed (Mark 8:29–31) – hardly an auspicious end to a messianic career. Paul made it clear to the Corinthian Christians that the very idea of "a crucified Messiah" (or "a crucified Christ") was scandalous to a Jew (1 Corinthians 1:23). From a very early stage, it is clear that Christians recognized a link between Jesus' Messiahship and the destiny of the mysterious "Suffering Servant":

He was despised, and rejected . . . A man of sorrows, acquainted with grief . . . He was despised, and we esteemed him not. Surely he has borne our griefs and carried our sorrows. Yet we esteemed him stricken, smitten by God, and afflicted. But he was wounded for our transgressions, he was bruised for our iniquities. Upon him was the chastisement that made us whole. And with his stripes we are healed . . . The Lord has laid upon him the iniquity of us all. (Isaiah 53:3–6)

## Lord

A second title which claims our attention is "Lord" (Greek: *kyrios*). The word is used in two main senses in the New Testament. It is used as a polite title of respect, particularly when addressing someone. Thus when Martha speaks to Jesus, and addresses him as "Lord" (John 11:21), she is probably, although not necessarily, merely treating Jesus with proper respect.

Of infinitely greater importance, however, are the frequent passages in the New Testament in which Jesus is referred to as "the Lord." The confession that "Jesus is Lord" (Romans 10:9; 1 Corinthians 12:3) was clearly regarded by Paul as a statement of the essential feature of the gospel. Christians are those who "call upon the name of the Lord" (Romans 10:13; 1 Corinthians 1:2). But what is implied by this? It is clear that there was a tendency in first-century Palestinian Judaism to use the word "Lord" (Greek: *kyrios*; Aramaic: *mare*) to designate a divine being, or at the very least a figure who is decidedly more than just human, in addition to its function as a polite or honorific title. But of particular importance is the use of this Greek word *kyrios* to translate the cypher of four letters used to refer to God in the Old Testament (often referred to as the "Tetragrammaton," from the Greek words for "four" and "letters"). As this point is important, we need to explore it in more detail.

The Old Testament writers were reluctant to refer to God directly, apparently regarding this as compromising his transcendence. On occasions where it was necessary to make reference to God, they tended to use a "cypher" of four letters, sometimes transliterated into English as YHWH. This group of letters, which lies behind the King James Version references to God as "Jehovah," and the Jerusalem Bible's references to God as "Yahweh," was used to represent the sacred name of God. Other Hebrew words could be used to refer to gods in general; this name was used to refer only to the "God of Abraham, Isaac, and Jacob."

This name is specific to God, almost acting as a proper name. It is never used to refer to any other divine or angelic being, unlike other Hebrew words for "god." These latter words act as common nouns, referring to "god" or "gods" in general, and can be used to refer to Israel's own God, or to other gods (such as the pagan gods of other nations). But the Tetragrammaton is used only to name the specific God which Israel knew and worshipped, and who is made known through the life, death, and resurrection of Jesus Christ. The best English translation is probably "Lord," although some translations use the term "Yahweh."

When the Old Testament was translated from Hebrew into Greek, the word *kyrios* was generally used to translate the sacred name of God. Of the 6,823 times that this name is used in the Hebrew, the Greek word *kyrios* ("Lord") is used to translate it on 6,156 occasions. This Greek word thus came to be an accepted way of referring directly and specifically to the God who had revealed himself to Israel at Sinai, and who had entered into a covenant with his people on that occasion. Jews would not use this term to refer to anyone or anything else. To do so would be to imply that this person or thing was of divine status. The historian Josephus tells us that the Jews refused to call the Roman Emperor *kyrios*, because they regarded this name as reserved for God alone.

Yet the writers of the New Testament had no hesitation in using this sacred name to refer to Jesus, with all that this implied. A name which was used exclusively to refer to God was regarded as referring equally to Jesus. This was not some error made by ill-informed writers, ignorant of the Jewish background to the name. After all, the first disciples were Jews. Those New Testament writers, such as Paul, who make most use of the term "Lord" to refer to Jesus were perfectly well aware of its implications. Yet they regarded the evidence concerning Jesus, especially his resurrection from the dead, as compelling them to make this statement concerning his identity. It was a deliberate, considered, informed, and justified decision, which is entirely appropriate in the light of the history of Jesus. He has been raised to glory and majesty, and sits at the right hand of God. He therefore shares the same status as God and is to be addressed accordingly.

# Son of God – angelic

A further title used by the New Testament to refer to Jesus is "Son of God." In the Old Testament, the term is occasionally used to refer to angelic or supernatural persons (see Psalm 8:6; Job 38:7; Daniel 3:25). Messianic texts in the Old Testament refer to the coming Messiah as the "Son of God" (2 Samuel 7:12–14; Psalm 2:7; Psalm 86:26–27). The New Testament use of the term seems to mark a development of its Old Testament meaning, with an increased emphasis upon its exclusiveness.

Although all people are children of God in some sense of the word, the New Testament holds that Jesus is *the* Son of God. Paul distinguishes between Jesus as the natural Son of God, and believers as adopted sons. Their relation to God is quite different from Jesus' relationship to him, even though both may be referred to as "sons of God." We shall explore this point further when we consider the idea of "adoption" as a way of thinking about the benefits which Christ obtained for us on the cross. Similarly, in the first letter of John, Jesus is referred to as "the Son," while believers are designated as "children." ) distinction There is something quite distinct about Jesus' relation to God, as expressed in the title "Son of God."

The New Testament understanding of Jesus' relationship to God, expressed in the Father–Son relationship, takes a number of forms. First, we note that Jesus directly addresses God as "Father," using the Aramaic word "Abba," often thought to reflect a particularly close relationship (Mark 14:36; see also Matthew 6:9; 11:25–26; 26:42; Luke 23:34, 46). Secondly, it is clear from a number of passages that the evangelists regard Jesus as the Son of God, or that Jesus treats God as his father, even if this is not stated explicitly (Mark 1:11; 9:7; 12:6; 13:32; 14:61–62; 15:39). Thirdly, John's gospel is permeated with the Father–Son relationship (note especially passages such as John 5:16–27; 17:1–26), with a remarkable emphasis upon the identity of will and purpose of the Father and Son, indicating how close the relationship between Jesus and God was understood to be by the first Christians. At every level in the New Testament – in the words of Jesus himself, or in the impression which was created among the first Christians – Jesus is clearly understood to have a unique and intimate relationship to God, which the resurrection demonstrated publicly (Romans 1:3–4).

## Son of Man   ~humanity

For many Christians, the term "Son of Man" stands as a natural counterpart to "Son of God." It is an affirmation of the humanity of Christ, just as the latter term is a complementary affirmation of his divinity. However, it is not quite as simple as this. The term "Son of Man" (Hebrew *ben adam* or Aramaic *bar nasha*) is used in three main contexts in the Old Testament:

1. As a form of address to the prophet Ezekiel.
2. To refer to a future eschatological figure (Daniel 7:13–14), whose coming signals the end of history and the coming of divine judgment.
3. To emphasize the contrast between the lowliness and frailty of human nature and the elevated status or permanence of God and the angels (Numbers 23:19; Psalm 8:14).

The third such meaning relates naturally to the humanity of Jesus, and may underlie at least some of its references in the synoptic gospels. It is, however, the second use of the term which has attracted most scholarly attention.

The German New Testament scholar Rudolf Bultmann argued that Daniel 7:13–14 pointed to the expectation of the coming of a "Son of Man" at the end of history, and argued that Jesus shared this expectation. References by Jesus to "the Son of Man coming in clouds with great power and glory" (Mark 13:26) are thus, according to Bultmann, to be understood to refer to a figure *other than* Jesus. Bultmann suggested that the early church subsequently merged "Jesus" and "Son of Man," understanding them to be the one and the same. The early church thus invented the application of the term to Jesus.

This view has not, however, commanded universal assent. Other scholars have argued that the term "Son of Man" carries a range of associations, including suffering, vindication, and judgment, thus making it natural and proper to apply it to Jesus. George Caird is one New Testament scholar to develop such an approach, arguing that Jesus used the term "to indicate his essential unity with mankind, and above all with the weak and humble, and also his special function as predestined representative of the new Israel and bearer of God's judgment and kingdom."

## God

Finally, we need to consider a group of New Testament texts which make the most important and exciting assertion of all: that Jesus is none other than God. All the other material we have considered in this chapter can be seen as pointing to this conclusion. The affirmation that Jesus is divine is the climax of the New Testament witness to the person of Jesus Christ. At least ten texts in the New Testament seem to speak explicitly of Jesus in this way (John 1:1; 1:18; 20:28; Romans 9:5; Titus 2:13; Hebrews 1:8–9; 2 Peter 1:1; 1 John 5:20). Others point in this direction, implying (though not explicitly stating) much the same conclusion (such as Matthew 1:23; John 17:3; Galatians 2:20; Ephesians 5:5; Colossians 2:2; 2 Thessalonians 1:12; and 1 Timothy 3:16).

We could continue this examination of the various titles which the New Testament employs to refer to Jesus, to illustrate the many facets of its complex witness to his identity and significance. There is, however, a danger that by doing this, we may miss seeing the wood for the trees. In other words, we will fail to see that these titles, together with the New Testament accounts of the impact Christ had upon those whom he encountered, build up to give a pattern. It is clear that the New Testament witnesses to Jesus as the embodiment of all God's promises, witnessed to in the Old Testament, brought to fulfillment and fruition.

The statements made about Jesus may be broadly listed under two classes. First, we have statements about Jesus' *function* – what God has done for us in Jesus. Second, we have statements about Jesus' *identity* – who Jesus is. The two are, of course, closely connected. His achievements are grounded in his identity; his identity is demonstrated in his achievements. As the pieces of a jigsaw puzzle build up to give a pattern, which no single piece can show on its own, so the New Testament "Christological titles" build up to give an overall picture, which no single title can adequately disclose. Taken collectively, they build

his purpose + who He is — who He is expresses His purpose

up into a rich, deep, and powerfully persuasive portrait of Christ as the divine Savior and Lord, who continues to exercise an enormous influence over, and appeal to, sinful and mortal human beings.

## Functional statements about Jesus

In addition to a wide range of New Testament statements concerning the *identity* of Jesus, there are several important passages which speak of the significance of Jesus in *functional* terms – that is to say, in terms which identify him as performing certain functions or tasks associated with God. Three groups of texts are of particular importance, as they identify the function of Jesus in terms which have clear implications for his identity.

1. *Jesus is the savior of humanity*. The Old Testament affirmed that there was only one savior of humanity – God. In the full knowledge that it was God alone who was Savior, that it was God alone who could save, the first Christians nevertheless affirmed that Jesus was Savior. As Athanasius of Alexandria (ca. 296–373) emphasized, no

*[handwritten margin notes: What He does that associates him w/ God = helping us understand His identity]*

**Figure 9**   Image of a carving of a fish as early Christian symbol, funerary graffito from Rome, 2nd–3rd century AD. Museo della Civiltà Romana, Rome. © The Art Archive/Alamy.

creature, no matter how great, can achieve this. If Jesus Christ has brought salvation to humanity, as the creed declares that he has, then he must be God. If Jesus Christ is something other than God – in other words, a creature – then whatever "salvation" he brings is not the same as that offered by God.

A fish came to be a symbol of faith to the early Christians, as the five Greek letters spelling out "fish" in Greek (I-CH-TH-U-S) came to represent the slogan "Jesus Christ, Son of God, Savior." For the New Testament, Jesus saves his people from their sins (Matthew 1:21); in his name alone is there salvation (Acts 4:12); he is the "captain of salvation" (Hebrews 2:10); he is the "Savior, who is Christ the Lord" (Luke 2:11). And in these affirmations, and others, Jesus is understood to function as God, doing something which, properly speaking, only God can do.

2. *Jesus is worshipped.* Within the Jewish context in which the first Christians operated, it was God and God alone who was to be worshipped. Paul warned the Christians at Rome that there was a constant danger that humans would worship creatures, when they ought to be worshipping their creator (Romans 1:23). Yet the early Christian church worshipped Christ as God – a practice which is clearly reflected even in the New Testament. Thus 1 Corinthians 1:2 speaks of Christians as those who "call upon the name of our Lord Jesus Christ," using language which reflects the Old Testament formulas for worshipping or adoring God (such as Genesis 4:26; 13:4; Psalm 105:1; Jeremiah 10:25; Joel 2:32). Jesus is thus clearly understood to function as God, in that he is an object of worship.

3. *Jesus reveals God.* "Anyone who has seen me, has seen the Father" (John 14:9). These remarkable words, so characteristic of John's gospel, emphasize the belief that the Father speaks and acts in the Son – in other words, that God is revealed in and by Jesus. To have seen Jesus is to have seen the Father – in other words, Jesus is understood, once more, to function as God.

These three groups of passages clearly point to an understanding of Jesus which transcends the category of pure humanity. Yet neither the New Testament writers, nor Christian theology, understand this to entail that Jesus is *not* a human being. For every biblical passage that explicitly affirms that Jesus was rather more than a human being, others can be brought forward that affirm that he was indeed a real human being. Jesus wept, suffered, became tired, and experienced human emotions.

One of the perennial tasks of Christian theology has been the clarification of the relationship between human and divine elements in the person of Jesus Christ. First, Jesus was a genuine human being. He was someone who felt pain, who wept, and who knew what it was like to be hungry and thirsty. Yet this insight, on its own, is not enough to do justice to the biblical portrait of Jesus. We must turn to the second conclusion to understand why.

In the second place, the New Testament insists that Jesus was far more than a human being. Without in any way denying the real humanity of Jesus, the New Testament declares him to be the "Son of God," "Lord," and so forth. It applies words to him which are reserved for God, and attributes actions to him which are the privilege of God alone.

## Early Christological models

From what has been said thus far, any attempt to integrate the biblical witness to the identity of Jesus of Nazareth will have to weave together a number of quite different – and, at least on the face of it, apparently contradictory – statements. On the one hand, a large group of texts affirmed that Jesus of Nazareth was indeed a human being, who knew what it was like to be thirsty, hungry, tired, and in pain. On the other hand, another large group of texts suggested that he was considerably more than a human being. What Jesus of Nazareth said and did pointed to his being, in some sense of the term, divine. The riddle that Christian theology is called to resolve is how these two elements can be held together. How could theology locate him on a conceptual map? How was it to place him along the coordinates of time and eternity, humanity and divinity, particularity and universality?

It was not an easy process, not least because the idea of someone being both God and a human being seemed completely illogical and incoherent. So what way of picturing Jesus was best adapted to safeguard and enfold the complex witness of the New Testament to his impact on people? As the church wrestled with the question of the identity of Jesus of Nazareth, there was a dawning, painful recognition that it was going to be impossible to do full justice to his identity and significance. A number of simple solutions were explored, only to be rejected, in the first period of Christian theologian reflection. We may briefly note three of these inadequate approaches.

\  *Adoptionism* maintained that Jesus was basically a human being who was anointed by the Holy Spirit in the same way as the prophets of the Old Testament, but to a greater extent. At his baptism by John the Baptist, Jesus was thus "adopted" by the Father and became God's Son. He was given a mission to preach the good news of the Kingdom, and empowered to work miracles. According to this view, Jesus belongs to the same lineage as all the prophets of the Old Testament – he was different in degree but not in kind. In one sense, this can be seen as the church taking an existing Jewish idea, and seeing if it could be adapted to make sense of Jesus of Nazareth. It did not take long to find that it was simply inadequate.

Others preferred an approach which emphasized the divinity of Jesus of Nazareth, playing down his humanity. *Docetism* (deriving from the Greek verb *dokein*, "to appear") argued that Jesus Christ was completely divine, but appeared also to be human. Although really divine, Christ presented himself to humanity as one who shared their condition. Although historians are not entirely sure that Docetism was a coherent school of thought in the early church, there are certainly grounds for suggesting that it represented some kind of theological trend or tendency, which increasingly came to be seen as inadequate. As the church came to appreciate the importance of affirming Christ's humanity – not least because of the link it secured with human nature in general – docetism came to be seen as theologically simplistic.

Perhaps the most important failed approach to the identity of Jesus was *Arianism* (which got its name from Arius (256–326), an Alexandrian writer of the fourth century). Arius held that Jesus Christ was not divine, but was supreme among God's creatures. A clear line could be drawn separating God and the creation. There were no alternatives, no "in-between" positions. And having insisted on this rigorous divide, Arius declared that Jesus of Nazareth was to be located on the creaturely, not the divine, side of this dividing line. Biblical passages that seemed to attribute divinity to Jesus were to be interpreted as honorific in intention.

His critics, including Athanasius, argued that Arius' interpretation of core biblical passages (especially some found in John's gospel) was faulty. In addition, Athanasius suggested, Arius had made the whole

~yes!.

gospel incoherent. Christian doctrines could not be isolated from each other and discussed on their own. They were like a web, with each strand connected to and supporting others. Only God could save. But the New Testament was clear that Jesus was the savior of humanity. If Jesus was not God, he could not save – and the gospel proclamation was thus inconsistent.

Again, Athanasius pointed out that Christians worshipped Jesus. But if Jesus was not God, this made them guilty of idolatry – worshipping something that was not God. Athanasius thus argued that Arius' attempt to make sense of Jesus of Nazareth was deeply flawed, failing to do justice either to the biblical witness to Jesus or to the church's actual experience of their Lord and Savior.

## The Council of Chalcedon

The Council of Chalcedon (451) was a landmark in Christian theology, bringing a long period of exploration and reflection to a close with its definitive resolution of centuries of discussion. The term "Chalcedonian Definition" is often used to refer to the fundamental idea of the two natures of Christ, which the Council stated in the following way:

> We all with one voice confess our Lord Jesus Christ to be one and the same Son, perfect in divinity and humanity, truly God and truly human, consisting of a rational soul and a body, being of one substance with the Father in relation to his divinity, and being of one substance with us in relation to his humanity, and is like us in all things apart from sin. (Hebrews 4:15)

Chalcedon allowed a generous degree of diversity on how this concept of the "two natures" of Christ was to be understood. Provided that it was recognized that Jesus Christ is both truly divine and truly human, the precise manner in which this is articulated or explored was not of fundamental importance. In part, Chalcedon's decision to insist upon the two natures of Christ, while accepting a plurality of interpretations regarding their relation, reflects the political situation of the period. At a time in which there was considerable disagreement within the church over the most reliable way of stating the "two natures of Christ," the Council was obliged to adopt a realistic approach, and give its weight to whatever consensus it could find. That consensus concerned the recognition that Christ was both divine and human, but *not* how the divine and human natures related to each other. )

The Christian doctrine of the person of Jesus Christ is often discussed in terms of "incarnation." "Incarnation" is a difficult yet important word, deriving from the Latin term for "flesh," summarizing and affirming the basic Christian belief that Jesus Christ is both divine and human. The idea of the incarnation is the climax of Christian reflection upon the mystery of Christ – the recognition that Jesus Christ reveals God; that he represents God; that he speaks as God and for God; that he acts as God and for God; that he is God. In short, we must, in the words of a first-century writer, learn to "think about Jesus as we do about God" (2 Clement 1:12). We are thus in a position to take the crucial step which underlies all Christian thinking on the incarnation – to say that, as Jesus Christ acts as God and for God in every context of importance, we should conclude that, for all intents and purposes, he is God.

## The incarnation and icons

One of the most interesting theological debates of the later patristic period took place in the eastern church, and concerned the place of icons in Christian worship and devotion. An "icon" (Greek: *eikon*) is a religious painting or picture, which is understood to act as a window through which the worshipper may catch a closer glimpse of the divine than would otherwise be possible. This practice was regarded with severe disapproval by some, who thought that the use of such images in worship was tantamount to idolatry – something that was explicitly forbidden by the Ten Commandments. A faction known as the "iconoclasts" (from the Greek words for "breaking images") wanted to eliminate icons altogether. To portray God in an image was to imply that God could be described or defined – and that was to imply an unthinkable limitation on the part of God.

Yet many writers of this age defended the use of icons on explicitly theological grounds – above all, the doctrine of the incarnation. Germanus, Patriarch of Constantinople (died ca. 733), argued vigorously for the use of icons in public worship and private devotion on the basis of the following incarnational argument. "I represent God, the invisible one, not as invisible, but in so far as God has become visible for us by participation in flesh and blood." Yet the most interesting theological argument in defense of icons is due to the theologian John of Damascus (ca. 675–ca. 749).

In a series of three treatises aimed against those who reject the use of icons, originally written in Greek in the first half of the eighth century, John of Damascus argued that the theological fact of the incarnation of Christ provides a solid foundation for the use of icons in devotion. John uses a strongly incarnational approach to defend the use of physical items – including icons – in worship and adoration. Exactly what is wrong, he asked, with using physical materials to depict or convey the spiritual? Don't Bibles use paper and ink – which are, after all, material substances – to convey divine truth? Did not Christ die on a wooden cross to save the world? In that case, material objects were implicated in the salvation of the world. And what about the incarnation? Was that not about the word becoming flesh – about the immaterial assuming materiality? And what about the bread and wine in the eucharist? They were material objects, yet capable of mediating spiritual realities. So it is with icons.

Yet John has another theological card to play, again involving the incarnation. The incarnation both legitimates the use of material objects as devotional aids, and allows us to depict God. Before the coming of Christ, this was impossible. Since Christ is the "image (Greek: *eikon*) of the invisible God" (Colossians 1:15), icons may be used to represent him. As John put it:

> [Before the incarnation] there was absolutely no way in which God, who has neither a body nor a face, could be represented by any image. But now that he has made himself visible in the flesh and has lived with people, I can make an image of what I have seen of God. I do not worship matter; I worship the Creator of matter, who became matter for my sake, and who worked out my salvation through matter.

## Christ as mediator

So how are we to conceive the identity of Christ? What models or analogies may be helpful as we try to visualize the place of Jesus Christ on the map of divine and human possibilities? In this section, we shall explore one New Testament title for Christ which is relatively easy to grasp, and consider its implications. The New Testament refers to Christ as a *mediator* between God and humanity at several points (Hebrews 9:15; 1 Timothy 2:5). Christ is here understood to mediate between a transcendent God and fallen humanity.

So what is mediated? Two basic complementary answers are given within the New Testament, and the long tradition of Christian theological engagement with scripture: *revelation* and *salvation*. Christ mediates both *knowledge of God* and *fellowship with God*. —— *knowing him relational*

The so-called "*Logos*-Christology" of Justin Martyr and other early patristic writers is an excellent instance of the notion of the mediation of knowledge of God through Christ. The *Logos* is understood to be a mediating principle which bridges the gap between a transcendent God and God's creation. Although present in a transient manner in the Old Testament prophets, the *Logos* becomes incarnate in Christ, and thus provides a point of mediation between God and humanity. A related approach is found in Emil Brunner's *The Mediator* (1927), and in a more developed form in his 1938 work *Truth as Encounter*. In the latter, Brunner argued that faith was primarily an encounter with the God who meets us personally in Jesus Christ.

Other writers have stressed the importance of Christ as the one who mediates salvation. This approach can be seen in John Calvin's *Institutes* (1559). Christ is here seen as a unique channel or focus, through which God's redeeming work is directed toward and made available to humanity. Humanity, as originally created by God, was good in every respect. On account of the Fall, natural human gifts and faculties have been radically impaired. As a consequence, both the human reason and human will are contaminated by sin. Unbelief is thus seen as an act of will as much as of reason; it is not simply a failure to discern the hand of God within the created order, but a deliberate decision *not* to discern it and *not* to obey God.

Calvin develops the consequences of this at two distinct, although clearly related, levels. At the revelational level, humans lack the necessary rational and volitional resources to discern God fully within the created order. There are obvious parallels here with the *Logos*-Christology of Justin Martyr. At the soteriological level, humans lack what is required in order to be saved; they do not *want* to be

**Figure 10**  Engraved portrait of John Calvin (1509–64), author of the *Institutes of the Christian Religion*. © Fred de Noyelle/ Godong/Corbis.

saved (on account of the debilitation of the mind and will through sin), and they are *incapable* of saving themselves (in that salvation presupposes obedience to God, now impossible on account of sin). True knowledge of God and salvation must both therefore come from outside the human situation. In such a manner, Calvin lays the foundations for his doctrine of the mediatorship of Jesus Christ.

Calvin's analysis of the knowledge of God and of human sin lays the foundation for his Christology. Jesus Christ is the mediator between God and humanity. In order to act as such a mediator, Jesus Christ must be both divine and human. In that it was impossible for us to ascend to God, on account of our sin, God chose to descend to us instead. Unless Jesus Christ was himself a human being, other human beings could not benefit from his presence or activity. "The Son of God became the Son of Man, and received what is ours in such a way that he transferred to us what is his, making that which is his by nature to become ours through grace."

Calvin's stress upon the mediatorial presence of God in Christ leads him to insist upon a close connection between the person and the work of Christ. Drawing on a tradition going back to Eusebius of Caesarea (ca. 260–ca. 340), Calvin argues that Christ's work may be summarized under three offices or ministries (the *munus triplex Christi*) – prophet, priest, and king. The basic argument is that Jesus Christ brings together in his person the three great mediatorial offices of the Old Testament. In his *prophetic* office, Christ is the herald and witness of God's grace. He is a teacher endowed with divine wisdom and authority. In his *kingly* office, Christ has inaugurated a kingship which is heavenly, not earthly; spiritual, not physical. This kingship is exercised over believers through the action of the Holy Spirit. Finally, through his *priestly* office, Christ is able to reinstate us within the divine favor, through offering his death as a satisfaction for our sin.

In all these respects, Christ brings to fulfillment the mediatorial ministries of the Old Covenant, allowing them to be seen in a new and clearer light as they find their fulfillment in his mediatorship.

## Engaging with a text

Dorothy L. Sayers (1893–1957) is perhaps best known for her crime novels, which introduced the world to Lord Peter Wimsey, an amateur aristocratic sleuth. However, she also developed a considerable interest in Christian theology, as many of her writings make clear. One of these takes the form of a lecture given in 1940, during World War II, on the importance of the creeds. Sayers offered an important and penetrating analysis of the relation of the divinity and humanity of Christ in this lecture, which was later published in a collection entitled *Creed or Chaos?* (1947).

Sayers' basic theme in this lecture is that it is not good enough to agree that Jesus had some useful ideas, unless we have good reasons for asserting that there is something distinctive about Jesus which requires us to take those ideas with compelling seriousness. Hence, Sayers argues, the great questions of Christology are inevitable, and must be addressed. Using the rise of Nazism in Germany under Adolf Hitler during the 1930s as an example, she argues that claims to moral or cultural authority must be grounded in something intrinsic to the person of Christ. Otherwise, Christ will be judged by moral and cultural principles, instead of judging them, by acting as their foundation and criterion.

> It is quite useless to say that it doesn't matter particularly who or what Christ was or by what authority He did those things, and that even if He was only a man, He was a very nice man and we ought to live by His principles: for that is merely Humanism, and if the "average man" in Germany chooses to think that Hitler is a nicer sort of man with still more attractive principles, the Christian Humanist has no answer to make...
> The central dogma of the Incarnation is that by which relevance stands or falls. If Christ was only man, then He is entirely irrelevant to any thought about God; if He is only God, then He is entirely irrelevant to any experience of human life... Teachers and preachers never, I think,

make it sufficiently clear that dogmas are not a set of arbitrary regulations invented *a priori* by a committee of theologians enjoying a bout of all-in dialectical wrestling. Most of them were hammered out under pressure of urgent practical necessity to provide an answer to heresy.

You may find the following questions helpful in interacting with this text, either on your own or in a group discussion.

1. Read through the opening paragraph. What point does Sayers make here? What is her fundamental criticism of "Christian Humanism"? How does she understand the question of the *identity* of Christ to shape our thinking on his relevance to life?
2. Consider this citation: "If Christ was only man, then He is entirely irrelevant to any thought about God; if He is only God, then He is entirely irrelevant to any experience of human life." Locate this statement within the text. How does Sayers arrive at this conclusion? And how does she further develop the ideas contained in it?
3. Read through the concluding section of the extract. Some argue that doctrines about Jesus – for example, that he is both divine and human – just make a simple gospel unnecessarily complicated. What do you think Sayers might say in response to such objections?

CHAPTER 5

# Salvation

A central theme of the Christian message is that the human situation
has, in some way, been transformed by the death and resurrection of
Jesus Christ. This is often described as "salvation." Although the word
"salvation" has a very specific meaning, as we shall see in a moment,
it is often used in a more general sense.

It is important to appreciate that the term "salvation" does not
necessarily have any specifically *Christian* reference. It can be used in a
thoroughly secular manner. For example, it was common for Soviet
writers, especially during the late 1920s, to speak of Lenin as the
"savior" of the Russian people. Military coups in African states during
the 1980s frequently resulted in the setting up of "councils of salvation," which would try to restore political and economic stability.
Salvation can thus be a purely secular notion, concerned with political
emancipation or the general human quest for liberation.

Even at the religious level, salvation is not a specifically Christian
idea. Many – but not, it must be stressed, all – of the world's religions
have concepts of salvation. They differ enormously, in relation to both
their understanding of how that salvation is achieved, and the shape or
form which it is understood to take.

In turning to explore the theology of salvation, we need to engage
with two questions. First, there is the question of how "salvation" itself is
to be understood. In what way is the Christian understanding of the
nature of salvation *distinctive*? Second, there is the question of how
salvation is possible, and in particular how it is grounded in the history
of Jesus Christ. Or, to put this another way: what is the basis of salvation,

*Theology: The Basics*, Third Edition. Alister E. McGrath.
© 2012 Alister E. McGrath. Published 2012 by Blackwell Publishing Ltd.

according to Christianity? Both these questions have been the subject of intense discussion throughout Christian history, and we shall briefly consider some themes to emerge from this debate in what follows.

We begin by considering the first of these questions: what *is* salvation? One way of beginning a discussion of this issue is to look at some images of salvation used in Paul's letters.

## Pauline images of salvation

Throughout his letters, Paul uses a rich range of images to illuminate and clarify what benefits Christ secures for believers. He clearly assumes that his readers will be able to grasp what these analogies were meant to convey. In what follows, we shall explore some of these, and try to appreciate their importance.

The first image is that of *salvation* itself. The term has a number of meanings, including release from danger or captivity, and being delivered from some form of fatal illness. Notions such as "healing" and "liberation" can be seen as embraced by this important Pauline term. Augustine of Hippo suggested that the church was like a hospital, in that it was full of people who were in the process of being healed. Paul sees salvation as having past (e.g., Romans 8:24), present (e.g., 1 Corinthians 1:18), and future (e.g., Romans 13:11) dimensions. The word "salvation" thus refers to something that has already happened in the past, to something that is happening in the present, and to something that will happen in the future.

A second image of importance is that of *adoption*. At several points, Paul speaks of Christians as having been "adopted" into the family of God (Romans 8:15, 23; Galatians 4:5). It is widely thought that Paul is here drawing on a legal practice, common in Greco-Roman culture (yet, interestingly, not recognized within traditional Jewish law). According to many interpreters of Paul, to speak of "believers" having been adopted into the family of God is to make the point that believers share the same inheritance rights as Jesus Christ, and will hence receive the glory which Christ achieved (although only after first sharing in his sufferings).

At the time of the Reformation in the sixteenth century, many came to place particular importance on the image of *justification*. Especially in those letters dealing with the relation of Christianity to

Judaism (such as Galatians and Romans), Paul affirms that believers have been "justified through faith" (e.g., Romans 5:1–2). This is widely held to involve a change in a believer's legal status in the sight of God, and their ultimate assurance of acquittal before God, despite their sinfulness. The term "justification" and the verb "to justify" thus came to signify "entering into a right relationship with God," or perhaps "being made righteous in the sight of God."

A fourth image is that of *redemption*. This term primarily bears the sense of "secure someone's release through payment." In the ancient world which acted as the backdrop to Paul's thought, the term could be used to refer to the liberation of prisoners of war, or to the securing of liberty of those who had sold themselves into slavery, often to pay off a family debt. Paul's basic idea appears to be that the death of Christ secures the freedom of believers from slavery to the law or to death, in order that they might become slaves of God instead (1 Corinthians 6:20; 7:23).

## The problem of analogy: salvation as ransom

In an earlier chapter, we noted how the theological use of analogies raised some interesting questions. How far can these analogies be pressed? For example, in thinking of God as "father," are we implying that God is male? A similar issue arises in connection with thinking about salvation, and we shall explore the question by looking at the image of salvation as a "ransom."

The image of Christ's death as a ransom came to be of central importance to Greek patristic writers, such as Irenaeus of Lyons. The New Testament speaks of Jesus giving his life as a "ransom" for sinners (Mark 10:45; 1 Timothy 2:6). So what are the implications of this image? The word "ransom" suggests three related ideas:

1. *Liberation.* A ransom is something which achieves freedom for a person who is held in captivity.
2. *Payment.* A ransom is a sum of money which is paid in order to achieve someone's liberation.
3. *Someone to whom the ransom is paid.* A ransom is usually paid to a person's captor.

There is no doubt that the New Testament proclaims that we have been liberated from captivity through the death and resurrection of Jesus. We have been set free from captivity to sin and the fear of death (Romans 8:21; Hebrews 2:15). It is also clear that the New Testament understands the death of Jesus as the price which had to be paid to achieve our liberation (1 Corinthians 6:20; 7:23). In both these respects, the scriptural use of "redemption" corresponds to the everyday use of the word. But what of the third aspect?

The New Testament nowhere suggests that Jesus' death was the price paid to someone (such as the devil) to achieve our liberation. Some patristic writers, however, assumed that they could press this analogy to its limits, and declared that God had delivered us from the power of the devil by offering him Jesus as the price of our liberation. *Who gives us access to Salvation?*

Origen (ca. 185–ca. 254), perhaps the most speculative of early patristic writers, was one such writer. If Christ's death was a ransom, Origen argued, it must have been paid to someone. But to whom? It could not have been paid to God, in that God was not holding sinners to ransom. Therefore, it had to be paid to the devil.

*Dibs on humanity* Gregory the Great (ca. 540–604) developed this idea still further. The devil had acquired rights over fallen humanity, which God was obliged to respect. The only means by which humanity could be released from this satanic domination and oppression was through the devil exceeding the limits of his authority, and thus being obliged to forfeit his rights. So how could this be achieved? Gregory suggests that it could come about if a sinless person were to enter the world, yet in the form of a normal sinful person. The devil would not notice until it was too late. In claiming authority over this sinless person, the devil would have overstepped the limits of his authority, and thus be obliged to forfeit his rights.

Gregory suggests the image of a baited hook, with Christ's humanity being the bait, and his divinity the hook. The devil, like a great sea-monster, snaps at the bait – and then discovers, too late, the hook. "The bait tempts in order that the hook may wound. Our Lord therefore, when coming for the redemption of humanity, made a kind of hook of himself for the death of the devil." Other writers explored other images for the same idea – that of trapping the devil. Christ's death was like a net for catching birds, or a trap for catching mice. It was this aspect of this approach to the meaning of the cross that caused the most disquiet subsequently. It seemed that God was guilty of deception.

*hooked the Devil*

This theme is probably best seen in the writings of Rufinus of Aquileia (ca. 345–410), particularly his exposition of the Apostles' Creed, which dates from around the year 400:

> [The purpose of the incarnation] was that the divine virtue of the Son of God might be like a kind of hook hidden beneath the form of human flesh . . . to lure on the prince of this world to a contest; that the Son might offer him his human flesh as a bait and that the divinity which lay underneath might catch him and hold him fast with its hook . . . Then, just as a fish when it seizes a baited hook not only fails to drag off the bait but is itself dragged out of the water to serve as food for others; so he that had the power of death seized the body of Jesus in death, unaware of the hook of divinity which lay hidden inside. Having swallowed it, he was immediately caught. The gates of hell were broken, and he was, as it were, drawn up from the pit, to become food for others.

The imagery of victory over the devil proved to have enormous popular appeal. The medieval idea of "the harrowing of hell" bears witness to its power. According to this, after dying upon the cross, Christ descended to hell, and broke down its gates in order that the imprisoned souls might go free. The idea rested (rather tenuously, it has to be said) upon 1 Peter 3:18–22, which makes reference to Christ "preaching to the spirits in prison."

The hymn "Ye Choirs of New Jerusalem," written by Fulbert of Chartres (died 1028), expresses this theme in two of its verses, picking up the theme of Christ as the "lion of Judah" (Revelation 5:5) defeating Satan, the serpent (Genesis 3:15):

> For Judah's lion bursts his chains
> Crushing the serpent's head;
> And cries aloud through death's domain
> To wake the imprisoned dead.
>
> Devouring depths of hell their prey
> At his command restore;
> His ransomed hosts pursue their way
> Where Jesus goes before.

**Figure 11**    Albrecht Dürer's *The Harrowing of Hell*, 1510 (or Christ's Descent into Hell/Christ in Limbo), woodcut, 39.2 × 28 cm. AKG Images.

A similar idea is found in *Piers the Plowman*, one of the most important English-language poems of the fourteenth century. In this poem, Piers falls asleep, and dreams of Christ throwing open the gates of Hell, and speaking the following words to Satan:

> Here is my soul as a ransom for all these sinful souls, to redeem those that are worthy. They are mine; they came from me, and therefore I have the better claim on them . . . You, by falsehood and crime and against all justice, took away what was mine, in my own domain; I, in fairness, recover them by paying the ransom, and by no other means. What you got by guile is won back by grace . . . And as a tree caused Adam and all mankind to die, so my gallows-tree shall bring them back to life.

# Theories of atonement

Having examined some biblical imagery for salvation, and how it is to be interpreted, we may now turn to consider how these themes have been explored and developed within the Christian theological tradition. This area of Christian theology is traditionally described as "theories of the atonement." The word "atonement" can be traced back to 1526, when the English writer William Tyndale (ca. 1494–1536) was confronted with the task of translating the New Testament into English. There was, at that time, no English word which meant "reconciliation." Tyndale thus had to invent such a word – "at-one-ment." This word soon came to bear the meaning "the benefits which Jesus Christ brings to believers through his death upon the cross." This unfamiliar word is rarely used in modern English, and has a distinctively old-fashioned feel to it. Rather than convey the impression that Christian thought is totally out of date, theologians now generally prefer to speak of this area as "the doctrine of the work of Christ."

In what follows, we shall look at three approaches to the cross which have played a significant role in Christian theology. They illustrate some aspects of Christian reflection on this important theme.

## The cross as sacrifice

In the first place, the New Testament, drawing on Old Testament imagery and expectations, presents Christ's death upon the cross as a sacrifice. This approach, which is especially associated with the Letter to the Hebrews, presents Christ's sacrificial offering as an effective and perfect sacrifice, which was able to accomplish that which the sacrifices of the Old Testament were only able to intimate, rather than achieve. In particular, Paul's use of the Greek term *hilasterion*, often translated as "mercy seat" (Romans 3:25), is also important here, as it is drawn from the Old Testament sacrificial rituals dealing with the purging of sin.

This idea is developed subsequently within the Christian tradition. In order for humanity to be restored to God, the mediator must sacrifice himself; without this sacrifice, such restoration is an impossibility. Athanasius argues that Christ's sacrifice was superior to those required under the Old Covenant in several respects:

> Christ offers a sacrifice which is trustworthy, of permanent effect, and which is unfailing in its nature. The sacrifices which were offered according to the Law were not trustworthy, since they had to be offered every day, and were again in need of purification. In contrast, the Savior's sacrifice was offered once only, and was accomplished in its entirety, and can thus be relied upon permanently.

This point is developed further in Athanasius' *Festal Letters*, written annually to celebrate the feast of Easter. In these letters, Athanasius develops the New Testament idea that there is an important analogy between the death of Christ on the cross and the sacrifice of a lamb during the Jewish festival of the Passover, commemorating Israel's deliverance from Egypt.

In his *Festal Letter VII* (written in 335), Athanasius explored the idea of Christ's sacrifice in terms of the passover sacrifice of the lamb:

> [Christ], being truly of God the Father, became incarnate for our sakes, so that he might offer himself to the Father in our place, and redeem us through his offering and sacrifice... This is he who, in former times, was sacrificed as a lamb, having been foreshadowed in that lamb. But afterwards, he was slain for us. "For Christ, our passover, is sacrificed." (1 Corinthians 5:7)

Augustine of Hippo brought new clarity to the whole discussion of the nature of Christ's sacrifice through his crisp and highly influential definition of a sacrifice, set out in *City of God*: "A true sacrifice is offered in every action which is designed to unite us to God in a holy fellowship." On the basis of this definition, Augustine has no difficulties in speaking of Christ's death as a sacrifice: "By his death, which is indeed the one and most true sacrifice offered for us, he purged, abolished, and extinguished whatever guilt there was by which the principalities and powers lawfully detained us to pay the penalty." In this sacrifice, Christ was both victim and priest; he offered himself up as a sacrifice: "He offered sacrifice for our sins. And where did he find that offering, the pure victim that he would offer? He offered himself, in that he could find no other."

This understanding of the sacrifice of Christ would become of decisive importance throughout the Middle Ages, and would shape western understandings of Christ's death. In view of Augustine's significance, we may cite in full the passage which is often singled out as the most succinct expression of his thoughts on this matter:

Thus the true Mediator, who "took the form of a servant" and was thus made "the mediator between God and humanity, the person Christ Jesus" (1 Timothy 2:5), receives the sacrifice in the "form of God" (Philippians 2:7, 8), in union with the Father, with whom he is one God. And yet, in the "form of a servant," he determined to be himself that sacrifice, rather than to receive it, in order to prevent anyone from thinking that such a sacrifice should be offered to any creature. Thus he is both the priest, who made the offering himself, and the oblation.

**Figure 12** Giovanni Bellini, *Crucifixion*, ca. 1470, wood, 71 × 63 cm. Musée du Louvre, Paris. AKG Images/Erich Lessing.

Hugh of St. Victor (died 1142), writing in the early twelfth century, found the imagery of "sacrifice" helpful in explaining the inner logic of the workings of Christ's death on the cross. Christ was able to be an effective sacrifice for human sin precisely because he was able to bring our fallen sinful nature before God:

> From our nature, he took a victim for our nature, so that the whole burnt offering which was offered up might come from that which is ours. He did this so that the redemption to be offered might have a connection with us, through its being taken from what is ours. We are truly made to be partakers in this redemption as we are united through faith to the redeemer who has entered into fellowship with us through his flesh.

The efficacy of Christ's sacrifice thus rested on his humanity, as well as his divinity.

## The cross as a victory

The second way of approaching the meaning of the cross integrates a series of biblical passages focusing upon the notion of a divine victory over hostile forces. The New Testament declares that God has given us a victory through the resurrection of Jesus Christ. "Thanks be to God, who gives us the victory through our Lord Jesus Christ" (1 Corinthians 15:57). The early church gloried in the triumph of Christ upon the cross, and the victory that he won over sin, death, and Satan. But in what way may this victory be understood? Who is it who has been defeated? And how?

Christian writers of the first five centuries were deeply attracted by the imagery of Christ gaining a victory through the cross. It was clear to them that Christ had defeated death, sin, and the devil. Just as David killed Goliath with his own weapons, so Christ defeated sin with its weapon – death. Through an apparent defeat, victory was gained over a host of hidden forces which tyrannized humanity.

Patristic writers such as Athanasius and Augustine of Hippo used a number of central images to explore the nature of human captivity to sin, and the manner in which we have been liberated by Christ's death and resurrection. We were held in bondage by the fear of death. We were imprisoned by sin. We were trapped by the power of the devil.

With great skill, these writers built up a coherent picture of the human dilemma. Human beings are held prisoner by hostile forces, and are unable to break free unaided. Someone was required who would break into their prison, and set them free. Someone from outside the human situation would have to enter into our predicament, and liberate us. Someone would have to cut the bonds which held us captive. Time and time again, the same theme is restated: we are trapped in our situation, and our only hope lies in liberation from outside.

According to this approach, through his death and resurrection, Christ has confronted and disarmed the host of hostile forces which collectively held us in captivity. The cross and resurrection represent a dramatic act of divine liberation, in which God delivers his people from captivity to hostile powers, as he once delivered his people Israel from bondage in Egypt. The second-century writer Irenaeus of Lyons put it like this: "The Word of God was made flesh in order that he might destroy death and bring us to life. For we were tied and bound in sin, we were born in sin, and we live under the dominion of death."

This note of triumph led to the appropriation of an image drawn from Roman culture of the late classical period in Christian depictions of the benefits won by Christ on the cross. The victory of Christ was depicted as a great triumphant procession, comparable to those of ancient Rome, in which the great military achievements of its heroes were celebrated. In its classical form, the triumphal parade proceeded the victorious hero from the Campus Martius through the streets of Rome, finally ending up at the temple of Jupiter on the Capitoline Hill. The parade was led by the general's soldiers, often carrying placards with slogans describing the general and his achievements, or showing maps of the territories he conquered. Other soldiers led carts containing booty that would be turned over to Rome's treasury. A section of the parade included prisoners, often the leaders of the defeated cities or countries, bound in chains.

It was a small step for Christian writers to transform this imagery into the proclamation of Christ as the conquering hero. This powerful symbolism was firmly grounded in the New Testament, which spoke of the victorious Christ as "making captivity a captive" (Ephesians 4:8). While this theme can be seen in some Christian art of this early period, its most dramatic impact was upon the hymnody of the time. One of the greatest hymns of the Christian church, dating from this period, portrays Christ's triumphant procession and celebrates his defeat of his foes.

The hymn-writer Venantius Honorius Clementianus Fortunatus (ca. 530–ca. 610) was born in Ceneda, near Treviso, in northern Italy. He became a Christian at an early age, and went on to study at Ravenna and Milan. He gained a reputation for excellence in poetry and rhetoric, and went on to become elected bishop of Poitiers around 599. He is chiefly remembered for his poem *Vexilla regis prodeunt* – "the royal banners go forth." According to a well-established tradition, in the year 569, St. Radegunde presented a large fragment of what was believed to be the true Cross to the town of Poitiers, in southern Gaul. Radegunde had obtained this fragment from the Emperor Justin II. Fortunatus was the one chosen to receive the relic on its arrival at Poitiers. When the bearers of the holy fragment were some two miles distant from the town, Fortunatus, with a great gathering of believers and enthusiasts – some of whom were carrying banners, crosses, and other sacred emblems – went forth to meet them. As they marched, they sang this hymn, which Fortunatus had composed for the occasion. This was soon incorporated into the passiontide office of the western church, and is still widely used today in marking Holy Week within western Christianity.

> The royal banners forward go,
> The cross shines forth in mystic glow;
> Where He in flesh, our flesh Who made,
> Our sentence bore, our ransom paid.
>
> O tree of glory, tree most fair,
> Ordained those holy limbs to bear,
> How bright in purple robe it stood,
> The purple of a Savior's blood!
>
> Upon its arms, like balance true,
> He weighed the price for sinners due,
> The price which none but He could pay,
> And spoiled the spoiler of his prey.

(Incidentally, we should note here the importance of Christian hymns and songs as means of making doctrinal statements memorable and accessible to congregations. The hymnbooks of the Christian church are often its most important and most memorable statements of doctrine.)

## The cross and forgiveness

A third approach to the meaning of the death of Christ integrates a series of biblical passages dealing with notions of judgment and forgiveness. The understanding of the work of Christ outlined above has enormous attractions, not least on account of its highly dramatic character. It also, however, has some serious weaknesses. For the eleventh-century writer Anselm of Canterbury, two weaknesses were of particular importance. In the first place, it failed to explain why God should wish to redeem us. And, in the second, it was of little value in understanding how Jesus Christ was involved in the process of redemption. Anselm felt that more explanation was required.

To meet this need, he developed an approach to the work of Christ which centers upon the rectitude of the created order. God created the world in a certain way, which expresses the divine nature. God also created human beings in order that they might have fellowship in eternity with their creator. This purpose, however, would seem to have been frustrated by human sin, which comes as a barrier between humanity and God. A fundamental disruption has thus been introduced into creation. Its moral ordering has been violated. The redemption of humanity is thus called for, in order that the natural rectitude of the created order may be restored. In this sense, Anselm understands redemption as a restoration of humanity to its original status within creation.

How, then, can we be redeemed? Anselm stresses that God is obliged to redeem us in a way that is consistent with the moral ordering of the creation, reflecting God's own nature. God cannot create the universe in one way, as an expression of God's will and nature, and then violate its moral order by acting in a completely different way in the redemption of humanity. God must redeem us in a way that is consistent with God's own nature and purposes. Redemption must, in the first place, be moral, and in the second, be *seen* to be moral. God cannot employ one standard of morality at one point, and another later on. God is therefore under a self-imposed obligation to respect the moral order of the creation.

Having established this point, Anselm then considers how redemption is possible. The basic dilemma can be summarized as follows. God cannot restore us to fellowship with him, without first dealing with human sin. Sin is a disruption of the moral ordering of the universe. It represents the rebellion of the creation against its creator. It represents an insult and an offense to God. The situation must therefore be made right before fellowship between God and humanity can be restored. God must therefore "make good" the situation in a way that is consistent with both the divine mercy and the divine righteousness. Anselm thus introduces the concept of a "satisfaction" – a payment or other action which compensates for the offense of human sin. Once this satisfaction has been made, the situation can revert to normal. But this satisfaction must first be made.

The problem, Anselm observes, is that human beings do not have the ability to make this satisfaction. It lies beyond their resources. They need to make it – but they cannot. Humanity ought to make satisfaction for its sins, but cannot. God is under no obligation to make satisfaction – but God could do this, if it was appropriate. Therefore, Anselm argues, if God were to become a human being, the resulting God-person would have both the *obligation* (as a human being) and the *ability* (as God) to make the necessary satisfaction. Thus the incarnation leads to a just solution to the human dilemma. The death of Jesus Christ upon the cross demonstrates God's total opposition to sin, while at the same time providing the means by which sin could be really and truly forgiven, and the way opened to renewed fellowship between humanity and God.

The basic idea is that the value of the satisfaction thus offered had to be equivalent to the weight of human sin. Anselm argued that the Son of God became incarnate in order that Christ, as God incarnate, would possess both the human *obligation* to pay the satisfaction, and the divine *ability* to pay a satisfaction of the magnitude necessary for redemption. This idea is faithfully reproduced by Mrs. Cecil F. Alexander (1818–95) in her famous nineteenth-century hymn *There Is a Green Hill Far Away*:

> There was no other good enough
> To pay the price of sin;
> He only could unlock the gate
> Of heaven, and let us in.

The theological basis of the notion of "satisfaction" was developed further in the thirteenth century by Thomas Aquinas. Aquinas grounds the adequacy of the "satisfaction of Christ" to compensate for human sin in three considerations.

A proper satisfaction comes about when someone offers to the person offended something which gives him a delight greater than his hatred of the offense. Now Christ by suffering as a result of love and obedience offered to God something greater than what might be exacted in compensation for the whole offense of humanity; firstly, because of the greatness of the love, as a result of which he suffered; secondly, because of the worth of the life which he laid down for a satisfaction, which was the life of God and of a human being; thirdly, because of the comprehensiveness of his passion and the greatness of the sorrow which he took upon himself.

Aquinas here follows Anselm in arguing that the inherent worth of Christ's death is grounded in his divinity. Why is Christ's death so significant, and possessed of a capacity to redeem us? Because, Aquinas argues, he – and he alone – is God incarnate. As Aquinas puts it, "the worth of Christ's flesh is to be reckoned, not just according to the nature of flesh but according to the person who assumed it, in that it was the flesh of God, from whom it gained an infinite worth." In response to the question of why the death of one person should have possessed such saving significance, Aquinas points out that Christ's significance in this matter does not rest on his humanity, but on his divinity.

Nevertheless, despite this emphasis on the divinity of Christ, it is clear that Aquinas has taken care to ensure that the importance of the humanity of Christ should not be overlooked. The first and third of his three considerations can each be argued to give a significant place to Christ's humanity in the process of redemption, by stressing the saving importance of Christ's love and suffering. Anselm tended to treat Christ's humanity as little more than the means by which Christ was able to justly bear the penalty due for human sin; Aquinas is thus able to offer a more positive assessment of the soteriological role of the humanity of Christ.

But how does Christ's achievement upon the cross affect us? In what way do we share in the benefits of his death and resurrection? Anselm felt that this point did not require discussion, and so gave no guidance on the matter. Later writers, however, felt that it needed to be addressed. Three main ways of understanding how believers relate to Christ in this manner may be noted.

*Participation.* Through faith, believers participate in Jesus Christ. They are "in Christ," to use Paul's famous phrase. They are caught up in him, and share in his risen life. As a result of this, they share in all the benefits won by Christ, through his obedience upon the cross.

*Representation.* Christ is the covenant representative of humanity. Through faith, we come to stand within the covenant between God and humanity. All that Christ has won for us is available to us, on account of the covenant. Just as God entered into a covenant with Israel, so God has entered into a similar covenant with his church. Christ, by his obedience upon the cross, represents God's covenant people, winning benefits for them as their representative. By coming to faith, individuals come to stand within the covenant, and thus participate in all its benefits, won by Christ.

*Substitution.* Christ is here understood to be our substitute. We ought to have been crucified, on account of our sins; Christ is crucified in our place. God allows Christ to stand in our place, taking his guilt upon himself, in order that Christ's righteousness, won by obedience upon the cross, might become ours.

## Salvation, sin, and Christ

What is sin? Although in everyday language the word "sin" means something like "a moral failing" or "an immoral act," the term has a more precise theological meaning. The fundamental sense of "sin" is something that separates humanity from God. Salvation is the breaking down of the barrier of separation between humanity and God on account of Christ. Many Christian theologians see this anticipated or symbolized in an incident that took place at the time of Christ's death – the rending of the temple curtain (Matthew 27:51). As this curtain separated the "holy of holies" from ordinary people, it could be taken to point to the removal of barriers between humanity and God through the death of Christ.

Sin is thus the antithesis of salvation. It is quite simple to develop a list of fundamental New Testament concepts of salvation, and link them with their corresponding concepts of sin. Some examples will help make this point.

| Sin | Salvation |
| --- | --- |
| Alienation | Reconciliation |
| Captivity | Liberation |
| Guilt | Forgiveness |
| Condemnation | Vindication |
| Illness | Healing |
| Being lost | Being found |

So how does this connection between sin and salvation show itself in the person of Jesus Christ, as the savior of humanity? How does the saving work of Christ relate to the human predicament? This question was addressed by the Byzantine theologian Nicholas Cabasilas (born ca. 1322), who argued that Christ's death took place in such a way that he was able to deal with each of the three afflictions of sinful humanity – namely, its transient and finite human nature, its sinful character, and its ultimate fate of death. In each of these respects, Cabasilas argued, Christ entered into the human situation, and transformed it. By becoming incarnate, he transformed human nature. By dying on the cross, he defeated sin. And through his resurrection, Christ defeated the power of death. By doing all these three things, Christ abolished the obstacles in the way of humanity returning to God, and sharing fellowship with its creator and redeemer.

A somewhat different approach emerged in reformed theology during the sixteenth and seventeenth centuries, although the ideas can be traced back much earlier than this. This approach is normally referred to as the "threefold office of Christ," referring to the three roles or functions that Christ plays in the drama of redemption. Christ, it is argued, brought to fulfillment the three great "offices" or "roles" of the Old Testament – the prophet, priest, and king.

These three categories were seen as a convenient summary of all that Jesus Christ had achieved in order to redeem his people. Jesus is prophet (Matthew 21:11; Luke 7:16), priest (Hebrews 2:17; 3:1), and king (Matthew 21:5; 27:11), bringing together in his one person the three great offices of the Old Testament. Jesus is the prophet who, like Moses, would see God face to face (Deuteronomy 17:15); he is the king who, like David, will establish a new people of God, and reign over them in justice and compassion (2 Samuel 7:12–16);

he is the priest who will cleanse his people of their sins. Thus the three gifts brought to Jesus by the Magi (or Wise Men: Matthew 2:1–12) were seen as reflecting these three functions.

The seventeenth-century Genevan theologian François Turrettini (1623–87) set out this approach with particular clarity. Identifying the threefold crisis of humanity as consisting of "ignorance, guilt, and bondage to sin," Turrettini argues that Christ meets each of these needs, and transforms them through the redemption that he achieved through his cross and resurrection.

> The threefold misery of humanity resulting from sin (that is, ignorance, guilt, and the oppression and bondage of sin) required this threefold office. Ignorance is healed through the prophetic office, guilt through the priestly, and the oppression and bondage of sin through the kingly. The prophetic light scatters the darkness of error; the merit of the priest removes guilt and obtains reconciliation for us; the power of the king takes away the bondage of sin and death. The prophet shows God to us; the priest leads us to God; and the king joins us together with God, and glorifies us with him. The prophet illuminates the mind by the spirit of enlightenment; the priest soothes the heart and conscience by the spirit of consolation; the king subdues rebellious inclinations by the spirit of sanctification.

This pattern became widespread in later reformed theology, as can be seen from the writings of the great nineteenth-century Princeton theologian, Charles Hodge (1797–1878). For Hodge, fallen humanity needs "a Savior who is a prophet to instruct us; a priest to atone and to make intercession for us; and a king to rule over and protect us."

## Salvation, Christ, and the redeemed life

As we have seen, one aspect of the Christian understanding of salvation is that it is specifically linked with the death and resurrection of Christ. This is one important way in which the Christian notion of salvation can be distinguished from the secular idea of liberation or self-fulfillment, or from the ideas of salvation found in other religions. There is, however, another way in which the Christian idea of salvation is specifically coupled to Jesus of Nazareth – namely, that

Christ provides a model or paradigm for the redeemed life. Christ in some sense gives shape or specification to Christian existence.

In general, mainstream Christianity affirms that the Christian life is made possible through Christ, while recognizing two quite distinct ways in which the resulting Christian life is "shaped" or "specified" by him:

1. The Christian life takes the form of the believer's sustained attempt to imitate Christ. Having become a Christian, the believer now treats Christ as an example of the ideal relationship to God and other people, and attempts to mimic this relationship. This "mimetic" approach may perhaps be seen at its best in the works of some later medieval spiritual writers. A particularly good example can be found in Thomas à Kempis' famous *Imitation of Christ*. This great work of monastic spirituality places emphasis upon the human responsibility to bring one's life into line with the example set by Christ, especially the idea of "bearing the cross."

2. The Christian life is a process of "being conformed to Christ," in which the outward aspects of the believer's life are brought into line with the inward relationship to Christ, established through faith. This approach is characteristic of writers such as Martin Luther and John Calvin, and is based on the idea of God conforming the believer to the likeness of Christ through the process of renewal and regeneration brought about by the Holy Spirit.

## Engaging with a text

Our text for further study is taken from a sermon preached by Augustine of Hippo, one of the Christian church's greatest theologians. Augustine had a reputation as a lucid and powerful preacher, and his sermons include detailed yet very accessible accounts of the major themes of Christian theology. Unsurprisingly, Augustine regularly preached on the meaning of the cross, and the means by which Christ's death and resurrection secured human salvation. The sermon is based on the opening section of the fifth chapter of the book of Revelation, which allows Augustine to explore how Christ can be thought of as both a lion and a lamb – the "lion of Judah" and the "lamb of God" who takes away the sin of the world.

If Christ had not been put to death, death would not have died. The devil was conquered by his own trophy of victory. The devil jumped for joy, when he seduced the first man, and cast him down to death. By seducing the first man, he killed him; by killing the last man, he lost the first from his snare. The victory of our Lord Jesus Christ came when he rose again from the dead, and ascended into heaven. It was at this point that the text from the Book of Revelation, which you heard read today, was fulfilled: "The lion of the tribe of Judah has won the day" (Revelation 5:5). The one who was slain as a lamb is now called a lion – a lion on account of his courage, a lamb on account of his innocence; a lion, because he was unconquered; a lamb, because of his gentleness. By his death, the slain lamb has conquered the lion who "goes around seeking someone to devour" (1 Peter 5:8). The devil, on the other hand, is here called a lion for his savagery, rather than his bravery . . . The devil jumped for joy when Christ died; and by the very death of Christ the devil was overcome: he took, as it were, the bait in the mousetrap. He rejoiced at Christ's death, believing himself to be the commander of death. But that which caused his joy dangled the bait before him. The Lord's cross was the devil's mousetrap: the bait which caught him was the death of the Lord.

After you have read through this text, try answering these questions, either on your own or in your discussion group.

1. Refresh your memory of the three major approaches to the meaning of the cross that we considered earlier in this chapter. Which of them seems to be the "best fit" for Augustine's approach?
2. Try to summarize, in your own words, the basic argument that Augustine sets out. In what way does Christ's death on the cross deliver humanity from its entanglement with the power of the devil, according to Augustine?
3. What does Augustine mean when he writes: "The Lord's cross was the devil's mousetrap"? What impact do you think this would have had on his audience? What point do you think he was trying to make?

# CHAPTER 6

# *Spirit*

One of the most important theological developments of the late twentieth century was the rise of the charismatic movement. The origins of this movement can be traced back to the early years of the century, particularly in the Azusa Street revival in Los Angeles in 1906. Today, the charismatic movement is a major influence in global Christianity, affecting most mainline Christian churches. Its emphasis on the role of the Holy Spirit in worship and the Christian life has given a much higher profile to theological reflections on role of the Spirit. Yet Christian theologians have always been aware of the importance of the Holy Spirit, even if recent developments have raised awareness of its significance. In this chapter, we shall consider some leading themes in this area of theology, which is often referred to as *pneumatology* (from the Greek word *pneuma*, "spirit").

## Biblical models of the Holy Spirit

"God is spirit" (John 4:24). But what does this tell us about God? The English language uses at least three words – "wind," "breath," and "spirit" – to translate a single Hebrew term, *ruach*. This important Hebrew word has a depth of meaning which it is virtually impossible to reproduce in English. *Ruach*, traditionally translated simply as "spirit," is associated with a range of meanings, each of which casts some light on the complex associations of the Christian notion of the Holy Spirit.

*Theology: The Basics*, Third Edition. Alister E. McGrath.
© 2012 Alister E. McGrath. Published 2012 by Blackwell Publishing Ltd.

**Figure 13**    A picture of the Day of Pentecost – Joseph Ignaz Mildorfer, *The Coming of the Holy Spirit*, 1750s, oil on canvas, 55 × 33 cm. The Day of Pentecost is traditionally seen as marking the coming of the Holy Spirit upon the early church. Hungarian National Gallery, Budapest.

1. *Spirit as wind*. The Old Testament writers are careful not to identify God with the wind and thus reduce God to the level of a natural force. Nevertheless, a parallel is drawn between the power of the wind and that of God. To speak of God as spirit is to call to mind the surging energy of the "Lord of Hosts," and remind Israel of the power and dynamism of the God who had called Israel out of Egypt. This image of the spirit as redemptive power is perhaps stated in its most significant form in the account of the exodus from Egypt in which a powerful wind divides the Red Sea (Exodus 14:21). Here, the idea of *ruach* conveys both the power and the redemptive purpose of God.

The image of the wind also allowed the pluriformity of human experience of God to be accounted for, and visualized in a genuinely helpful manner. The Old Testament writers were conscious of experiencing the presence and activity of God in two quite distinct manners. Sometimes, God was experienced as a judge, one who condemned Israel for its waywardness; yet at other times, God is experienced as one who refreshes the chosen people, like water in a dry land. The image of the wind conveyed both these ideas in a powerful manner.

It must be remembered that Israel bordered the Mediterranean Sea to the west and the great deserts to the east. When the wind blew from the east, it was experienced as a mist of fine sand which scorched vegetation and parched the land. Travelers' accounts of these winds speak of their remarkable force and power. Even the light of the sun is obliterated by the sandstorm thrown up by the wind. This wind was seen by the biblical writers as a model for the way in which God demonstrated the finitude and transitoriness of the creation. "The grass withers and the flowers fall, when the breath of the Lord blows on them" (Isaiah 40:7). Just as the scorching east wind, like the Arabian sirocco, destroyed plants and grass, so God was understood to destroy human pride (see Psalm 103:15–18; Jeremiah 4:11). Just as a plant springs up, fresh and green, only to be withered before the blast of the hot desert wind, so human empires rise, only to fall before the face of God.

At the time when the prophet Isaiah was writing, Israel was held captive in Babylon. The "Babylonian Captivity" or "Exile" began in 597 BC, and continued until the fall of the Babylonian empire in 538 BC. To many, it seemed that the great Babylonian empire was a permanent historical feature, which nothing could change. Yet the transitoriness of human achievements when the "breath of the Lord" blows upon them is asserted by the prophet, as he proclaims the pending destruction of that empire. God alone is permanent, and all else is in a state of flux and change.

The western winds, however, were totally different. In the winter, the west and southwest winds brought rain to the dry land as they blew in from the sea. In the summer, the western winds did not bring rain, but coolness. The intensity of the desert heat was mitigated through these gentle cooling breezes. And just as this wind brought refreshment, by moistening the dry ground in winter and cooling the heat of the day in summer, so God was understood to refresh human spiritual needs. In a series of powerful images, God is compared by the Old Testament writers to the rain brought by the western wind (Hosea 6:3), refreshing the land.

2. *Spirit as breath.* The idea of spirit is associated with life. When God created Adam, God breathed into him the breath of life, as a result of which he became a "living being" (Genesis 2:7). The basic difference between a living and a dead human being is that the former breathes and the latter does not. This led to the idea that life was dependent upon breath. God is the one who breathes the breath of life into empty shells, and brings them to life. God brought Adam to life by breathing into him. The famous vision of the valley of the dry bones (Ezekiel 37:1–14) also illustrates this point. Can these dry bones live? The bones only come to life when breath enters into them (Ezekiel 37:9–10).

The model of God as spirit thus conveys the fundamental insight that God is the one who gives life, even the one who is able to bring the dead back to life. It is thus important to note that *ruach* is often linked with God's work of creation (e.g., Genesis 1:2; Job 26:12–13; 33:4; Psalm 104:27–31), even if the precise role of the Spirit is left unspecified. There is clearly an association between "Spirit" and the giving of life through creation. This point was made clearly by the English theologian Charles Gore (1853–1932), reflecting on the role of the spirit in the animation or "vitalization" of creation.

> "I believe in the Holy Ghost, the giver of life." All life is His operation. Wherever the Holy Spirit is, there is also life; and wherever life, is, there is also the Holy Spirit. Thus if creation takes its rise in the will of the Father, if it finds its law in the being of the Word or Son, yet the effective instrument of creation, the finger of God, the moving principle of vitalization is the Holy Spirit, the divider and distributor of the gifts of life.

3. *Spirit as charism.* The technical term "charism" refers to the "filling of an individual with the spirit of God," by which the person in question is enabled to perform tasks which would otherwise be impossible. The gift of wisdom is often portrayed as a consequence of the endowment of the Spirit (Genesis 41:38–39; Exodus 28:3; 35:31;

Deuteronomy 34:9). At times, the Old Testament attributes gifts of leadership or military prowess to the influence of the Spirit (Judges 14:6, 19; 15:14, 15). However, the most pervasive aspect of this feature of the Spirit relates to the question of prophecy.

The Old Testament does not offer much in the way of clarification concerning the manner in which the prophets were inspired, guided, or motivated by the Holy Spirit. In the period before the Israelites were exiled in Babylon, prophecy was often associated with ecstatic experiences of God, linked with wild behavior (1 Samuel 10:6; 19:24). Nevertheless, the activity of prophecy gradually became associated with the *message* rather than the *behavior* of the prophet. The prophet's credentials rest upon an endowment with the Spirit (Isaiah 61:1; Ezekiel 2:1–2; Micah 3:8; Zechariah 7:12), which authenticates the prophet's message – a message which is usually described as "the word (*dabhar*) of the Lord."

The New Testament is rich in references to the Spirit, which plays a particularly significant role in the Pauline letters. For Paul, the Spirit has been poured out on all believers, and dwells in their hearts. This allows Paul to distinguish the Christian "life in the Spirit" from an unchristian "life in the flesh" (Romans 5:5; 8:9–11; 1 Corinthians 12:13; Galatians 4:5). While it is difficult to give a brief synopsis of Paul's understanding of the role of the Holy Spirit in the life of the believer and the church, the following points are generally regarded as being of particular importance.

1. The Spirit provides a proof or demonstration that believers are indeed children of God (Romans 8:16; 2 Corinthians 1:22; 5:5).
2. The Spirit is the ground or source of spiritual gifts in the life of the individual and church, including discernment, obedience, wisdom, interpretation, and ecstatic utterances (Romans 12:3–8; 1 Corinthians 12:4–11).

## The debate over the divinity of the Holy Spirit

As we saw earlier, biblical writers clearly saw the spirit as an aspect of God's power, presence, and activity in the world. But is the Holy Spirit itself *divine*? The early church found itself puzzled by the Spirit, and unable to make much in the way of theological sense of this area of doctrine. This is not to say that the Holy Spirit did not place a prominent role in the early church. The second-century writer Montanus, who is known to have been active during the period 135–75, placed considerable emphasis on the activity of the Spirit, particularly in relation to dreams, visions, and prophetic revelations.

The relative absence of extensive discussion of the role of the Holy Spirit in the first three centuries reflects the fact that theological debate centered elsewhere. The Greek patristic writers had, in their view, more important things to do than worry about formalizing a doctrine of the Holy Spirit, when vital political and Christological debates were raging all around them. This point was made by the fourth-century writer Amphilochius of Iconium, who pointed out that the Arian controversy had first to be resolved before any serious discussion over the status of the Holy Spirit could get under way. The theological development of the early church was generally a response to public debates; once a serious debate got under way, doctrinal clarification was the inevitable outcome. The Nicene Creed, as set out in 325, offers surprisingly little affirmation or explanation of the Holy Spirit. Yet the theological groundwork for the expansion of the church's vision of the Spirit had been laid by this stage.

Athanasius and Basil of Caesarea (ca. 330–79) made a powerful case for the recognition of the divinity of the Holy Spirit, and made an appeal to the formula which had by then become universally accepted for baptism. Since the time of the New Testament (see Matthew 28:18–20), Christians were baptized in the name of "the Father, Son, and Holy Spirit." Athanasius argued that this had momentous implications for an understanding of the status of the person of the Holy Spirit. In his *Letter to Serapion*, Athanasius declared that the baptismal formula clearly pointed to the Spirit sharing the same divinity as the Father and the Son. This argument eventually prevailed.

It is instructive to compare the statements of the Council of Nicea (325) and Constantinople (381) on the person and work of the Spirit, which indicates how much more confident the church felt about its understanding of this area of theology as a result of the discussions and debates of the fourth century.

325: [I believe] in the Holy Spirit.

381: [I believe] in the Holy Spirit, the Lord and giver of life, who proceeds from the Father, and is worshipped and glorified together with the Father and Son, who spoke by the prophets.

However, we must note that patristic writers were hesitant to speak openly of the Spirit as "God," in that this practice was not sanctioned by scripture – a point discussed at some length by Basil of Caesarea in his treatise on the Holy Spirit (374–75). Even as late as 380, Gregory of Nazianzus conceded that many Orthodox Christian theologians were uncertain as to whether to treat the Holy Spirit "as an activity, as a creator, or as God."

This caution can be seen in the final statement of the doctrine of the Holy Spirit formulated by a Council of Constantinople. The Spirit was here described, not as "God," but as "the Lord and giver of life, who proceeds from the Father, and is worshipped and glorified together with the Father and Son." Yet despite this slight theological ambiguity, the Council was clear that the Spirit was to be treated as having the same dignity and rank as the Father and Son, even if the term "God" was not to be used explicitly in speaking of the Spirit.

Three factors were of special importance in establishing the divinity of the Holy Spirit during the later fourth century. First, as Gregory of Nazianzus stressed, scripture applied all the titles of God to the Spirit, with the exception of "unbegotten." Gregory drew particular attention to the use of the word "holy" to refer to the Spirit, arguing that this holiness did not result from any external source, but was the direct consequence of the nature of the Spirit. The Spirit was to be considered as the one who sanctifies, rather than the one who requires to be sanctified.

Second, the functions which are specific to the Holy Spirit establish the divinity of the Spirit. Didymus the Blind (died 398) was one of many writers to point out that the Spirit was responsible for the creating, renewing, and sanctification of God's creatures. Yet how could one creature renew or sanctify another creature? Only if the Spirit was divine could sense be made of these functions. If the Holy Spirit performed functions which were specific to God, it must follow that the Holy Spirit shares in the divine nature. This point is stated with particular clarity by Basil of Caesarea:

> All who are in need of sanctification turn to the Spirit; all those seek him who live by virtue, for his breath refreshes them and comes to their aid in the pursuit of their natural and proper end. Capable of perfecting others, the Spirit himself lacks nothing. He is not a being who needs to restore his strength, but himself supplies life ... and shares the gifts of grace, heavenly citizenship, a place in the chorus of angels, joy without end, abiding in God, being made like God and – the greatest of them all – being made God.

For Basil, the Spirit makes creatures both to be like God and to be God – and only one who is divine can bring this about. (In chapter 4, we explored how this same argument was also used to infer the divinity of Christ from the fact that the New Testament recognized him as "savior.")

Third, the reference to the Spirit in the baptismal formula of the church was interpreted as supporting the divinity of the Spirit. Baptism took place in the name of the "Father, Son, and Holy Spirit" (Matthew 28:17–20). Athanasius and others argued that this formula established the closest of connections between the three members of the Trinity, making it impossible to suggest that the Father and Son shared in the substance of the Godhead, while the Spirit was nothing other than a creature. In a similar way, Basil of Caesarea argued that the baptismal formula clearly implied the inseparability of Father, Son, and Spirit. This verbal association, according to Basil, clearly had considerable theological implications.

These arguments have commanded wide support within Christian theology, and have had a significant impact on both eastern and western Christian theologies of the Holy Spirit. Yet divergences remain, one of which we shall consider in what follows.

## The *filioque* debate

One of the most significant events in the early history of the church was the achievement of broad agreement throughout the Roman empire, both east and west, on the text and leading ideas of the Nicene Creed (325). This document was intended to bring doctrinal stability to the church in a period of considerable importance in its history. Part of that agreed text referred to the Holy Spirit "proceeding from the Father," drawing on the language of John 15.26. By the ninth century, however, the western church routinely altered this phrase, speaking of the Holy Spirit "proceeding from the Father and the Son." The origins of this addition are generally agreed to originate in Spain, with the third Council of Toledo (589), which included the following statement: "I believe in the Holy Spirit who proceeds from the Father and Son (*qui ex patre filioque procedit*)."

So what difference does this addition make? Is it simply a matter of words? Or does it express something much deeper? The *filioque* debates often focus on the different concepts of the Trinity which are held by the eastern and western churches, focusing particularly on their understandings of the Holy Spirit.

Greek patristic writers insisted that there was only one source of being within the Trinity. The Father alone was the sole and supreme cause of all things, including the Son and the Spirit within the Trinity. The Son and the Spirit derive from the Father, but in different manners. In searching for suitable terms to express this relationship, theologians eventually fixed on two quite distinct images: the Son is begotten of the Father, while the Spirit proceeds from the Father. These two terms are intended to express the idea that both Son and Spirit derive from the Father, but in different ways.

The Cappadocian fathers, along with other Greek theologians, believed it was important to distinguish the identities and functions of Son and Spirit. A failure to distinguish the ways in which Son and Spirit derive from the one and the same Father would lead to God having two sons, which would have raised insurmountable problems. Identical functions would seem to imply identical essences.

There is thus no question of the Holy Spirit being *subordinate* to the Son. The Son is the Word of God, and the Spirit is the breath of God. The Father pronounces his word; at the same time as he utters this word, he breathes out in order to make this word capable of being heard and received. The visual imagery of a spoken word being propelled throughout the world thus helps illuminate both the distinctiveness of Son and Spirit, while at the same time affirming their mutual involvement in the work of the Father.

Within this context, it is unthinkable that the Holy Spirit should proceed from the Father and the Son. This would totally compromise the principle of the Father as the sole origin and source of all divinity. It would amount to affirming that there were two sources of divinity within the one Godhead, with all the internal contradictions and tensions that this would generate. If the Son were to share in the exclusive ability of the Father to be the source of all divinity, this ability would no longer be exclusive. For this reason, leading writers of the Greek church – such as Gregory of Palamas and Photius the Great – regarded the western idea of a "double procession" of the Spirit with intense suspicion.

Western writers, however, took a different position. Augustine of Hippo argued that the Spirit had to be thought of as proceeding from Father *and* the Son – a notion of double procession. One of his main proof texts was John 20:22, in which the risen Christ is reported as having breathed upon his disciples, and said: "Receive the Holy Spirit." Augustine explains this as follows in his major treatise *On the Trinity*:

> Nor can we say that the Holy Spirit does not also proceed from the Son. After all, the Spirit is said to be the Spirit of both the Father and the Son. [John 20:22 is then cited] The Holy Spirit proceeds not only from the Father, but also from the Son.

So what understanding of role of the Spirit does Augustine adopt? The answer lies in his distinctive understanding of the Spirit as the "bond of love" between Father and Son. The Spirit is to be thought of as the "bond of the Father and the Son (*patris et filii copula*)." The Father is only the Father of the Son, and the Son only the Son of the Father; the Spirit, however, is the Spirit of both Father and Son, binding them together in a bond of love.

Augustine develops this understanding of the person and work of the Holy Spirit further. Not only is the Spirit the bond of unity between Father and Son on the one hand; the same Spirit is also the bond of unity between God and believers on the other. The Spirit is a gift, given by God, which unites believers both to God and to other believers. The Holy Spirit forges bonds of unity between believers, upon which the unity of the church ultimately depends. The church is the "temple of the Holy Spirit," within which the Holy Spirit dwells. The same Spirit which binds together the Father and Son in the unity of the Godhead also binds together believers in the unity of the church. Yet eastern critics of this approach argue that it essentially reduces the role of the Spirit. Augustine, they complained, was really talking about the "Spirit of Christ," not the "Spirit of God."

This controversy remains important in ecumenical dialogues to the present day. It is now generally agreed that the eastern and western theological traditions have developed categories and conceptions that differ in substantial ways from one another, and which cannot easily be reconciled or declared to be equivalent. Recent ecumenical dialogues – such as the North American Orthodox-Catholic Theological Consultation (2003) – have taken considerable care to emphasize their shared theological beliefs, while noting that certain beliefs remain contested, as does the language used to express these beliefs. Some closing words of that consultation merit further study:

> Gregory Nazianzen reminds us, in his Fifth Theological Oration on the divinity of the Holy Spirit, that the Church's slow discovery of the Spirit's true status and identity is simply part of the "order of theology," by which "lights break upon us gradually" in our understanding of the saving Mystery of God. Only if we "listen to what the Spirit is saying to the Churches" (Revelation 3:22), will we be able to remain faithful to the Good News preached by the Apostles, while growing in the understanding of that faith, which is theology's task.

What difference does this make? While the issues remain debates, there is a reasonable degree of clarity concerning the strengths and weaknesses of each position. The pneumatological advantages of the eastern position – that is, a single procession of the Spirit – include the avoidance of a "Christomonism" which limits God's work of revelation and salvation to Christ; a defense against dualism, modalism, and subordinationism; and the safeguarding of a panoramic vision of the work and activity of the Spirit. The pneumatological advantages of the western position – that is, a double procession of the Spirit – include the explicit recognition that the Spirit is a personal being rather than an impersonal force, power, or activity; a defense against pantheism and imprecise forms of mysticism; and the provision of a specific Christological criterion for the evaluation of allegedly "spiritual" phenomena.

## The functions of the Spirit

What does the Holy Spirit do? Many theologians have tried to provide brief summaries of the work of the Spirit. A good example is found in Basil of Caesarea's succinct statement: "Through the Holy Spirit we are restored to paradise, led back to the Kingdom of heaven, adopted as children, given confidence to call God 'Father' and to share in Christ's grace, called children of light, and given a share in eternal glory."

Another classic statement of the work of the Holy Spirit is found in the liturgical sequence *Veni Sancte Spiritus* ("Come Holy Spirit"), traditionally attributed to the medieval theologian Stephen Langton (ca. 1150–1228). This hymn speaks of the work of the spirit using a number of images, all focusing on the Spirit's role in recreating, renewing, healing, and redirecting human nature. The Latin text of this sequence will be familiar to some readers, and is difficult to translate into English without losing its rhyme and rhythm. A few stanzas of the original Latin are printed out below, along with my translation, to give an idea of the comprehensive vision of the function of the Spirit found in this famous liturgical piece.

> Lava quod est sordidum,
> riga quod est aridum,
> sana quod est saucium.
>
> Flecte quod est rigidum,
> fove quod est frigidum,
> rege quod est devium.

"Wash what is dirty; refresh what is dry; heal what is wounded; bend what is stubborn; melt what is frozen; direct what is wandering."

The Christian tradition has generally understood the work of the Holy Spirit to focus on three broad areas: revelation, salvation, and the Christian life. In what follows, we shall provide a brief indication of the richness of the Christian understanding of the role of the Spirit in each of these three areas.

1. The revelation of God to humanity

There has been a widespread recognition of the pivotal role of the Spirit in relation to the making of God known to humanity. In the second century, Irenaeus wrote of the "Holy Spirit, through whom the prophets prophesied, and our forebears learned of God and the righteous were led in the paths of justice." Similarly, in his 1536 commentary on the gospels, Martin Bucer (1491–1551) argues that revelation cannot occur without the assistance of God's Spirit:

> Before we believe in God and are inspired by the Holy Spirit, we are unspiritual and for that reason we are completely unable to apprehend anything relating to God. So all the wisdom and righteousness which we possess in the absence of the Holy Spirit are the darkness and shadow of death.

**Figure 14**    Meeting of the Second Vatican Council, St. Peters, Rome. David Lees/Time & Life Pictures/Getty Images.

The task of the Holy Spirit is to lead the faithful into God's truth; without that Spirit, truth remains elusive. This idea is developed further in the notion of the "inspiration of Scripture," which affirms that the Bible has a God-given authority by virtue of its origins. This doctrine, in various forms, is the common tradition of Christianity, and has its origins in the Bible itself, most notably the affirmation that "every Scripture is God-breathed (*theopneustos*)" (2 Timothy 3:16). Most Christian theologians affirm the activity of the Holy Spirit both in the inspiration of Scripture, and in the subsequent responsibility of the church to interpret and apply this text. The Dogmatic Constitution on Revelation of the Second Vatican Council illustrates this well.

> Sacred Scripture is the word of God inasmuch as it is consigned to writing under the inspiration of the divine Spirit, while sacred tradition takes the word of God entrusted by Christ the Lord and the Holy Spirit to the Apostles, and hands it on to their successors in its full purity, so that led by the light of the Spirit of truth, they may in proclaiming it preserve this word of God faithfully, explain it, and make it more widely known.

In Protestant theology, however, the doctrine of the inspiration of Scripture often serves an additional purpose – that of insisting on the primacy of Scripture over the church. Whereas more Catholic writers point to the formation of the canon of Scripture as indicating the authority of the church over that of Scripture, Protestant writers argue that the church merely recognized an authority which was already present within Scripture itself. The *Gallic Confession* (1559) illustrates this point well.

> We know these books to be canonical, and the sure rule of our faith, not so much by the common accord and consent of the Church, as by the testimony and inward persuasion of the Holy Spirit, which enables us to distinguish them from other ecclesiastical books which, however useful, can never become the basis for any articles of faith.

Yet it is not simply God's revelation which is linked with the work of the Spirit; the Spirit is also widely regarded as being involved in the human response to that revelation. Most Christian theologians have regarded faith itself as the result of the work of the Holy Spirit. John Calvin is one writer who draws attention to the pivotal role of the Spirit in revealing God's truth and applying or "sealing" this truth to humanity, as we noted earlier (see pp. 17–18).

> Now we shall have a right definition of faith if we say that it is a steady and certain knowledge of the divine benevolence towards us, which is founded upon the truth of the gracious promise of God in Christ, and is both revealed to our minds and sealed in our hearts by the Holy Spirit.

2. The appropriation of salvation

We have already noted how patristic writers justified the divinity of the Spirit with reference to the functions of the Spirit. Many of those functions relate directly to the doctrine of salvation; for example, the role of the Spirit in sanctification, making humanity like God, and divinization. This point is particularly important within the eastern Christian churches, with their traditional emphasis on deification; the western concept of salvation, which tends to be relational rather than ontological, nevertheless finds room for a role for the Spirit. The Holy Spirit plays a critical role in illuminating, healing, and enabling humanity to take hold of Christ, and thus benefit from his identity and his work.

Protestant theologians of the sixteenth century placed particular emphasis upon this point. In Calvin's doctrine of the application of salvation, the Holy Spirit plays a major role in relation to the establishment of a living relationship between Christ and believer. This can be seen more clearly in some of the Reformed confessions of this age, such as the Belgic Confession.

> We believe that, to attain the true knowledge of this great mystery, the Holy Spirit creates in our hearts an upright faith, which embraces Jesus Christ with all his merits, takes hold of him, and seeks nothing more besides him.

A similar point is made in Catholic theology. For example, the Dogmatic Constitution on Revelation of the Second Vatican Council regularly affirms the critical role of the Spirit in preparing the human mind and heart for revelation and salvation. "To make this act of faith, the grace of God and the interior help of the Holy Spirit must precede and assist, moving the heart and turning it to God, opening the eyes of the mind and giving joy and ease to everyone in assenting to the truth and believing it."

### 3. The energization of the Christian life

For many writers, the Holy Spirit plays an especially important role in relation to the Christian life, both the individual and the corporate life. The fifth-century writer Cyril of Alexandria is one of many to stress the role of the Spirit in bringing unity within the church.

> All of us who have received the one and the same Spirit, that is, the Holy Spirit, are in a sense merged together with one another and with God. [ . . . ] Just as the power of the holy flesh of Christ united those in whom it dwells into one body, I think that, in much the same way, the one and undivided Spirit of God, who dwells in us all, leads us all into spiritual unity.

However, any properly Christian understanding of the role of the Spirit will go far beyond this, and will include reference to at least two other areas. First, the "making real" of God in personal and corporate worship and devotion. The importance of the role of the Spirit in relation to Christian prayer, spirituality, and worship has been stressed by many writers, classic and modern. Second, the enabling of believers to lead a Christian life, particularly in relation to morality. Martin Bucer thus draws attention to the necessity of the Spirit, if believers are to be able to keep the law.

> So those who believe are not under the law, because they have the Spirit within them, teaching them everything more perfectly than the law ever could, and motivating them much more powerfully to obey it. In other words, the Holy Spirit moves the heart, so that believers wish to live by those things which the law commands, but which the law could not achieve by itself.

Yet the Christian life is corporate, not just individual, and it is important to note the ecclesiological dimensions of the work of the Holy Spirit. Since the Second Vatican Council (1962–65), many Catholic theologians have explored the role of the Spirit in shaping and sustaining Christian community, and fostering its witness in the world. The *Catechism of the Catholic Church* (1994) thus speaks of the church as both "the Body of Christ and the Temple of the Holy Spirit."

> The Spirit prepares people, and goes out to them with his grace, in order to draw them to Christ. The Spirit manifests the risen Lord to them, recalls his word to them and opens their minds to the understanding of his Death and Resurrection.

This compressed statement highlights many aspects of the classic understanding of the role of the Spirit in the Christian life – not least the important theme, especially associated with the Fourth Gospel, of the Spirit's role in "calling to mind" the person and words of Jesus of Nazareth (John 15:26).

Other aspects of pneumatology merit attention, even if they cannot be addressed in the limited space of this chapter. For example, growing interest in the theology of mission, linked with an increasing awareness of the importance of tracing God's imprints in other cultures and faiths, has led many to explore the role of the Spirit in the world, preparing the way for the proclamation of Christ. The activity of the Holy Spirit has never been understood to be limited to the church; it extends throughout the world. This can be seen particularly in the so-called "Turn to Pneumatology," evident at meetings of the World Council of Churches in 1990 and 1991.

## Engaging with a text

Throughout this chapter, we have considered questions about the identity and role of the Holy Spirit. For many theologians, this identity and role has a particularly significant connection with Christian existence – for example, with preaching, worship, and prayer. One recent theological writer to make this point is Sarah Coakley, presently Norris-Hulse Professor of Divinity at Cambridge University, England. Coakley's work has focused on the relation of systematic theology and Christian spirituality. In the extract below from a 1998 article on the link between a Trinitarian theology and spirituality, Coakley explores the role of the Spirit in an illuminating way.

Coakley bases her analysis here on Romans 8:14–17; 26–27, which you should read before approaching the passage. This section of Paul's letter includes the following statement, which is of particular importance to Coakley's reflections: "Likewise the Spirit helps us in our weakness; for we do not know how to pray as we ought, but that very Spirit intercedes with sighs too deep for words." You might like to spend a few moments thinking about this passage before approaching Coakley's reflections on its implications for a theology of the Holy Spirit.

> What is being described in Paul is *one* experience of an activity of prayer that is nonetheless ineluctably, though obscurely, triadic. It is *one* experience of God, but God as simultaneously (i) doing the praying in me, (ii) receiving that prayer, and (iii) in that exchange, consented to in me, inviting me into the Christian life of redeemed sonship. Or to put it another way: the "Father" (so-called here) is both source and ultimate object of divine longing in us; the "Spirit" is that irreducibly – though obscurely – distinct enabler and incorporator of that longing in creation – that which *makes* the creation divine; and the "Son" is that divine and perfected creation, into whose life I, as pray-er, am caught up ... As John of the Cross puts it in a lovely passage in *The Spiritual Canticle* (39.3.4), not coincidentally quoting Romans 8: "the Holy Spirit raises the soul most sublimely with that His divine breath ... that she may breathe in God the same breath of love that the Father breathes in the Son and the Son in the Father."

> The Spirit, on this view, note, is no redundant third, no hypostatized afterthought, no cooing "feminine" adjunct to an established male household. Rather, experientially speaking, the Spirit is *primary,* just as Pentecost is primary for the church; and leaving noncluttered space for the Spirit is the absolute precondition for the unimpeded flowing of this divine exchange in us, the "breathing of the divine breath," as John of the Cross puts it.

The passage can be understood in a number of ways, but has a particular focus on the theological foundations and implications of prayer. Coakley emphasizes that Paul's statements about what happens in prayer are easily accommodated within a Trinitarian or "triadic" framework. Although these statements are not fully developed, they point toward a way of making sense of the activity and experience of prayer within a theological matrix. Although primarily concerned to reflect on the theme of "Living into the Mystery of the Holy Trinity," Coakley spends some time teasing out the distinctive identity and function of the Holy Spirit.

You may find the following questions helpful in interacting with this text, either on your own or in a group discussion.

1. Try to set out in your own words Coakley's analysis of the role of Father, Son, and Spirit in prayer. Why does she see this as being so important?

2. Coakley cites the sixteenth-century Spanish writer John of the Cross in developing her thesis about the role of the Spirit. What specific points does she draw out from his writings?

3. "The Spirit is *primary*." What does Coakley mean by this? What is the point of her allusion to the Day of Pentecost?

# CHAPTER 7

# Trinity

For many people, the doctrine of the Trinity is one of the most baffling areas of Christian theology. How can we think of God as "three persons"? There are many who suspect that this is simply an attempt by theologians to make their subject inaccessible to outsiders. Thomas Jefferson (1743–1826), third president of the United States of America, was severely critical of what he termed the "incomprehensible jargon of the Trinitarian arithmetic." Why on earth do we need to speak of God in this convoluted and puzzling way? Might it suggest that theology is thoroughly irrational?

More recently, Christians have become aware of the Islamic critique of the doctrine, which holds that it compromises the unity of God. Many Christians neglected the notion, partly because it was seen as obscure. Karl Rahner remarked that modern Christians were "almost mere monotheists," paying lip service to the Trinity in theory, but ignoring it in practice. "We must be willing to admit," he remarked, "that, should the doctrine of the Trinity have to be dropped as false, the major part of religious literature could well remain virtually unchanged."

Yet despite these difficulties, there has been a massive revival of interest in the doctrine of the Trinity in Christian theology in the late twentieth and early twenty-first century. The foundations of this revival of interest were laid by Karl Barth and others in the period before the Second World War. Since then, there has been a remarkable surge of interest in developing Trinitarian approaches across the life and thought of the church. Catholics, Protestants, and Orthodox alike have been involved in the exploration of the Trinitarian geography of faith.

*Theology: The Basics*, Third Edition. Alister E. McGrath.
© 2012 Alister E. McGrath. Published 2012 by Blackwell Publishing Ltd.

The importance of this development was emphasized by the British theologian Colin Gunton (1941–2003), one of the most important recent advocates of the "promise of trinitarian theology":

> Because God is triune, we must respond to him in a particular way, or rather set of ways, corresponding to the richness of his being ... In turn, that means that everything looks – and, indeed, is – different in the life of the Trinity.

In this chapter, we shall consider some of the leading themes of the Christian doctrine of the Trinity, beginning with some of its conceptual foundations.

## Belief in the Trinity

Why do Christians believe in the Trinity? Surely a simpler way of thinking and speaking about God would make things a lot easier? The best way of understanding the basis of this seemingly baffling doctrine is to consider it as being the inevitable and legitimate way of thinking about God which emerges from a sustained engagement with the biblical witness to the words and works of God. The doctrine of the Trinity can be regarded as the outcome of a process of sustained and critical reflection on the pattern of divine activity revealed in scripture, and continued in Christian experience. This is not to say that scripture contains or sets out an explicit doctrine of the Trinity; rather, scripture bears witness to a God who demands to be understood in a Trinitarian manner.

At first sight, there are only two biblical verses which are open to a Trinitarian interpretation: Matthew 28:19 and 2 Corinthians 13:14. The first commands the disciples to baptize people "in the name of the Father, Son, and Holy Spirit"; the second speaks of the Father, Son, and Spirit in the familiar words of "the grace." Both these verses have become deeply rooted in the Christian consciousness, the former on account of its baptismal associations, and the latter through the common use of the formula in Christian prayer and devotion. Yet these two verses, taken together or in isolation, can hardly be thought of as constituting a doctrine of the Trinity.

The ultimate grounds of the doctrine of the Trinity do not lie in the two verses noted above. Rather, the foundations of the doctrine are to be found in the pattern of divine activity to which the New Testament bears witness. The Father is revealed in Christ through the Spirit. There is the closest of connections between the Father, Son, and Spirit in the New Testament writings. Time after time, New Testament passages link together these three elements as part of a greater whole. The totality of God's saving presence and power can only, it would seem, be expressed by involving all three elements (for example, see 1 Corinthians 12:4–6; 2 Corinthians 1:21–22; Galatians 4:6; Ephesians 2:20–22; 2 Thessalonians 2:13–14; Titus 3:4–6; 1 Peter 1:2).

The best way of beginning to think about the doctrine of the Trinity is to think of the Christian Bible as setting out the nature and actions of one God – the god that Christians refer to as the "God and Father of our Lord Jesus Christ." While insisting that there is only one God, Christianity affirms a rich, complex vision of God, which is extremely difficult to put into words. Down the ages, Christian theologians have realized that they have two basic options here. They could set out a very simple concept of God, which is easily grasped – but fails to do justice to the profound and multifaceted witness to God found in the Bible, and then in Christian worship and experience. Or they could do their best to remain faithful to this witness to God – even though the end result was difficult to understand. Orthodox Christian theology has always adopted the second of these two courses. A quotation from Augustine of Hippo is often noted here: "If you can fully grasp it, it's not God."

The starting point for Christian reflections on the Trinity is, as we have seen, the New Testament witness to the presence and activity of God in Christ and through the Spirit. For Irenaeus, the whole process of salvation, from its beginning to its end, bore witness to the action of Father, Son, and Holy Spirit. Irenaeus made use of a term which would feature prominently in future discussions of the Trinity: "the economy of salvation." The use of the term "economy" here needs a little explanation. The Greek word *oikonomia* basically means "the way in which one's affairs are ordered" (the relation to the modern sense of the word will thus be clear). For Irenaeus, the "economy of salvation" meant "the way in which God has ordered the salvation of humanity in history."

**Figure 15**   Andrei Rublev (1360–ca. 1430). *Icon with the Trinity.*
Tretyakov State Gallery, Moscow. Photo Scala, Florence.

At the time, Irenaeus was under considerable pressure from Gnostic
critics, who argued that the creator God was quite distinct from
(and inferior to) the redeemer God (see chapter 3). Marcion of
Sinope (ca. 110–60) argued that the Old Testament God was merely a
creator God, and totally different from the redeemer God of the
New Testament. As a result, the Old Testament should be shunned by
Christians, who should concentrate their attention upon the
New Testament. Irenaeus vigorously rejected this idea. He insisted that
the entire process of salvation, from the first moment of creation to the
last moment of history, was the work of the one and the same God.
There was a single economy of salvation, in which the one God – who
was both creator and redeemer – was at work to redeem the creation.

In his *Demonstration of the Apostolic Preaching*, Irenaeus insisted upon the distinct yet related roles of Father, Son, and Spirit within the economy of salvation. He affirmed his faith in:

> *God the Father uncreated*, who is uncontained, invisible, one God, creator of the universe; this is the first article of our faith . . . And the *Word of God*, the Son of God, our Lord Jesus Christ, . . . who, in the fulness of time, in order to gather all things to himself, he became a human being amongst human beings, capable of being seen and touched, to destroy death, bring life, and restore fellowship between God and humanity. And the *Holy Spirit* . . . who, in the fulness of time, was poured out in a new way on our human nature in order to renew humanity throughout the entire world in the sight of God.

This passage brings out clearly the idea of the Godhead in which each person is responsible for an aspect of the economy of salvation. Far from being a rather pointless piece of theological speculation, the doctrine of the Trinity is grounded directly in the complex human experience of redemption in Christ, and is concerned with the explanation of this experience. This point has been made repeatedly by later theologians, who see it as the starting point for authentic Trinitarian theology. As the American theologian Catherine Mowry LaCugna (1952–97) put it, "the shape of trinitarian doctrine is dictated by the pattern of redemption; everything comes from God, is made known and redeemed through Jesus Christ, and is consummated by the power of the Holy Spirit."

Tertullian argued that God's action within the economy of salvation is complex, revealing both a *unity* and a *distinctiveness*. The doctrine of the Trinity thus affirms the unity of God, while recognizing the complexity and profundity of the Christian vision of God. Tertullian thus argues that *substance* is what unites the three aspects of the economy of salvation; *person* is what distinguishes them. The three persons of the Trinity are distinct, yet not divided (*distincti non divisi*), different yet not separate or independent of each other (*discreti non separati*). The complexity of the human experience of redemption is thus the result of the three persons of the Godhead acting in distinct yet coordinated manners in human history, without any loss of the total unity of the Godhead.

So what are the basic elements of the Christian vision of God that are formally set out in the doctrine of the Trinity? The three main elements are the following:

1. God created the world, establishing it with order and form.
2. God redeemed the world in Jesus Christ.
3. God is present in the world here and now, guiding and encouraging believers.

It is easy to set out a simple understanding of God which is able to incorporate one of these elements. For example, speaking of God as creator or lawgiver causes no fundamental intellectual problems. Yet this is only part of the Christian vision of God, which omits more than it affirms.

The doctrine of the Trinity weaves together the strands of the Christian understanding of God, giving a vision of God which is faithful to the Christian experience of that God, even though it poses an intellectual challenge. Omitting anything may make the doctrine easier to understand – but it is a distorted, inaccurate, and inadequate representation of God, which fails to do justice to the way that God actually is. In the end, the doctrine of the Trinity can be seen as an admission that human words are simply inadequate to express the glory and wonder of God. The English theologian Charles Gore (1853–1932) made this point as follows:

> Human language never can express adequately divine realities. A constant tendency to apologize for human speech, a great element of agnosticism, an awful sense of unfathomed depths beyond the little that is made known, is always present to the mind of theologians who know what they are about, in conceiving or expressing God. "We see," says St. Paul, "in a mirror, in terms of a riddle"; "we know in part." "We are compelled," complains St. Hilary [of Poitiers] "to attempt what is unattainable, to climb where we cannot reach, to speak what we cannot utter; instead of the mere adoration of faith, we are compelled to entrust the deep things of religion to the perils of human expression."

The second of the three elements we have just noticed has been of particular importance to the development of the doctrine of the Trinity.

It can be seen as being directly related to the evolution of Christology. The more emphatic the church became that Christ was God, the more it came under pressure to clarify how Christ related to God. The development of the doctrine of the Trinity took place in three stages, and was essentially complete by the end of the fourth century:

> Stage 1: the recognition of the full divinity of Jesus Christ.
> Stage 2: the recognition of the full divinity of the Spirit.
> Stage 3: the definitive formulation of the doctrine of the Trinity, embedding and clarifying these central insights, and determining their mutual relationship.

With the full recognition of the divinity of the Holy Spirit in the fourth century, the scene was set for the final development of the Christian doctrine of the Trinity. This sequential development of the doctrine of the Trinity is acknowledged by Gregory of Nazianzus (329–89), who pointed to a gradual progress in clarification and understanding of the mystery of God's revelation in the course of time. It was, he argued, impossible to deal with the question of the divinity of the Spirit until the issue of the divinity of Christ had been settled.

> The Old Testament preached the Father openly and the Son more obscurely. The New Testament revealed the Son, and hinted at the divinity of the Holy Spirit. Now the Spirit dwells in us, and is revealed more clearly to us. It was not proper to preach the Son openly, while the divinity of the Father had not yet been admitted. Nor was it proper to accept the Holy Spirit before [the divinity of] the Son had been acknowledged . . . Instead, by gradual advances and . . . partial ascents, we should move forward and increase in clarity, so that the light of the Trinity should shine.

## A Trinitarian heresy: modalism

The term "modalism" was introduced by the German historian of dogma, Adolf von Harnack, to describe the common element of a group of Trinitarian heresies, associated with Noetus and Praxeas in the late second century, and Sabellius in the third. Each of these writers was concerned to safeguard the unity of the Godhead, fearing a lapse into some form of tritheism as a result of the doctrine of the Trinity.

This vigorous defense of the absolute unity of God (often referred to as "monarchianism," from the Greek word *monarchia*, meaning "a single principle of authority") led these writers to insist that the self-revelation of the one and only God took place in different ways at different times. The divinity of Christ and the Holy Spirit is to be explained in terms of three different ways or "modes" of divine self-revelation (hence the term "modalism"). This all too easily becomes an essentially Unitarian notion of God whom we call Father, Son, or Spirit only because this one God self-discloses in three different modes or manners.

Although various forms of "modalism" have emerged within the Christian tradition over time, they are generally based upon much the same understandings of the dynamics of the Trinity:

1. The one God is revealed in the manner of creator and lawgiver. This aspect of God is referred to as "the Father."
2. The same God is also revealed in the manner of savior, in the person of Jesus Christ. This aspect of God is referred to as "the Son."
3. The same God is also revealed in the manner of the one who sanctifies and gives eternal life. This aspect of God is referred to as "the Spirit."

There is thus no fundamental difference between the three persons of the Trinity, except for appearance and chronological location. Two main types of modalism should be noted: those which understand the difference between the three persons in a *chronological* way, and those which understand them in a *functional* way. It is important to appreciate this distinction, as it is frequently encountered in theological discussions. Chronological modalism holds that God was Father at one point in history; that God was then Son at another point; and finally, that God was Spirit. God thus appears in different modes at different times. The classic example of this form of modalism is Sabellianism, which we will discuss in more detail below. Functional modalism, on the other hand, holds that God operates in different ways at the present moment, and that the three persons refer to these different modes of action.

*" top heresy hunter "*

Perhaps the most important Trinitarian heresy is known as "Sabellianism". Its main features were set out by Epiphanius of Constantia in the late fourth century, as follows:

*ousia*

*main source for early heresy*

> Their doctrine is that Father, Son, and Holy Spirit are one and the same being, in the sense that three names are attached to one substance. It is just like the body, soul and spirit in a human being. The body is as it were the Father; the soul is the Son; while the Spirit is to the Godhead as his spirit is to a human being. Or it is like the sun, being one substance but having three manifestations: light, heat, and the orb itself. The heat [ . . . ] is analogous to the Spirit; the light to the Son; while the Father himself is represented by the essence of each substance. The Son was at one time emitted, like a ray of light; he accomplished in the world all that related to the dispensation of the gospel and the salvation of humanity, and was then taken back into heaven, as a ray is emitted by the sun and then withdrawn again into the sun. The Holy Spirit is still being sent forth into the world and into those individuals who are worthy to receive it.

It is clear from the analysis presented by Epiphanius that Sabellianism is a form of chronological modalism. Its basic feature is the belief that the one supreme God acts in different ways at different points in history. In contrast, functional modalism designates the general belief that the same God acts in three different manners at any given point in history. The three persons of the Trinity thus designate different aspects of the activity of the one God. In its simplest forms, functional modalism could be set out as follows.

1. God the Father is the creator;
2. God the Son is the redeemer;
3. God the Holy Spirit is the sanctifier.

Here, the three persons of the Trinity are held to designate three actions of the one supreme God. God acts as creator (and we call this "Father"); God acts as redeemer (and we call this "Son"); God acts as sanctifier (and we call this the "Holy Spirit." The persons of the Trinity thus refer to different divine functions. The approach to the doctrine of the Trinity set out by Karl Barth could be interpreted as a variant of this form of modalism, as it can be understood to mean that God operates in different ways in the present. Many Barth scholars, however, dispute this.

## Visualizing the Trinity

As we have emphasized, the doctrine of the Trinity seems counterintuitive to many people. Partly, this difficulty arises from the problem of the *visualization* of the Trinity. How can we make sense of such a complex and abstract idea? How can we picture it in our minds? St. Patrick (ca. 391–ca. 461), the patron saint of Ireland, is rumored to have used the leaf of a shamrock to illustrate how a single leaf could have three different elements. Gregory of Nyssa uses a series of analogies in his letters to help his readers grasp the reality of the Trinity, including:

1. The analogy of a spring, fount and stream of water. The one flows from the other and they share the same substance – water. Although different aspects of the stream of water may be *distinguished*, they cannot be *separated*.

2. The analogy of a chain. There are many links in a chain; yet to be connected to one is to be connected to all of them. In the same way, Gregory argues, someone who encounters the Holy Spirit also encounters the Father and the Son.

3. The analogy of a rainbow. Drawing on the Nicene statement that Christ is "light from light," Gregory argues that the rainbow allows us to distinguish and appreciate the different colors of a sunbeam. There is only one beam of light, yet the colors blend seamlessly into one another.

In what follows, we shall explore one more recent way of thinking about the Trinity which has proved very helpful to many. It is associated with the contemporary American theologian Robert Jenson (born 1930), and is set out in his work *The Triune Identity: God According to the Gospel* (1982).

## The Trinity and the naming of God

To understand Jenson's approach, we may ask a simple question: who is the God of Israel? One answer might be that God is God; as there is no other god, there is nothing further to discuss. But remember that ancient Israel existed in a polytheistic context. There were many "gods." The God whom Israel knew and worshipped thus needed to be identified – to be *named*. The Old Testament declares that the God of Israel is the God of Abraham, Isaac, and Jacob; the God who led the people of Israel out of Egypt into the promised land with great signs and wonders. We thus identify and name God by telling the story of God.

You might do the same sort of thing when trying to identify a person. Your conversation with someone might go like this: "You know John Brown? You don't? Well, do you remember reading about a man who managed to row a boat all the way across the Atlantic Ocean about a year ago? The boat nearly sank at one point. And when he finished the journey, he wrote a book about it. Ah! You *do* know who I mean!" What you are doing here is telling a story which centers on John Brown. You are identifying him in this way. John Brown is the person at the center of the story. And so it is with God and the Old Testament. The Old Testament identifies God from the history of God's people – the great stories of Abraham, Isaac, and Jacob, of the exodus from Egypt, and so on, are told, in order to identify God. The God of Israel is the one who acted in this way.

This is made clear in a number of Old Testament passages (e.g., Exodus 19:4–5; Deuteronomy 26:5–9; Ezekiel 20:5–26). Question: who is God? Answer: God is the one who delivered Israel from Egypt. Of course, God has a name as well – a name which proves difficult to translate into English, "Yahweh," "the Lord," and "Jehovah" being three of the best-known translations. But the fact remains that God is usually thought of in terms of God's actions.

Now we turn to the God whom Christians worship and adore. Who is this God? To answer this question, the New Testament tells a story – perhaps the most famous story in the world – the story of Jesus Christ. And as that story reaches its climax in the account of the resurrection of Jesus from the dead, we learn that God, for Christians, is the one who acted in this way to raise Jesus. Question: who is the God whom Christians worship and adore? Answer: whoever "raised Jesus our Lord from the dead" (Romans 4:24). Of course, the New Testament writers make it abundantly clear that the one who "raised Jesus our Lord from the dead" is the same God who delivered Israel from Egypt, thus affirming the continuity between the Old and New Testaments, between Israel and the church.

As Jenson points out, this approach can be taken further without difficulty. The resurrection of Jesus and the pouring out of the Spirit at Pentecost are treated as closely related by the New Testament. The complexity of the New Testament's statements concerning the relationship of God, Jesus, and the Spirit defies neat categorization. It is, however, clear that "God" is the one who raised Jesus from the dead, and is now present in the church through the Holy Spirit. In many ways, the Christian slogan "Father, Son, and Holy Spirit" (Matthew 28:19; 2 Corinthians 13:14) corresponds to the Old Testament slogan "the God of Abraham, Isaac, and Jacob" – it *identifies* the God in question. Question: what God are you talking about? Answer: the God who raised Jesus Christ from the dead, and is now present through the Spirit.

The Trinitarian formula can thus be thought of as a *proper name* – a shorthand way of identifying exactly what God we are talking about. Christianity packs into this one neat phrase the high points of salvation history, the big moments (resurrection and Pentecost) when God was so clearly present and active. It specifically links God with these events, just as Israel specifically linked God with the exodus from Egypt. It focuses our attention on certain specific events, in which God's presence and activity were to be found concentrated and publicly demonstrated.

The doctrine of the Trinity can thus be seen as a summary of the story of God's dealings with Israel and the church. It narrates the story of how God created and redeemed humanity, affirming that it is the story of the one and the same God throughout. If you were talking about a great modern statesman, such as Winston Churchill or John F. Kennedy, you'd concentrate upon the high points of their careers – the moments when they stepped on to the stage of history, in order to change its direction. And the doctrine of the Trinity identifies those great moments in the history of salvation, when God was active and was seen to be active. It affirms that God is active in the world, that God is made known by God's actions, and points to the creation, the death and resurrection of Jesus Christ, and Pentecost as turning points in God's dealings with us. The doctrine of the Trinity thus spells out exactly who the God we are dealing with actually is.

Jenson develops this approach in a fresh and helpful direction, offering a creative restatement of the traditional doctrine of the

Trinity. In *The Triune Identity*, Jenson argues that "Father, Son, and Holy Spirit" is the proper name for the God whom Christians know in and through Jesus Christ. It is imperative, he argues, that God should have a proper name. "Trinitarian discourse is Christianity's effort to identify the God who has claimed us. The doctrine of the Trinity comprises both a proper name, 'Father, Son and Holy Spirit' . . . and an elaborate development and analysis of corresponding identifying descriptions." Jenson points out that ancient Israel was set in a polytheistic context, in which the term "god" conveyed relatively little information. It was necessary to *name* the god in question. A similar situation was confronted by the writers of the New Testament, who were obliged to identify the god at the heart of their faith, and distinguish this god from the many other gods worshipped and acknowledged in the region, especially in Asia Minor.

The doctrine of the Trinity thus *identifies* and *names* the Christian God – but identifies and names this God in a manner consistent with the biblical witness. It is not a name which we have chosen; it is a name which has been chosen for us, and which we are authorized to use. In this way, Jenson defends the priority of God's self-revelation against human constructions of concepts of divinity. "The gospel identifies its God thus: God is the one who raised Israel's Jesus from the dead. The whole task of theology can be described as the unpacking of this sentence in various ways. One of these produces the church's trinitarian language and thought." The doctrine of the Trinity, Jenson affirms, allows the church to discover the distinctiveness of its creed, and avoid becoming absorbed by rival conceptions of God.

The doctrine of the Trinity thus centers on the recognition that God is named by scripture, and within the witness of the church. Within the Hebraic tradition, God is identified by historical events. Jenson notes how many Old Testament texts identify God with reference to divine acts in history – such as the liberation of Israel from its captivity in Egypt. The same pattern is evident in the New Testament: God is identified with reference to specific historical events, supremely the resurrection of Jesus Christ. God comes to be identified in relation to Jesus Christ. Who is God? Which god are we talking about? The God who raised Christ from the dead. As Jenson puts it, "the emergence of a semantic pattern in which the uses of

'God' and 'Jesus Christ' are mutually determining" is of fundamental importance within the New Testament.

> The gospel of the New Testament is the provision of a new identifying description for this same God [as that of Israel]. The coming-to-apply of this new description is the event, the witness to which is the whole point of the New Testament. God, in the gospel, is "whoever raised Jesus from the dead." Identification of God by the resurrection did not replace identification by the exodus; it is essential to the God who raised Jesus that he is the same one who freed Israel. But the new thing that is the content of the gospel is that God has now identified himself also as "him that raised from the dead Jesus our Lord" (Romans 4:24). In the New Testament such phrases become the standard way of referring to God.

Jenson thus recovers a personal conception of God from metaphysical speculation. "Father, Son, and Holy Spirit" is a *proper name*, which we are asked to use in naming and addressing God. "Linguistic means of identification – proper names, identifying descriptions, or both – are a necessity of religion. Prayers, like other requests and praises, must be addressed." The Trinity is thus an instrument of theological precision, which forces us to be explicit about the God under discussion. Christians do not believe in a generic god, but in a very specific God who is known in and through a series of actions in history.

## Communicating the Trinity: hymns

Our discussion thus far may well have created the impression that the doctrine of the Trinity is highly inaccessible, having little to do with the realities of Christian life. Yet, as we noted earlier in this book, many theologians realized the importance of congregational hymns as a means of communicating theology to ordinary believers. For Charles Wesley (1707–88), hymns were not merely a means of praising God; they were an instrument of theological education. So what should be more natural than to try to set out the basic themes of the doctrine of the Trinity in the form of a hymn?

In 1746, Wesley published a collection of 24 short hymns concerning the Trinity. Individually and collectively, they manage to

**Figure 16** Charles Wesley preaching to the Indians in 1745, engraving. The Art Archive/Eileen Tweedy.

communicate and explain central Trinitarian ideas without technical language or theological fuss. This is one of the most effective of these hymns:

1. Father of Mankind be ever ador'd:
   Thy Mercy we find, In sending our Lord,
   To ransom and bless us; Thy Goodness we praise,
   For sending in Jesus, Salvation by Grace.

2. O Son of His Love, Who deignest to die,
   Our Curse to remove, Our Pardon to buy;
   Accept our Thanksgiving, Almighty to save,
   Who openest Heaven, To all that believe.

3. O Spirit of Love, Of Health, and of Power,
   Thy working we prove; Thy Grace we adore,
   Whose inward Revealing applies our Lord's Blood,
   Attesting and sealing us Children of God.

The hymn sets out the idea of the "economy of salvation" – the distinctively Christian understanding of the way in which salvation is effected in history. Wesley's concern is to identify its leading aspects, and show how the action of one and the same triune God can be seen in action throughout. Each person of the Trinity has its own distinctive role to play – a notion usually referred to as "appropriation." Every aspect of the great drama of redemption is shown to be interlocked. Father, Son, and Spirit are woven into this great tapestry of divine salvation in a continuous narrative. Although Wesley's theology needs a little elaboration at points, the fundamental purpose of the hymn is clear – to help congregations appreciate the manner in which the doctrine of the Trinity weaves together into a seamless garment the great threads of redemption.

## The "social Trinity": Jürgen Moltmann

One of the most influential recent ways of understanding the doctrine of the Trinity and establish its relevance is a *social* understanding of the Trinity. Advocates of this approach hold that Christians should not imagine God on basis of a model of some individual person or thing which has three aspects, aspects, dimensions, or modes of being – for example, Patrick's image of the shamrock leaf, or Anselm of Canterbury's model of the River Nile as spring, river and lake (Anselm's knowledge of African geography is not very reliable!). Social approaches to the Trinity insist that God is instead to be thought of as a collective reality – a group, or a society, bound together by the mutual love, accord, and self-giving of its members. Cornelius Plantinga, for example, spoke of the Trinity as "a zestful, wondrous community of divine light, love, joy, mutuality and verve."

In *The Trinity and the Kingdom of God* (1980), Jürgen Moltmann attempts to liberate the Christian doctrine of God from the confines both of the ancient Greek metaphysics of substance and of the modern metaphysics of transcendental subjectivity. Moltmann's analysis is of particular importance on account of its social doctrine of the Trinity, which emphasizes the relative independence of the person and work of the Holy Spirit in its community with the Father and the Son. Developing this in a way that might cause anxiety to some, Moltmann emphasizes that there is no fixed order in the Trinity. The unity of God is the unity of persons in relationship, as expressed in the Cappadocian doctrine of perichoresis. On this reading of this concept, Moltmann argues that "the trinitarian persons form their own unity by themselves in the circulation of the divine life."

Moltmann develops this point with reference to the notion of *perichoresis*. This Greek term (often translated as "mutual interpenetration") came into general use in the sixth century. It refers to the manner in which the three persons of the Trinity relate to one another. The concept of *perichoresis* allows the individuality of the persons to be maintained, while insisting that each person shares in the life of the other two. Moltmann's development of the idea proved particularly influential. The Trinity is to be conceived as "a community of being," in which each person, while maintaining its distinctive identity, penetrates the others and is penetrated by them. This notion has important implications for Christian political thought, as the liberation theologian Leonardo Boff and other theologians concerned with political theology have made subsequently clear. The mutual relationships among three coequal persons within the Godhead have been argued to provide a model both for human relationships within communities and for Christian political and social theorizing.

The doctrine of *perichoresis*, according to Moltmann, "links together in a brilliant way the threeness and the unity, without reducing the threeness to the unity, or dissolving the unity in the threeness." Moltmann understands this perichoresis as a process by which each person of the Trinity, by virtue of their eternal mutual love, lives *in* the other two as a fellowship through a "process of most perfect and intense empathy." This conception of God is radically opposed, Moltmann insists, to any "monotheistic" or "monarchical" doctrine of God which would reduce the real subjectivity of the three persons. Of particular interest is how Moltmann uses this notion to develop a fundamentally theological understanding of human society.

"The trinity is our social program." For Moltmann, the doctrine of the Trinity is to be understood to provide a vision of God as a union of three divine persons or distinct, but related subjects. This specific understanding of God as a mutually loving, interacting, and sustaining society allows Christian theology to develop a theory of society. Moltmann therefore sees the social view of the Trinity as having both a theological and a social function: theologically, it offers a penetrating critique of a false idea of God; socially, it articulates a notion of God as a social being, capable of functioning as a proper paradigm for society as a whole.

> The triune God is reflected only in a united and uniting community of Christians without domination and subjection and a united and uniting humanity without class rule and without dictatorial oppression. That is the world in which people are defined by their social relationships and not by their power or their property. That is the world in which human beings have all things in common and share everything with one another except their personal qualities.

## Engaging with a text

Karl Barth is widely regarded as one of the greatest theologians of the twentieth century, and is widely credited with the rediscovery of interest in the doctrine of the Trinity in recent decades. Barth's ideas on the Trinity are important for an understanding of recent theological debates. Unfortunately, they are a little difficult to grasp for those who are new to theology, and this section will therefore offer much more explanation than normal.

Barth's reflections on the Trinity are anchored in his fundamental belief that divine self-revelation has actually taken place. What, Barth asks towards the beginning of his *Church Dogmatics*, must be true, if God is able to be known in this way? Read this text slowly, and try to appreciate the issues Barth is raising.

> The question of the self-revealing God which thus forces itself upon us as the first question cannot, if we follow the witness of Scripture, be separated in any way from the second question: How does it come about, how is it actual, that this God reveals Himself? Nor can it be separated from the third question: What is the result? What does this event do to the man to whom it happens? Conversely the second and third questions cannot possibly be separated from the first . . . *God* reveals Himself. He reveals Himself *through Himself*. He reveals *Himself*. If we really want to understand revelation in terms of its subject, i.e., God, then the first thing that we have to realize is that this subject,

God, the revealer, is identical with His act in revelation, and also with its effect. It is from this fact, which in the first instance we are merely indicating, that we learn we must begin the doctrine of revelation with the doctrine of the triune God.

"*God* reveals Himself. He reveals Himself *through Himself*. He reveals *Himself*." With these words (which are very difficult to translate into inclusive English) Barth sets up the revelational framework which leads to the formulation of the doctrine of the Trinity. Barth often quotes the Latin phrase *Deus dixit!* – "God has spoken" – in his discussion of revelation. For Barth, God *has* spoken, and it is the task of theology to inquire concerning what this revelation presupposes and implies. For Barth, theology is a process of "thinking afterwards" about what is contained in God's self-revelation. We have to "inquire carefully into the relation between our knowing of God, and God himself in his being and nature."

With such statements, Barth sets up the context of the doctrine of the Trinity: given that God's self-revelation has taken place, what must be true of God if this can have happened? What does the actuality of revelation have to tell us about the being of God? Barth's starting point for his discussion of the Trinity is not a doctrine or an idea, but the actuality of God's speaking and God's being heard. For how can God be heard, when sinful humanity is incapable of hearing the Word of God?

The above is simply a paraphrase of sections of the first half-volume of Barth's *Church Dogmatics*, entitled "The Doctrine of the Word of God," punctuated by occasional quotations. There is an enormous amount being said in this, and it requires unpacking. Two themes need to be carefully noted.

1. Sinful humanity is fundamentally incapable of hearing the Word of God.
2. Nevertheless, sinful humanity has heard the Word of God, in that this Word makes its sinfulness known to it.

The very fact that revelation takes place thus requires explanation. For Barth, this implies that humanity is passive in the process of reception; the process of revelation is, from its beginning to its end, subject to the sovereignty of God as Lord. For revelation to *be* revelation, God must be capable of effecting self-revelation to sinful humanity, despite their sinfulness.

Once this paradox has been appreciated, the general structure of Barth's doctrine of the Trinity can be followed. In revelation, Barth argues, God must be as shown in the divine self-revelation. There must be a direct correspondence between the revealer and the revelation. If "God reveals himself as Lord" (a characteristically Barthian assertion), then God must be Lord "antecedently in himself." Revelation is the reiteration in time of what God actually is in eternity. There is thus a direct correspondence between:

1. the revealing God;
2. the self-revelation of God.

To put this in the language of Trinitarian theology, the Father is revealed in the Son.

So what about the Spirit? Here we come to what is perhaps the most difficult aspect of Barth's doctrine of the Trinity: the idea of "revealedness" (*Offenbarsein*). To explore this, we will have to use an illustration not used by Barth himself. Imagine two individuals walking outside Jerusalem on a spring day around the year AD 30. They see three men being crucified, and pause to watch. The first points to the central figure, and says, "There is a common criminal being executed." The second, pointing to the same man, replies, "There is the Son of God dying for me." To say that Jesus is the self-revelation of God will not do in itself; there must be some means by which Jesus is *recognized* as the self-revelation of God. It is this recognition of revelation *as* revelation that constitutes the idea of *Offenbarsein*.

How is this insight achieved? Barth is quite clear: sinful humanity is not capable of reaching this insight unaided. Barth is not prepared to allow humanity any positive role in the interpretation of revelation, believing that this is to subject divine revelation to human theories of knowledge. The recognition of revelation *as* revelation must itself be the work of God – more accurately, the work of the Spirit. Humanity does not become capable of hearing the word of the Lord (*capax verbi domini*), and then act in response to having heard that word; both the hearing and capacity to hear are given in the one act by the Spirit.

Barth's achievement was to demonstrate that the concepts of revelation and the Trinity were so completely interlocked and interwoven that neither could be affirmed without the other. To believe in a revealing God is implicitly to believe in a Trinitarian conception of God, which it is the task of theology to unfold and explore. For Barth, the doctrine of the Trinity is thus presupposed by the entire project of Christian theology. While many would express reservations at aspects of his approach, few would deny that Barth's achievement represents a massive theological landmark.

You may find the following questions helpful in interacting with this text, either on your own or in a group discussion.

1. Try to set out in your own words the argument that links the actuality of revelation with the doctrine of the Trinity.
2. Try to answer this hypothetical question. Has revelation taken place, if we do not recognize it as revelation? You might like to use the example given above (the scene at Calvary) to answer this question.
3. On the basis of the extracted passage from the *Church Dogmatics* reproduced above, set out how Barth understands Father, Son, and Spirit to be involved in the process of divine revelation. You might like to reproduce Barth's own discussion, and then restate this in your own words.

CHAPTER 8

# Church

The Apostles' Creed includes a clause which declares that Christians believe in the church. So what is meant by this? How is the church to be defined, and what is its purpose? This area of theology is traditionally designated "ecclesiology" (from the Greek word for "church," *ekklesia*). It is one of the more delicate areas of theology, as it raises awkward denominational questions which are of central importance to the identity of churches. In this chapter, we shall explore a number of aspects of the doctrine of the church. As always, limits on space restrict the extent to which certain ideas can be discussed, and prevent us from looking at some issues which are of considerable interest.

## The church: local or universal?

The New Testament uses the word "church" in two somewhat different manners. At many points, the term "church" is used to designate individual Christian congregations – local visible gatherings of believers. For example, Paul wrote letters to churches in the cities of Corinth and Philippi. The book of Revelation makes reference to the "seven churches of Asia," probably meaning seven local Christian communities in the region of Asia Minor (modern-day Turkey). Yet, at other points, we find the term being used in a wider, more general sense, meaning something like "the total body of Christian believers." The tension between the local and universal senses of the

*Theology: The Basics*, Third Edition. Alister E. McGrath.
© 2012 Alister E. McGrath. Published 2012 by Blackwell Publishing Ltd.

word "church" is of considerable importance, and needs careful examination. How could both aspects be maintained?

Traditionally, this tension is resolved through arguing that there is one, universal church which exists in local communities. On the basis of this approach, there is one universal church, consisting of all Christian believers, which takes the form of individual local churches in a given region. One influential way of conceiving this distinction is due to John Calvin, who drew an important distinction between the *visible* and the *invisible* church. At one level, the church is the community of Christian believers, a visible group. It is also, however, the fellowship of saints and the company of the elect – an *invisible* entity.

For Calvin, the distinction between the invisible and visible churches is basically eschatological (that is, to do with the end times). The invisible church is the church which will come into being at the end of time, as God ushers in the final judgment of humanity. The relation between the visible and invisible churches can be summarized as follows:

| Visible church | Invisible church |
|---|---|
| The church is the observable community of believers on earth | The church is the assembly of the elect, known only to God |
| The church is an object of present experience | The church is an object of present faith and future hope |
| The church includes both good and evil, elect and reprobate | The church consists only of the elect |

Calvin's ideas were given more formal expression in the *Westminster Confession of Faith*, a document which has had considerable influence in Puritan and Reformed church circles:

> The catholic or universal church, which is invisible, consists of the whole number of the elect that have been, are, or shall be gathered into one, under Christ the head thereof... The visible church, which is also catholic or universal under the gospel (not confined to one nation as before under the law), consists of all those throughout the world that profess the true religion, together with their children.

The importance of this model, and others like it, is best appreciated by considering the following question. How can we talk about "one" Christian church, when there are so many different Christian denominations?

## Only one church?

Faced with this apparent tension between a theoretical belief in "one church" and the brute observable reality of a plurality of churches, Christian writers developed approaches to allow the later observation to be incorporated within the framework of the former. Four major approaches to the issue of the unity of the church may be noted, each of which possesses distinctive strengths and weaknesses:

1. An *imperialist* approach, which declares that there is only one empirical – that is, observable – church which deserves to be known and treated as the true church. All others are fraudulent pretenders to this title, or are at best little more than approximations to the real thing. This position was maintained by the Roman Catholic church prior to the Second Vatican Council (1962–65), which took the momentous step of recognizing other Christian churches as "separated" Christian brothers and sisters.

2. A *Platonic* approach, which draws a fundamental distinction between the empirical church (that is, the church as a visible historical reality) and the ideal church. This has found relatively little support in mainstream Christian theology, although some scholars have suggested that some such idea may lie behind Calvin's distinction between the "visible" and "invisible" church. However, as we noted above, this distinction is better interpreted along eschatological lines.

3. An *eschatological* approach, which suggests that the present disunity of the church will be abolished on the last day. The present situation is temporary, and will be resolved on the day of judgment. This understanding lies behind Calvin's distinction between the "visible" and "invisible" churches, which we considered above.

4. A *biological* approach, which likens the historical evolution of the church to the development of the branches of a tree. This image,

**Figure 17** Hans Küng (born 1928). Sean Gallup/Getty Images.

developed by the eighteenth-century German Pietist writer Nicolas von Zinzendorf (1700–60), and taken up with enthusiasm by Anglican writers of the following century, allows the different empirical churches (e.g., the Roman Catholic, Orthodox, and Anglican churches) to be seen as possessing an organic unity, despite their institutional differences.

In recent years, many theologians concerned with ecumenism (deriving from the Greek word *oecumene*, "the whole world," and now generally understood to mean "the movement concerned with the fostering of Christian unity") argued that the true basis of the "unity of the church" required to be recovered, after centuries of distortion. The maxim *ubi Christus, ibi ecclesia* ("where Christ is, there is also the church"), which derives from Ignatius of Antioch (ca. 50–ca. 107), pointed to the unity of the church lying in Christ, rather than in any historical or cultural factor. The New Testament does not even suggest that the diversity of local churches poses any threat to, or is inconsistent with, the unity of the church. The church already possesses a unity through its common calling from God, which expresses itself in different communities in different cultures and situations.

It therefore follows that "unity" must not be understood *sociologically* or *organizationally*, but *theologically*. As the Roman Catholic theologian Hans Küng (born 1928) argued in his magisterial study *The Church*:

> The unity of the church is a spiritual entity. It is one and the same God who gathers the scattered from all places and all ages and makes them into one people of God. It is one and the same Christ who through his word and Spirit unites all together in the same bond of fellowship of the same body of Christ … The Church *is* one, and therefore *should be* one.

Küng's point is that the unity of the church is grounded in the saving work of God in Christ. This is in no way inconsistent with that one church adapting itself to local cultural conditions, leading to the formation of local churches. As Küng puts it:

> The unity of the church presupposes a multiplicity of churches; the various churches do not need to deny their origins or their specific situations; their language, their history, their customs and traditions, their way of life and thought, their personal structure will differ fundamentally, and no one has the right to take this from them. The same thing is not suitable for everyone, at every time, and in every place.

Discussion of the universality of the church has often focused on the idea of "catholicity," which needs more detailed explanation.

## The catholicity of the church

In modern English, the term "catholic" is often confused, especially in non-religious circles, with "Roman Catholic" – that is, the branch of Christianity that accepts the authority of the pope, and places particular emphasis on historical and institutional continuity between the present-day church and that of the period of the apostles. Although this confusion is understandable, it must be pointed out that it is not only Roman Catholics who are "catholic," just as it is by no means only Eastern Orthodox writers who are "orthodox" in their theology. Indeed, many Protestant churches, more than a little embarrassed by the use of the term "catholic" in the creeds, have replaced it with the less contentious word "universal," arguing that this brings greater intelligibility to belief in "one holy universal and apostolic church."

The term "catholic" derives from the Greek phrase *kath' holou* ("referring to the whole"). The Greek words subsequently found their way into the Latin word *catholicus*, which came to have the meaning "universal or general." This sense of the word is retained in the English phrase "catholic taste," meaning a "wide-ranging taste" rather than a "taste for things that are Roman Catholic." Older versions of the English Bible often refer to some of the New Testament letters (such as those of James and John) as "catholic epistles," meaning that they are directed to all Christians (rather than those of Paul, which are directed to the needs and situations of individual identified churches, such as those at Rome or Corinth).

The developed sense of the word is perhaps best seen in the fourth-century catechetical writings of Cyril of Jerusalem (ca. 315–86). In his eighteenth catechetical lecture, Cyril teases out a number of senses of the word "catholic":

> The church is thus called "catholic" because it is spread throughout the entire inhabited world, from one end to the other, and because it teaches in its totality (*katholikos*) and without leaving anything out every doctrine which people need to know relating to things visible and invisible, whether in heaven and earth. It is also called "catholic" because it brings to obedience every sort of person – whether rulers or their subjects, the educated and the unlearned. It also makes available a universal (*katholikos*) remedy and cure to every kind of sin.

It will be clear that Cyril is using the term "catholic" in four ways, each of which deserves comment.

1. "Catholic" is to be understood as "spread throughout the entire inhabited world." Here, Cyril notes the geographical sense of the word. The notion of "wholeness" or "universality" is thus understood to mandate the church to spread into every region of the world.

2. "Catholic" means "without leaving anything out." With this phrase, Cyril stresses that the "catholicity" of the church involves the complete proclamation and explanation of the Christian faith. It is an invitation to ensure that the totality of the gospel is preached and taught.

3. "Catholic" means that the church extends its mission and ministry to "every sort of person." Cyril here makes an essentially sociological point. The gospel and the church are for all kinds of human beings, irrespective of their race, gender, or social status. We can see here a clear echo of St. Paul's famous declaration that "there is neither Jew nor Greek, there is neither slave nor free, there is neither male nor female; for you are all one in Christ Jesus" (Galatians 3:28).

4. "Catholic" means that the church offers and proclaims "a universal remedy and cure to every kind of sin." Here, Cyril makes a soteriological statement: the gospel, and the church which proclaims that gospel, can meet every human need and distress. Whatever sins there may be, the church is able to offer an antidote.

The various senses of the term "catholic" are also brought out clearly by Thomas Aquinas, in his discussion of the section of the Apostles' Creed dealing with the doctrine of the church. In this analysis, Aquinas singles out three essential aspects of the idea of "catholicity."

> The church is catholic, i.e., universal, first with respect to place, because it is throughout the entire world (*per totum mundum*), against the Donatists. See Romans 1:8: "Your faith is proclaimed in all the world"; Mark 16:15: "Go into all the world and preach the gospel to the whole creation." . . . Secondly, the church is universal with respect to the condition of people, because no one is rejected, whether master or slave, male or female. See Galatians 3:28: "There is neither male nor female." Thirdly, it is universal with respect to time. For some have said that the church should last until a certain time, but this is false, because this church began from the time of Abel and will last to the end of the world. See Matthew 28:20: "And I am with you always, to the close of the age." And after the close of the age it will remain in heaven.

Note how catholicity is here understood in terms of geographical, anthropological, and chronological universality.

## The church: holy or just human?

One of the most interesting debates concerning the doctrine of the church concerns whether its members are required to be holy. The debate is seen at its most intense during the Donatist controversy of the fourth century, which focused on the question of whether church leaders were required to be morally pure. Under the Roman emperor Diocletian (284–313), the Christian church was subject to various degrees of persecution. The origins of the persecution date from 303; it finally ended with the conversion of Constantine, and the issuing of the Edict of Milan in 313. Under an edict of February 303, Christian books were ordered to be burned and churches demolished. Those Christian leaders who handed over their books to be burned came to be known as *traditores* – "those who handed over [their books]." The modern word "traitor" derives from the same root. One such *traditor* was Felix of Aptunga, who later consecrated Caecilian as Bishop of the great North African city of Carthage in 311.

Many local Christians were outraged that such a person should have been allowed to be involved in this consecration, and declared that they could not accept the authority of Caecilian as a result. The new bishop's authority was compromised, it was argued, on account of the fact that the bishop who had consecrated him had lapsed under the pressure of persecution. The hierarchy of the Catholic church was thus tainted as a result of this development. The church ought to be pure, and should not be permitted to include such people. By the time Augustine – destined to be a central figure in the controversy – returned to North Africa from Rome in 388, a breakaway faction had established itself as the leading Christian body in the region, with especially strong support from the local African population.

The Donatists believed that the entire sacramental system of the Catholic church had become corrupted on account of the lapse of its leaders. How could the sacraments be validly administered by people who were tainted in this way? It was therefore necessary to replace these people with more acceptable leaders, who had remained firm in their faith under persecution. It was also necessary to rebaptize and re-ordain all those who had been baptized and ordained by those who had lapsed. Inevitably, this resulted in the formation of a breakaway faction. By the time Augustine returned to Africa, the breakaway faction was larger than the church from which it had originally broken away.

Augustine responded by putting forward a theory of the church which he believed was more firmly grounded in the New Testament than the Donatist teaching. In particular, Augustine emphasized the *sinfulness of Christians*. The church is not meant to be a "pure body," a society of saints, but a "mixed body" (*corpus permixtum*) of saints and sinners. Augustine finds this image in two biblical parables: the parable of the net which catches many fishes, and the parable of the wheat and the weeds (or "tares," to use an older word familiar to readers of the King James Bible). It is this latter parable (Matthew 13:24–31) which is of especial importance, and requires further discussion.

The parable tells of a farmer who sowed seed, and discovered that the resulting crop included both wheat and weeds. What could be done

**Figure 18**   Augustine of Hippo by Benozzo de Gozzoli, 1465, fresco. Museo Civico San Gimignano. The Art Archive/Museo Civico San Gimignano/Gianni Dagli Orti.

about it? To attempt to separate the wheat and the weeds while both were still growing would be to court disaster, probably involving damaging the wheat while trying to get rid of the weeds. But at the harvest, all the plants – whether wheat or weeds – are cut down and sorted out, thus avoiding damaging the wheat. The separation of the good and the evil thus takes place at the end of time, not in history.

For Augustine, this parable refers to the church in the world. It must expect to find itself including both saints and sinners. To attempt a separation in this world is premature and improper. That separation will take place in God's own time, at the end of history. No human can make that judgment or separation in God's place.

So in what sense is the church holy? For Augustine, the holiness in question is not that of its members, but of Christ. The church cannot be a congregation of saints in this world, in that its members are contaminated with original sin. However, the church is sanctified and made holy by Christ – a holiness which will be perfected and finally realized at the last judgment. In addition to this theological analysis, Augustine makes the practical observation that the Donatists failed to live up to their own high standards of morality. The Donatists, Augustine suggests, were just as capable as Catholics of getting drunk or beating people up.

Yet the Donatist vision of a "pure body" remains attractive to many. As is so often the case with theological debates, the evidence is never entirely on one side of the argument. A strong case continues to be made for the idea of the church as a "pure body," especially in denominations which trace their identity back to the more radical wing of the Protestant Reformation, often known as "anabaptism." The radical Reformation conceived of the church as an "alternative society" within the mainstream of sixteenth-century European culture.

For the radical Protestant writer and church leader Menno Simmons (1492–1559), the church was "an assembly of the righteous," at odds with the world, and not a "mixed body," as Augustine argued:

> In truth, those who merely boast of his name are not the true congregation of Christ. The true congregation of Christ is those who are truly converted, who are born from above of God, who are of a regenerate mind by the operation of the Holy Spirit through the hearing of the Word of God, and have become the children of God.

It will be clear that there are strong parallels with the Donatist view of the church as a holy and pure body, isolated from the corrupting influences of the world, and prepared to maintain its purity and distinctiveness by whatever disciplinary means proved necessary.

Anabaptism maintained discipline within its communities through "the ban" – a means by which church members could be excluded from Anabaptist congregations. This means of discipline was regarded as essential to the identity of a true church. Part of the Anabaptist case for radical separation from the mainstream churches (a practice which continues to this day among the Amish of Lancaster County, Pennsylvania) was the failure of those churches to maintain proper discipline within their ranks. The Schleitheim Confession (1529) grounded its doctrine of the "ban" on Christ's words, as they are recorded in Matthew 18:15–20:

The ban shall be used in the case of all those who have given themselves to the Lord, to walk in his commandments, and with all those who are baptized into the one body of Christ and are called brothers or sisters, yet who lapse on occasion, and inadvertently fall into error and sin. Such people shall be admonished twice in secret, and on the third occasion, they shall be disciplined publicly, or banned according to the command of Christ. (Matthew 18)

The "ban" was seen as being both deterrent and remedial in its effects, providing both an incentive for banned individuals to amend their way of life and a disincentive for others to imitate them in their sin. The Polish Racovian Catechism (1605) lists five reasons for maintaining rigorous discipline within Anabaptist communities, most of which reflect its policy of radical separation:

1. So that the fallen church member may be healed, and brought back into fellowship with the church.
2. To deter others from committing the same offense.
3. To eliminate scandal and disorder from the church.
4. To prevent the word of the Lord falling into disrepute outside the congregation.
5. To prevent the glory of the Lord being profaned.

Despite its pastoral intentions, the "ban" often came to be interpreted harshly, with congregation members often avoiding all social contact (known as "shunning") with both the banned individual and his or her family.

Other writers have pointed out how the term "holy" is often equated with "morality," "sanctity," or "purity," which often seem to bear little relation to the behavior of fallen human beings. Yet the Hebrew term *kadad*, which underlies the New Testament concept of "holiness," has a rather different meaning, bearing the sense of "being cut off," or "being separated." There are strong overtones of *dedication*: to be "holy" is to be set apart for and dedicated to the service of God.

A fundamental element – indeed, perhaps *the* fundamental element – of the Old Testament idea of holiness is that of "something or someone whom God has set apart." The New Testament restricts the idea almost entirely to personal holiness. It refers the idea to individuals, declining to pick up the idea of "holy places" or "holy things." People are "holy" in that they are dedicated to God, and distinguished from the world on account of their calling by God. A number of theologians have suggested a correlation between the idea of "the church" (the Greek word for which can bear the meaning of "those who are called out") and "holy" (that is, those who have been separated from the world, on account of their having been called by God).

To speak of the "holiness of the church" is thus primarily to speak of the holiness of the one who called that church and its members. The church has been separated from the world, in order to bear witness to the grace and salvation of God. In this sense, there are obvious connections between the church being "holy" and the church being "apostolic." The term "holy" is theological, not moral, in its connotations, affirming the calling of the church and its members, and the hope that the church will one day share in the life and glory of God.

So if the church is not defined by holiness, what is its distinguishing feature? A number of responses have been offered to this question, and we shall consider one of them in what follows.

## The church as constituted by the Word of God

It will be clear from our discussion thus far that Christian theologians insist that the term "church" is to be defined theologically, not sociologically. To "believe in the church" is not to trust in the institution of the church, but to affirm that the church is ultimately called into being by God, with a mission and authorization which derives from God. A central theme of Protestant understanding of the nature and mission of the church focuses on the presence of Christ resulting from the proclamation of the "Word of God," in preaching and the sacraments. For Martin Luther, the church is the community called into being by the preaching of God's Word:

> Now, anywhere you hear or see [the Word of God] preached, believed, confessed, and acted upon, do not doubt that the true holy catholic church, a "holy Christian people" must be there, even though there are very few of them. For God's word "shall not return empty" (Isaiah 55:11), but must possess at least a fourth or a part of the field.

> And even if there were no other sign than this alone, it would be enough
> to prove that a holy Christian people must exist there, for God's word
> cannot be without God's people and conversely, God's people cannot
> be without God's word. For who would preach the word, or hear it
> preached, if there were no people of God? And what could or would
> God's people believe, if there were no word of God?

Luther thus concludes that an episcopally ordained ministry is therefore
not actually necessary to safeguard the existence of the church. What
really matters is the preaching of the gospel, which Luther holds to be
essential to the identity of that church. "Where the word is, there is
faith; and where faith is, there is the true church." The visible church is
constituted and upheld by the preaching of the Word of God. No
human assembly may claim to be the "church of God" unless it is
founded on this gospel. It is more important to preach the same gospel
as the apostles than to be a member of an institution which is historically
derived from them.

John Calvin took a similar line, again stressing the importance of
the proclamation of God's Word as definitive of the identity of a
church.

> Wherever we see the Word of God purely preached and listened to,
> and the sacraments administered according to Christ's institution, it
> is in no way to be doubted that a church of God exists. For his promise
> cannot fail: "Wherever two or three are gathered in my name, there
> I am in the midst of them" (Matthew 18:20) ... If the ministry has
> the Word and honors it, if it has the administration of the sacraments,
> it deserves without doubt to be held and considered a church.

For Calvin, the preaching of the Word and right administration of the
sacrament are linked with the presence of Christ − and wherever
Christ is, there his church is to be found as well.

This theme has continued to be of major importance in the
twentieth century, particularly in the writings of Karl Barth. For
Barth, the church is the community which comes into being in
response to the preaching of the Word of God. The church is seen
as a community which proclaims the good news of what God has
done for humanity in Christ, and which comes into being wherever
the Word of God is faithfully proclaimed and accepted.

As Barth put it in his 1948 address to the World Council of Churches, the church consists of "the gathering together (*congregatio*) of those men and women (*fidelium*) whom the living Lord Jesus Christ chooses and calls to be witnesses of the victory he has already won, and heralds of its future manifestation." Barth's ecclesiology is thoroughly Trinitarian at this point, involving Father, Son, and Spirit in a dynamic understanding of the nature of the church. For Barth, the church is not an extension of Christ, but is united with Christ, and called and commissioned by him to serve the world. Christ is present within his church, through the Holy Spirit.

The role of the Holy Spirit is particularly important. Although it would not be correct to say that Barth has a "charismatic" understanding of the church, his Christological approach to the identity of the church allocates a definite and distinctive role to the Holy Spirit, which Barth summarized as follows in his *Dogmatics in Outline*:

> *Credo ecclesiam* ["I believe in the church"] means that I believe that here, at this place, in this assembly, the work of the Holy Spirit takes place. By that is not intended a deification of the creature; the church is not the object of faith, we do not believe *in* the church; but we do believe that in this congregation the work of the Holy Spirit becomes an event.

The church is thus seen as an event, not an institution. Barth does not identify the Holy Spirit with the church, nor limit the operation of the Spirit to the bounds of the institution of the church. He argues that the Spirit empowers and renews the church, unites it with Christ's redemptive work on the cross, and is the means by which the risen Christ is made present to the people of God. In this way, the Spirit safeguards the church from lapsing into purely secular ways of understanding its identity and mission.

For many Protestant theologians, the key concept of "apostolicity" means *conforming to the teaching of the apostles* – in other words, maintaining doctrinal continuity with the apostles through grounding belief and practice in scripture. Others, however, would place the emphasis elsewhere. Many Catholic theologians, for example, would argue that *institutional continuity* is essential to the identity of the church. More radical Protestant voices, especially within Anabaptism, argued that it was essential to include discipline in any definition of the church. How else could the purity and distinctiveness of the church be maintained?

## Pure or mixed body: what difference does it make?

Earlier in this chapter, we explored two rather different understandings of the observable or "empirical" church. One of these argues that the church is a "mixed body" of saints and sinners; the other that the church is (or ought to be) a pure body. So what difference does this make to ministry? How does theology impact on practice? We may note some points briefly.

A pure-body ecclesiology assumes that the members of the church are doctrinally and morally pure. It is therefore able to assume a very high level of commitment on their part. Evangelism is something that church members do outside the church. Preaching is primarily about deepening their knowledge of their faith, and encouraging them in their social and personal responsibilities as believers. For the same reason, such ecclesiologies often lead to an emphasis being placed on discipline. If a church is defined by doctrinal and moral purity, there must be means of enforcing this purity – otherwise, the existence and integrity of the church is called into question. Earlier, we noted the "Ban" as a means of securing this discipline; other approaches are, of course, possible.

A mixed-body ecclesiology must assume much less commitment on the part of its members. Evangelism is now something that must be done within the congregation itself. Preaching may take the form of encouraging congregational members in their social and personal responsibilities as believers; it must also, however, deal with the fact that some members will not be converted. Correspondingly, a lesser degree of commitment can be expected from the congregation as a whole, even though many individual members will be very committed to their faith. Since this ecclesiology does not demand moral or doctrinal purity on the part of its members, there is no need for means of enforcing this within the congregation. Most churches adopting this ecclesiology demand such purity from their ministers, but not from their members.

## Ministry within the church: the Second Vatican Council

So what of ministry within the church? What theological defense might be offered for the existence of a distinct priestly order within the church? And how does this relate to the laity as a whole? In the western medieval church, a well-defined hierarchical model of ministry developed, which placed particular emphasis upon the priest as the *alter Christus* ("other Christ") whose task was to represent Christ to the people of God, especially through the sacraments. A sharp distinction was recognized between the "sacred" and "secular." On ordination, a priest was distinguished from lay believers by an "indelible character," bestowed upon him by virtue of the sacrament of ordination.

This view was challenged by the rise of the Reformation, which sought to abolish the distinction between the sacred and secular. (Although some historians represent early Protestantism as eliminating the sacred, it is perhaps more accurate to suggest that the movement sacralized the secular.) The basic distinction between the sacramentally ordained priesthood and the universal priesthood of the laity was denied. Furthermore, the cultic aspect of priesthood was replaced by a new emphasis on the priest as one entrusted with the ministry of the Word. The Protestant rejection of the hierarchical structure of the priesthood and the jurisdiction derived from it led it to argue that its ministers should be elected by the church community.

Martin Luther argued for the abolition of any distinction between a sacramentally ordained priesthood and the universal priesthood of the laity. Every believer, Luther argued, shared in the corporate priesthood of the people of God by virtue of their baptism. Every believer was a priest; but not every believer was called to exercise the "office and work" of a priest. For Luther, ordained clergy were essentially office-holders, who were elected (and could be removed from office) by the local congregation.

The Council of Trent responded by reaffirming the hierarchical nature of offices within the church, and insisted that these were endowed with a specific spiritual jurisdiction. Responding to

Protestant denials of the idea of a "priestly character" that was conferred on an individual through sacramental ordination, Trent reemphasized the link between priestly authority and the role of the priest as *alter Christus* in offering the sacrifice of the Mass. The celebration of the Mass was thus seen as the key to a priest's distinct role and identity, with the church being understood primarily as a hierarchical structure with governing authority.

This model was reinforced by the First Vatican Council, which insisted that the church of Christ is not a community of equals in which all the faithful have the same rights. It is a society of unequals, some of whom are clergy and some of whom are laity. This was often expressed in terms of the distinction between *ecclesia docens* ("the teaching church," referring to the hierarchy) and *ecclesia discens* ("the learning church," referring to the laity, whose responsibilities were primarily to obey their superiors).

Yet, by the middle of the twentieth century, many Catholic theologians believed that reconsideration was necessary. Yves Congar (1904–95) and others laid the groundwork for the recovery of a theology of the laity, who they believed had been marginalized in traditional institutional models of the church. (Congar once asked this question: "What is the position of the laity in the church?" His answer? They kneel before the altar, sit under the pulpit, and put their hands in their wallets.) Prophetically, as it proved, Congar declared that the reappropriation or development of a theology of the laity would lead to far more than some minor adjustments of inherited ecclesiological views; it would lead to a reorientation of the whole vision of what it meant to be a Christian church.

The Second Vatican Council reviewed this question, and in doing so, opened up a highly creative theological discussion of the relation between priests and laity. The document normally referred to as the "Dogmatic Constitution of the Church" (occasionally referred to by the Latin title *Lumen Gentium*) reaffirmed the basic relationship between ministerial priesthood and the common or universal priesthood of the laity. The church has received a unique mission from Jesus Christ, which is entrusted to all the members of the people of God – not just its ordained members.

*Lumen Gentium* argued that the laity shared in the priesthood of Christ, so that they were all called to offer God a spiritual sacrifice, to bear witness to Christ in the sight of the world, and to build up the church, each according to his own vocation. The mission of the Church extends to all people in all times. To fulfill this mandate, God has established one priesthood – Christ's priesthood – in which all the members of the people of God share, albeit in different ways. God has willed that there also be a ministerial priesthood which is at the service of the entire body of the faithful. Its primary purpose is to activate and empower the priesthood of all the baptized. While affirming the distinct nature and theological legitimacy of this ordained priesthood, the Second Vatican Council stressed that it was there to serve the people of God as a whole.

In certain respects, the Second Vatican Council can be seen to echo themes associated with the Reformation. The laity, it affirmed, by virtue of their baptism, shared in their own distinct way in Christ's threefold office as priest, prophet, and king. As a result they shared in the mission of the church, especially in a way that was specific to their secular calling and their capacity to engage in temporal affairs. "They are called in a special way to make the Church present and operative where only through them can she become the salt of the earth."

This new approach has led to the revisiting of the history of the priesthood. For the Belgian Catholic writer Edward Schillebeeckx (1914–2009), the origins of Christian priesthood are to be found in the social dynamics of the earliest Christian communities. This ministry gradually developed a cultic dimension, which subsequently became its dominant characteristic. Yet this, according to Schillebeeckx, was a matter of historical contingency, and need not be seen as binding on the church. The sacramental needs of the community could, in certain situations, make it appropriate for a designated, non-ordained member of the church to celebrate the eucharist. Schillebeeckx's approach has caused controversy within Catholicism, not least because it leads to the loss of any clear sense of priestly identity. Some have argued that the recent difficulties in recruiting to the Catholic priesthood in the western world are at least partly due to the priesthood not clearly involving or demanding functions distinct from those which can be performed by the laity.

This debate will continue, as will others concerning the role of ministers within the church. Debates over the ordination of women to the priesthood or consecration to the episcopacy raise similar or related questions. In the end, many of these debates reduce to a single, yet far from simple, theological question: in what sense is a priest different from an ordinary Christian? The answer given to that question determines the answer given to many of the questions raised in this tantalizingly brief section.

## Engaging with a text

One way of understanding the church is to see it as the sphere of God's transforming love for humanity. Some theologians argued that the church could be seen as a walled garden – rather like the original garden of Eden – in which believers could grow in grace and holiness, protected from the world around them. This approach to the Christian church develops the notion of a closed and protected community, within which faith, hope, and love may blossom, and individuals may live in tranquility with each other and with God. The church is called and fashioned out of the world in much the same way as a garden is an enclosed portion of wilderness, which can be watered, cultivated, and tended. The church is thus an Edenic community, seeking to recover the values of paradise within its own bounds. This idea is found in the writings of Ephrem the Syrian (died 373), who regularly asserted that the church was not merely the gateway to paradise; in some way, a paradisiacal realm was established within its walls.

This idea is also found in a hymn by the great English writer Isaac Watts (1674–1748). Although Watts is probably best known for *When I survey the wondrous Cross*, he also penned a hymn which deals with the nature of the church:

> We are a garden walled around,
> Chosen and made peculiar ground;
> A little spot enclosed by grace
> Out of the world's wide wilderness.

> Like trees of myrrh and spice we stand,
> Planted by God the Father's hand;
> And all his springs in Zion flow,
> To make the young plantation grow.

Awake, O, heavenly wind! and come,
Blow on this garden of perfume;
Spirit divine! descend and breathe
A gracious gale on plants beneath.

The imagery derives from Augustine of Hippo, who pointed out that, in the Old Testament book of the Song of Songs, the church is described as "an enclosed garden, my sister and bride, a sealed fountain, a well of living water, an orchard of choice fruit" (Song of Songs 4:12–13). Watts develops this imagery.

You may find the following questions helpful in interacting with Watts' text.

1. In the first verse, Watts uses the phrase "peculiar ground." What do you think he means by this? At this time, the English word "peculiar" bore the meaning of "special." In what way does Watts' text help identify what is distinctive about the church?

2. Note the use of wilderness imagery in this verse. This was popular at the time: John Bunyan's famous work *Pilgrim's Progress* refers to a journey through the "wilderness of the world." What do you think Watts hopes to demonstrate by contrasting the garden of the church with the wilderness of the world? How does this imagery help us understand his views on the nature and ministry of the church?

3. How do you think that the image of a garden helps Watts unfold the idea that the church is a place of spiritual growth and development? Does he see this process as something that we achieve, or something that is enabled and guided by God? What is the significance of his reference to the "heavenly wind" in the final verse?

CHAPTER 9

# Sacraments

The term "sacrament" is widely used within Christianity to refer to certain rites or church ceremonies which are understood to possess a special spiritual significance. At its heart, a sacrament is an outward and visible sign of an inward and spiritual grace. The Roman Catholic and Eastern Orthodox churches recognize seven sacraments: baptism, the eucharist, confirmation (or chrismation), confession, anointing of the sick, marriage, and ordination. Protestants recognize only baptism and the eucharist as having been instituted by Christ.

There is no agreement within Christianity over how best to refer to the sacrament which focuses on bread and wine, following Christ's command to do so at the Last Supper. The following ways of referring to it are widely encountered in theological works:

- *The eucharist.* This term was widely used in Greek-speaking Christianity, and has also found wide acceptance in the west. The basic meaning of the Greek word *eucharistia* is "giving thanks" or "thanksgiving."
- *The Mass.* This term arose in the Latin-speaking western church during the third century. Its original meaning was "dismissal," referring to the sending out of the congregation into the world after the service was completed. Gradually, the name for this specific aspect of the service came to be applied to the service as a whole.
- *Holy Communion.* This name for the sacrament reflects the basic Christian conviction that it enables or encourages a deeper fellowship or "communion" between the believer and Christ.

*Theology: The Basics*, Third Edition. Alister E. McGrath.
© 2012 Alister E. McGrath. Published 2012 by Blackwell Publishing Ltd.

- *Lord's Supper.* This term is particularly associated with Protestant-ism, and reflects the belief that the fundamental purpose of the sacrament is to recall this pivotal moment in Christ's life, immedi-ately preceding his betrayal, arrest, trial, and crucifixion.

A number of theological debates have centered on the sacraments, and will be considered in this chapter:

1. What is a sacrament?
2. What does a sacrament actually do?
3. What factors affect the effectiveness of sacraments?
4. Is infant baptism justified?
5. In what way, if any, is Christ present at the eucharist?

## What is a sacrament?

The New Testament does not make use of the specific term *sacrament*. Instead, we find the Greek word *mysterion* (which is naturally translated as "mystery"), used to refer to the saving work of God in general. This Greek word is never used to refer to what would now be regarded as a sacrament (for example, baptism). However, it is clear from what we know of the history of the early church that a connection was made at an early stage between the "mystery" of God's saving work in Christ and the "sacraments" of baptism and the eucharist.

The Latin term *sacramentum* came to be widely used in the western church during the third and fourth centuries. The third-century Roman theologian Tertullian pointed out that, in normal Latin use, the word *sacramentum* meant "a sacred oath," referring to the oath of allegiance and loyalty which was required of Roman soldiers. Tertullian used this parallel as a means of bringing out the importance of sacraments in relation to Christian commitment and loyalty within the church. This theme would become of fundamental importance in the sacramental theology of the Swiss reformer Huldrych Zwingli (1484–1531).

So how are sacraments to be defined? Augustine of Hippo argued that the defining characteristic of a sacrament was that it was a sign of sacred realities. "Signs, when applied to divine things, are called sacraments." Yet these signs are not arbitrary: there is some connection between the sign itself and what is being represented. "If sacraments did not bear some resemblance to the things of which they are the sacraments, they would not be sacraments at all." For example, baptism involves water, which is a sign of cleansing or purification – thus pointing to the cleansing and purification of the human soul through the grace of Christ.

The medieval period saw Augustine's ideas being developed and consolidated. Hugh of St. Victor offered the following definition: "a sacrament is a physical or material element set before the external senses, representing by likeness, signifying by its institution, and containing by sanctification, some invisible and spiritual grace." It was an important development of Augustine's thinking, which had been a little vague on precisely which "signs" counted as sacraments. There are four aspects of Hugh's definition:

1.  A "physical or material" element – such as the water of baptism, the bread and wine of the eucharist, or the oil of extreme unction.

2.  A "likeness" to the thing which is signified, so that it can represent the thing signified. Thus the water of baptism can be argued to have a "likeness" to the cleansing power of the grace of Christ, allowing it to represent that grace in this context.

3.  There must be a good reason for believing that the sign in question is *authorized* to represent the spiritual reality to which it points.

4.  The sacrament is somehow capable of conferring the benefits which it signifies to those who partake in it.

But there was a problem. Hugh's definition excluded penance as a sacrament, as it contained no material element. By this stage, penance was firmly established as an integral element of the sacramental system of the church. Theory and practice were thus seriously out of line. A resolution of this difficulty became a matter of urgency. The problem was solved by Peter Lombard (ca. 1100–60), who – by omitting one vital aspect of Hugh's definition – was able to bring theory into line with practice.

Peter's achievement was to omit reference to any "physical or material element" in his definition of a sacrament as "a sign of the grace of God and a form of invisible grace, so that it bears its image and exists as its cause." This definition was included in Peter

Lombard's highly influential and authoritative theological textbook *The Four Books of the Sentences*, and so passed into general use in later medieval theology, remaining virtually unchallenged until the time of the Reformation.

In the sixteenth century, Protestantism challenged this definition on a number of grounds, offering a narrower definition of the essential feature of a sacrament. Martin Luther, writing in 1520, declared that the essential feature of a sacrament was that it was a physical sign of a promise of God, the use of which was sanctioned by Christ himself.

> It has seemed right to restrict the name of sacrament to those promises of God which have signs attached to them. The remainder, not being connected to signs, are merely promises. Hence, strictly speaking, there are only two sacraments in the church of God – baptism and the bread. For only in these two do we find the divinely instituted sign and the promise of the forgiveness of sins.

Luther thus restricted the number of sacraments to two – baptism and eucharist. This fundamental distinction between Protestantism and Catholicism remains in place to this day.

## What do sacraments do?

From what has already been said, sacraments have universally been understood as *signs* within Christian theology. So what do sacraments do? *They signify divine grace.* But this is only a partial answer. Do sacraments do *more* than simply signify the grace of God? Are the sacraments merely signs, or are they a special kind of sign – such as an effective sign, which causes what is being signified?

Traces of this view may be found in the second century. Ignatius of Antioch declared that the eucharist was "the medicine of immortality and the antidote that we should not die, but live for ever in Jesus Christ." The idea is clearly that the eucharist does not merely *signify* eternal life, but is somehow instrumental in *effecting* it. The idea is developed subsequently by many writers, especially Ambrose of Milan (ca. 340–97). Writing in the fourth century, Ambrose argued that in baptism, the Holy Spirit, "coming upon the font or upon those who are to be baptized, effects the reality of regeneration."

In medieval theology, a careful distinction was drawn between the "sacraments of the Old Covenant" (such as circumcision) and the "sacraments of the New Covenant." The essential distinction which early medieval theologians identified as lying between them is that the sacraments of the Old Covenant merely *signified* spiritual realities, whereas the sacraments of the New Covenant *actualized* what they signified. The thirteenth-century Franciscan writer Bona-venture (1221–74) made this point as follows, using a medical analogy:

> In the Old Law, there were ointments of a kind, but they were figurative and did not heal. The disease was lethal, but the anointings were super-ficial . . . Genuinely healing ointments must bring both spiritual anointing and a life-giving power; it was only Christ our Lord who did this, since through his death, the sacraments have the power to bring to life.

These views remain characteristic of modern Catholicism. Sacraments convey the grace that they represent. However, many theologians add a qualifier here, noting that it is possible for an individual to resist this grace, by placing an obstacle in its path. Thus the Council of Trent's *Decree on the Sacraments* condemns the teaching "that sacraments of the new law do not contain the grace which they signify, or that they do not confer this grace to those who present no obstacle." The second phrase is important, as it reflects an awareness that obstacles can be placed in the way of the effectiveness of the sacraments by individual believers.

The Second Vatican Council, while continuing to emphasize the effective causality of sacraments, noted the importance of believers responding appropriately to them:

> Because [sacraments] are signs, they also instruct. They not only presuppose faith, but by words and objects they also nourish, strengthen, and express it. That is why they are called "sacraments of faith." They do indeed confer grace, but in addition the very act of celebrating them most effectively disposes the faithful to receive this grace to their profit, to worship God duly, and to practice charity.

Protestantism found itself divided over the question of what the sacraments achieved. Luther was prepared to allow that sacraments caused what they signified. In his *Shorter Catechism* (1529), he made it clear that baptism brought about both the signification and causation of divine forgiveness:

> Q.  What gifts or benefits does Baptism bring?
> A.  It brings about the forgiveness of sins, saves us from death and the devil, and grants eternal blessedness to all who believe, as the Word and promise of God declare.
> Q.  How can water bring about such a great thing?
> A.  Water does not; but it is the Word of God with and through the water, and our faith which trusts in the Word of God in the water. For without the Word of God, that water is nothing but water, and there is no Baptism. But when it is linked with the Word of God, it is a Baptism, that is, a gracious water of life, and a bath of new birth in the Holy Spirit.

These views remain generally characteristic of Lutheranism to this day. Other Protestant writers, however, were suspicious of such an approach, which they regarded as approaching a magical view of sacraments. The Swiss reformer Huldrych Zwingli insisted that sacraments were signs, and nothing more:

> Sacraments are simply the signs of holy things. Baptism is a sign which pledges us to the Lord Jesus Christ. The Remembrance shows us that Christ suffered death for our sake. They are the signs and pledges of these holy things.

Zwingli therefore argues that both baptism and the eucharist (which he refers to as "the Remembrance") are external signs of spiritual realities, which have no power in themselves to bring about what they signify. Baptism is thus a sign, but not a cause, of God's forgiveness of sins. This viewpoint remains influential within Protestantism, and is especially found within modern evangelicalism.

Yet a third Protestant approach was set out by John Calvin and his successors within the Reformed tradition. Calvin's approach can be seen as a mediating approach, roughly halfway between Luther's causative view and Zwingli's representationalist view of the sacraments. Calvin defines a sacrament as "an external symbol by which the Lord seals on our consciences his promises of good will

towards us, in order to sustain the weakness of our faith."
Yet although the sacraments are external signs, he argues that there
is such a close connection between the symbol and the gift which it
symbolizes that we can "easily pass from one to the other."
The sign is visible and physical, whereas the thing signified is invisible and spiritual – yet the connection between the sign and the
thing signified is so intimate that it is permissible to apply the one to
the other.

> Why should the Lord put in your hand the symbol of his body, unless it
> was to assure you that you really participate in it? And if it is true that a
> visible sign is given to us to seal the gift of an invisible thing, when we
> have received the symbol of the body, let us rest assured that the body
> itself is also given to us.

Calvin can thus maintain the difference between sign and
thing signified, while insisting that the sign really points to the gift
it signifies.

One of the most characteristic features of Protestantism was
its insistence upon the laity being allowed to receive communion
"in both kinds" – in other words, receiving both the bread and
the wine. There had been a longstanding tradition within the western
church, whose origins are somewhat obscure, which held that
only priests should be allowed to receive both elements; the laity
were only allowed bread. (Some historians speculate that early medieval
problems with an enthusiastic but intoxicated laity may lie behind
the practice.)

Luther was adamant that the laity should be allowed to receive the
wine. The bread and wine were both signs of God's grace and love.
To deny the laity access to both sacramental signs was to imply that
they were also denied access to the divine realities they signified.
The practice of "communion in both kinds" would henceforth be
characteristic of the Reformation. It is important to appreciate the
theological defense of this practice – namely, that to exclude
people from sharing in the sign of a divine reality is tantamount to
declaring that they are also excluded from that reality itself.

A related theological debate is also of importance here – the question
of the worthiness of the person who presides over the sacraments.

## What factors affect the effectiveness of sacraments?

In the previous chapter, we noted some of the issues which lay behind the Donatist controversy. One of these concerns the personal worthiness or holiness of the minister who administers the sacraments. The Donatists refused to recognize that a *traditor* – that is to say, a Christian minister whose personal credentials had been compromised or tainted through collaboration with the Roman authorities during the Diocletian persecution – could administer the sacraments. Subjective imperfections on the part of the person administering the sacraments rendered them invalid. Accordingly, they argued that baptisms, ordinations, and eucharists administered by such ministers were of no spiritual value.

Responding to this approach, Augustine argued that Donatism laid excessive emphasis upon the qualities of the human agent, and gave insufficient weight to the grace of Jesus Christ. It is, he argued, impossible for fallen human beings to make distinctions concerning who is pure and impure, worthy or unworthy. This view, which is totally consistent with his understanding of the church as a "mixed body" of saints and sinners, holds that the efficacy of a sacrament rests, not upon the merits of the individual administering it, but upon the merits of the one who instituted them in the first place – Jesus Christ. The validity of sacraments is independent of the merits of those who administer them.

The theological issue at stake has come to be represented by two Latin slogans, each reflecting a different understanding of the grounds of the efficacy of the sacraments.

1. Sacraments are efficacious *ex opere operantis* – literally, "on account of the work of the one who works." Here, the efficacy of the sacrament is understood to be dependent upon the personal qualities of the minister.

2. Sacraments are efficacious *ex opere operato* – literally, "on account of the work which is done." Here, the efficacy of the sacrament is understood to be dependent upon the grace of Christ, which the sacraments represent and convey.

The Donatist position is best described as reflecting an *ex opere operantis*, and Augustine's as reflecting an *ex opere operato*, understanding of sacramental causality. The latter view became normative within the western church, and was maintained by the mainstream reformers during the sixteenth century.

The *ex opere operato* approach to the efficacy of the sacraments was vigorously defended by Pope Innocent III (1160–1216) in the late twelfth century. For Innocent, the merits or demerits of the priest are of no consequence in relation to the efficacy of the eucharist. In the end, the sacraments are grounded in the Word of God, which is not restricted by human weakness or failing:

> Nothing more is accomplished by a good priest and nothing less by a wicked priest, because it is accomplished by the word of the creator and not the merit of the priest. Thus the wickedness of the priest does not nullify the effect of the sacrament, just as the sickness of a doctor does not destroy the power of his medicine. Although the "doing of the thing (*opus operans*)" may be unclean, nevertheless the "thing which is done (*opus operatum*)" is always clean.

A similar approach was adopted by mainline Protestant writers during the sixteenth century. The Thirty-Nine Articles of the Church of England (1563) state this point clearly:

> For those who receive the sacraments which are administered to them by faith and in proper fashion, the effect of Christ's ordinances is not taken away by the wickedness of the minister, nor is the grace of God's gifts diminished. These are effective on account of the institution and promise of Christ, even if they are administered by wicked people.

The *Catechism of the Catholic Church* offers a definitive statement of what is to be understood by an *ex opere operato* understanding of how the sacraments function:

> Celebrated worthily in faith, the sacraments confer the grace that they signify. They are *efficacious* because in them Christ himself is at work: it is he who baptizes, he who acts in his sacraments in order to commu-nicate the grace that each sacrament signifies . . . This is the meaning of the Church's affirmation that the sacraments act *ex opere operato* (liter-ally: "by the very fact of the action's being performed"), i.e., by virtue

of the saving work of Christ, accomplished once for all. It follows that "the sacrament is not wrought by the righteousness of either the celebrant or the recipient, but by the power of God." From the moment that a sacrament is celebrated in accordance with the intention of the Church, the power of Christ and his Spirit acts in and through it, independently of the personal holiness of the minister. Nevertheless, the fruits of the sacraments also depend on the disposition of the one who receives them.

We now turn to consider two theological questions that have caused considerable debate within Christianity. One relates to baptism; the other to the eucharist. We begin by considering what theological defense can be given of the church's longstanding practice of baptizing infants.

## Is infant baptism justified?

The New Testament includes no specific references to the baptism of infants. However, it does not explicitly forbid the practice, and there are also a number of passages which could be interpreted as condoning it – for example, references to the baptizing of entire households (which would probably have included infants) – at several points (Acts 16:15, 33; 1 Corinthians 1:16). Paul treats baptism as a spiritual counterpart to circumcision (Colossians 2:11–12), suggesting that the parallel may extend to its application to infants.

The practice of baptizing infants born to Christian parents – often referred to as *paedobaptism* – appears to have been a response to a number of pressures. It is possible that the parallel with the Jewish rite of circumcision led Christians to devise an equivalent rite of passage for Christian infants. More generally, there seems to have been a pastoral need for Christian parents to celebrate the birth of a child within a believing household. Infant baptism may well have had its origins partly in response to this concern. However, it must be stressed that there is genuine uncertainty concerning both the historical origins and the social or theological causes of the practice. What can be said is that the practice had become normal, if not universal, by the second or third century.

**Figure 19**    Perugino, *The Baptism of Christ*, ca. 1498–1500, oil on olivewood, 30 × 23.3 cm. Kunsthistorisches Museum, Vienna. The Baptism of Christ is seen by many theologians as a mandate for the baptism of Christians. AKG Images/Erich Lessing.

So what theological defense can be offered for this? In what follows, we shall explore a number of theological rationalizations of the practice of infant baptism, along with some criticisms of the practice.

1. Infant baptism is grounded in the efficacy of the sacrament
One obvious question associated with infant baptism is this: as the infant has no conscious faith of its own, how can it be considered to make an informed response to the Christian gospel? As the *Catechism of the Catholic Church* points out, "Always, Baptism is seen as connected with faith: 'Believe in the Lord Jesus, and you will be saved, you and your household,' St. Paul declared to his jailer in Philippi.

And the narrative continues, the jailer 'was baptized at once, with all his family.'" Is not the baptism of infants based on a mechanical or "magical" view of the sacraments?

Catholicism has always taken the view that an *ex opere operato* view of baptism avoids this difficulty. The effectiveness of baptism is not dependent upon human comprehension of the mode of its operation. As the *Catechism* puts it: "The sheer gratuitousness of the grace of salvation is particularly manifest in infant Baptism." Additionally, the weakness of individual faith is supplemented by the corporate faith of the church. "It is only within the faith of the Church that each of the faithful can believe." Baptism thus initiates a process of development in faith.

As we shall see, some Protestants reject infant baptism. In particular, many evangelicals hold that baptism is not a sacrament (in the strict sense of the word), but is rather to be seen as an "ordinance." On this view, baptism does not in any way convey the grace it symbolizes; rather, it is simply a public manifestation of the person's conversion. Since only adults can be converted, baptism is inappropriate for infants or for children who have not yet reached maturity.

Yet this viewpoint is not universal within Protestantism. Lutherans, following Luther himself, insist that the efficacy of baptism as a sacrament means that it has an effect on infants, even if this cannot be discerned. A statement issued recently by the Missouri Lutheran Synod (an American Lutheran denomination) makes this point clearly:

> Lutherans believe that the Bible teaches that a person is saved by God's grace alone through faith alone in Jesus Christ. Baptism, we believe, is one of the miraculous means of grace (together with God's written and spoken Word) through which God creates the gift of faith in a person's heart. Although we do not claim to understand how this happens or how it is possible, we believe (because of what the Bible says about baptism) that when an infant is baptized God creates faith in the heart of that infant. This faith cannot yet, of course, be expressed or articulated, yet it is real and present all the same.

2. Infant baptism remits the guilt of original sin
One of Augustine of Hippo's most significant contributions to the theology of baptism was his argument that humans are born into the world already contaminated by original sin. By "original sin,"

Augustine meant a flaw, defect, or infection from the moment of birth, rather than something that was acquired later in life through a sinful action. For Augustine, sinful human nature gives rise to individual sinful actions. Sin causes sins. Or, to use a medical analogy, sin is an illness, while individual sins are its symptoms. For Augustine, baptism remits the guilt of original sin.

So what happens to those who die without having been baptized, whether in infancy or later in life? If baptism remits the guilt of original sin, people who die without being baptized remain guilty. So what happens to them? Augustine's position demands that such people cannot be saved. Augustine himself certainly held to this belief, and argued forcefully that unbaptized infants were condemned to eternal damnation.

Augustine's position was modified in the light of popular pressure, apparently based upon a belief that his doctrine was unjust. Peter Lombard argued that unbaptized infants receive only "the penalty of being condemned" and do not receive the more painful "penalty of the senses." Although they are condemned, that condemnation does not include the experience of the physical pain of hell. This idea is sometimes referred to as "limbo," although this has never become part of the official teaching of any Christian body, including Roman Catholicism.

The *Catechism of the Catholic Church* can be seen as retaining this Augustinian emphasis upon the necessity of baptism for salvation, while at the same time not wishing to exclude God's special graciousness towards those infants who have died outside baptism.

> As regards children who have died without Baptism, the Church can only entrust them to the mercy of God, as she does in her funeral rites for them. Indeed, the great mercy of God who desires that all men should be saved, and Jesus' tenderness toward children which caused him to say: "Let the children come to me, do not hinder them," allow us to hope that there is a way of salvation for children who have died without Baptism.

3. Infant baptism is a sign of the covenant between God and the church
Christian theology has always seen baptism as the Christian equivalent of circumcision. In the New Testament, Paul notes that baptism has replaced circumcision (Colossians 2:11–12). In this passage, Paul refers to baptism as "the circumcision of Christ." Since only infants were normally circumcised under the Old Law, a parallel seemed to exist

between the circumcision of male infants in Judaism, and the baptism of infants in the church.

Developing this idea, Zwingli argued that baptism is to be seen as the New Testament equivalent of the Old Testament rite of circumcision. It is gentler than circumcision, in that it involves no pain or shedding of blood, and more inclusive, in that it embraces both male and female infants. The more *gentle* character of the gospel was publicly demonstrated by the absence of pain or the shedding of blood in the sacrament. Christ suffered – in being circumcised himself in addition to his death on the cross – in order that his people need not suffer in this manner. Further, Zwingli stressed that baptism was the sign of belonging to a community – the church. The fact that the child was not conscious of this belonging was irrelevant: whether the child knew it or not, it *was* a member of the Christian community, and baptism was the public demonstration of this membership.

Yet not all Christians are persuaded of the merits of infant baptism. In the early church, Tertullian argued that the baptism of children should be deferred until such time as they "know Christ." Anabaptism – a movement within the Protestant Reformation of the sixteenth century – insisted that baptism was to be reserved for those who understood what it meant, and had consented to be baptized.

Perhaps the most significant theological critique of infant baptism is due to the great twentieth-century Protestant theologian Karl Barth, who registered three fundamental areas of concern and criticism:

1. Infant baptism is without biblical foundation. All the evidence points to infant baptism having become the norm in the post-apostolic period, not the period of the New Testament itself.
2. The practice of infant baptism has led to the disastrous assumption that individuals are Christians as a result of their birth. Barth argues, in terms which remind many of Dietrich Bonhoeffer's idea of "cheap grace," that infant baptism devalues the grace of God, and reduces Christianity to a purely social phenomenon.
3. The practice of infant baptism weakens the central link between baptism and Christian discipleship. Baptism is a witness to the grace of God, and marks the beginning of the human response to this grace. In that infants cannot meaningfully make this response, the theological meaning of baptism is obscured.

## In what way, if any, is Christ present at the eucharist?

The phrase "the real presence" has come to denote the idea that Christ is present, in some way and to some extent, at the eucharist. *The Catechism of the Catholic Church* sets out this basic belief with clarity and precision:

> The mode of Christ's presence under the Eucharistic species is unique . . . In the most blessed sacrament of the Eucharist the body and blood, together with the soul and divinity, of our Lord Jesus Christ and, therefore, *the whole Christ is truly, really, and substantially contained.* This presence is called "real" – by which is not intended to exclude the other types of presence as if they could not be "real" too, but because it is presence in the fullest sense: that is to say, it is a *substantial* presence by which Christ, God and man, makes himself wholly and entirely present.

At the Last Supper, Jesus of Nazareth is recorded as speaking these words as he broke the bread in the presence of his disciples: "this is my

**Figure 20**   Juan de Juanes, *The Last Supper,* 1570, oil on canvas, 116 × 191 cm. Museo del Prado, Madrid. AKG Images/ Erich Lessing.

body" (Matthew 26:26). The doctrine of the "real presence" is grounded in the basic idea that the eucharistic bread and the wine either are transformed into the body and blood of Christ, or that they represent him in such an efficacious manner that he may be regarded as present. The words spoken by Jesus Christ over the bread at the Last Supper, and repeated in the liturgy of the church, were clearly of foundational importance in relation to the emergence of this idea. It was therefore inevitable and entirely proper that considerable theological attention should be given to the explanation of the meaning of this practice. What did it achieve? And in what way did the eucharistic bread and wine differ from ordinary bread and wine?

In what follows, we shall consider four main approaches to such questions that have been significant in theological debates.

## 1. Transubstantiation

This approach, endorsed by the Fourth Lateran Council (1215), rests on Aristotle's distinction between "substance" and "accident." The *substance* of something is its essential nature, whereas its *accidents* are its outward appearances (for example, its color, shape, smell, and so forth). The doctrine of transubstantiation affirms that the accidents of the bread and wine (their outward appearance, taste, smell, and so forth) remain unchanged at the moment of consecration, while their substance changes from that of bread and wine to that of the body and blood of Jesus Christ.

This doctrine underlies one of the Catholic church's best-known eucharistic hymns – Thomas Aquinas' *Pange lingua* ("Sing, my tongue"), dating from the middle of the thirteenth century. The hymn sets out a theology of the real presence, which identifies both its historical and theological significance. The fourth of its six verses sets out the idea of transubstantiation. As the Latin text is difficult to translate without losing its rhyming scheme, I have reproduced the original Latin text below, followed by my very literal English translation:

> Verbum caro, panem verum
> Verbo carnem efficit:
> Fitque sanguis Christi merum,
> Et si sensus deficit,
> Ad firmandum cor sincerum
> Sola fides sufficit.

"The Word in flesh makes real bread into his flesh with a word; and also wine into the blood of Christ; And if the senses are not sufficient to confirm the sincere heart, faith alone is sufficient."

This approach, often criticized by Protestant theologians, was re-affirmed by the Council of Trent: "After the consecration of the bread and wine, our Lord Jesus Christ is truly, really, and substantially contained in the venerable sacrament of the holy eucharist under the appearance of those physical things." The Council vigorously defended both the doctrine and the terminology of transubstantiation. "By the consecration of the bread and wine a change is brought about of the whole substance of the bread into the substance of the body of Christ and of the whole substance of the wine into the blood of Christ. This change the holy catholic church properly and appropriately calls transubstantiation."

## 2. Transsignification and transfinalization

In more recent times, the idea of transubstantiation has been reworked by Roman Catholic theologians, such as the Belgian writer Edward Schillebeeckx. In his important study *The Eucharist* (1968), Schillebeeckx argued that the Aristotelian philosophical framework underlying the notion of transubstantiation caused difficulties for many modern people. A new approach was needed, he argued, which would retain the essential theological insights of the Council of Trent, without embodying these in an outdated and vulnerable philosophical framework.

Schillebeeckx noted that a growing hostility towards the use of ontological or "physical" interpretations of the eucharist within Catholic circles after World War II was matched by a "rediscovery of the sacramental symbolic activity" – that is, a realization that "the sacraments are first and foremost symbolic acts or activity as signs." Schillebeeckx thus introduced the terms "transfunctionalism," "transfinalization," and "transsignification" to express the idea that the "bread and wine become the subject of a new *establishment of meaning*, not by men, but by the living Lord *in* the Church, through which they become the *sign* of the real presence of Christ giving himself to us."

Schillebeeckx's point is that interpretation of the signification of the eucharistic bread and wine is not arbitrary, nor a human impos-ition upon them; it is an act of discernment by the church, which it has been *authorized* to undertake by Christ. There is, for Schillebeeckx, no need to invoke the notion of a physical change of substance of the bread and wine. Christ's intention was not to alter the metaphysics of the eucharistic elements, but to ensure that these pointed to his continuing presence within the church, as the community of the faithful.

The official response of the Catholic Church to these developments was to affirm that they were acceptable, provided that they were upheld within the context of the traditional understanding of transubstantiation. If the bread and the wine were indeed changed in the manner that this traditional teaching affirmed, it followed that both the goal and the signification of the bread and wine were changed as well.

### 3. Sacramental union, or consubstantiation

A third view is especially associated with Martin Luther, and is characteristic of much contemporary Lutheran theology. This approach – sometimes referred to as "consubstantiation," but more accurately known as "the sacramental union" – insists upon the simultaneous presence of both bread and the body of Christ at one and the same time. There is no change in substance; the substance of both bread and the body of Christ are present together. The doctrine of transubstantiation seemed to Luther to be an absurdity, an attempt to rationalize a mystery.

For Luther, the crucial point was that Christ was really present at the eucharist – not some particular theory as to how he was present. Luther borrowed an image from the patristic writer Origen to make his point: if iron is placed in a fire and heated, it glows – and in that glowing iron, both the iron and heat are present. Why not use some simple everyday analogy such as this to illustrate the mystery of the presence of Christ at the eucharist, instead of rationalizing it using some scholastic subtlety? It is not the doctrine of transubstantiation which is to be believed, but simply that Christ really is present at the eucharist. It is more important to affirm this fact than to offer any theory or explanation of it. This is reflected in the contemporary Lutheran belief that Christ's true body and blood are present in, with, and under the external elements of bread and wine – even though this must be recognized as a divine mystery beyond human comprehension or explanation.

4. Memorialism

For some Protestant writers, particularly within evangelical traditions, Christ is remembered in his absence at the Lord's Supper. The intellectual roots of this approach are often identified as lying in the writings of Huldrych Zwingli. Zwingli's approach involved challenging the traditional interpretation of the words "this is my body." Up to this point, most Christians had seen these as a direct affirmation of the identity of the eucharistic bread with the body of Christ. Zwingli believed otherwise. He argued that scripture employed many figures of speech. Thus the word "is" might at one point mean "is absolutely identical with," and at another it might mean "represents" or "signifies."

Zwingli concludes that "there are innumerable passages in Scripture where the word 'is' means 'signifies.'" The question that must therefore be addressed, he declares, is whether Christ's words "this is my body" are to be taken literally or metaphorically. He has little doubt of the answer.

> In the words "This is my body," the word "this" means the bread, and the word "body" means the body which was put to death for us. Therefore the word "is" cannot be taken literally, for the bread is not the body.

Zwingli had another argument to deploy. He pointed out that both scripture and the creeds affirm that Christ is now "seated at the right hand of God." Now Zwingli has not the slightest idea where this might be, and wastes no time speculating on its location – but, he argues, it does mean that wherever Christ is now, he cannot be present in the eucharist. How could he be in two places at once? For this reason, Zwingli proposes a doctrine of the "real absence" of Christ at the eucharist. Christ, who is somewhere else, is remembered in his absence, and the hope of his future return is reaffirmed. For Zwingli, the eucharist was about "proclaiming the Lord's death until he comes again" (1 Corinthians 11:26).

## Engaging with a text

In 1982 the Faith and Order Commission of the Protestant World Council of Churches published a highly influential theological statement entitled "Baptism, Eucharist and Ministry." This World

Council of Churches paper (sometimes known as the "Lima Text," after the Peruvian city which hosted this meeting) is widely regarded as a landmark in ecumenical discussions of its themes. The statement was the outcome of several years of ecumenical study and dialogue, mainly between Protestant denominations, to identify what basic principles could be affirmed together by the churches of the Reformed, Lutheran, Methodist, Anglican, and Orthodox traditions. The document proved highly influential in catalyzing ecumenical discussions on issues relating to the sacraments and Christian ministry.

The document sets out a justification for baptism, and sketches an understanding of the differences that it makes. What follows is a statement concerning the identity of baptism. Read it through, and take time to follow through the biblical references embedded within the text.

> Baptism is the sign of new life through Jesus Christ. It unites the one baptized with Christ and with his people. The New Testament scriptures and the liturgy of the Church unfold the meaning of baptism in various images which express the riches of Christ and the gifts of his salvation. These images are sometimes linked with the symbolic uses of water in the Old Testament. Baptism is participation in Christ's death and resurrection (Romans 6:3–5; Colossians 2:12); a washing away of sin (1 Corinthians 6:11); a new birth (John 3:5); an enlightenment by Christ (Ephesians 5:14); a reclothing in Christ (Galatians 3:27); a renewal by the Spirit (Titus 3:5); the experience of salvation from the flood (1 Peter 3:20–21); an exodus from bondage (1 Corinthians 10:1–2) and a liberation into a new humanity in which barriers of division, whether of sex or race or social status, are transcended (Galatians 3:27–28; 1 Corinthians 12:13). The images are many but the reality is one.

1. Work through the biblical passages incorporated within this statement. The basic point being made in the document is that baptism weaves together some of the major themes and emphases of the Christian faith. Baptism is a multifaceted entity, with many different dimensions and levels of meaning. This is what the document means when it affirms that "the images are many but the reality is one."

2. Note how baptism is referred to as a "sign." Look again at the list of meanings of baptism that you drew up in response to the previous question. Which of these seem to have an obvious link with the symbolism of water?

3. Remember that this document was intended to be ecumenical, aiming to help the churches draw closer to each other. Read the text again, and reflect on whether any particular Christian denominations or groups might find it difficult or controversial at any point.

# CHAPTER 10

# *Heaven*

Most works of Christian theology follow the pattern of the creeds, and end with a discussion of eternal life. This traditional approach has been followed in this basic introduction to the themes of Christian theology. The term "eschatology" (from the Greek words *ta eschata*, meaning "the last things") is widely used in Christian theology to refer to beliefs about judgment, heaven, and so forth. In this final chapter, we shall explore some aspects of Christian thinking about one eschatological theme – heaven.

## The hope of heaven

Christianity is a religion of hope, which focuses on the resurrection of Jesus as the grounds for believing and trusting in a God who is able to triumph over death, and give hope to all those who suffer and die. The word "eschatology" is used to refer to Christian teachings about the "last things." Just as "Christology" refers to the Christian understanding of the nature and identity of Jesus Christ, so "eschatology" refers to the Christian understanding of such things as heaven and eternal life.

The eschatology of the New Testament is complex. However, one of its leading themes is that something which happened in the past has inaugurated something new, which will reach its final consummation in the future. The Christian believer is thus caught up in this tension between the "now" and the "not yet." In one sense, heaven has not

*Theology: The Basics*, Third Edition. Alister E. McGrath.
© 2012 Alister E. McGrath. Published 2012 by Blackwell Publishing Ltd.

yet happened; in another, its powerful lure already impacts upon us in a dramatic and complex fashion, in which we are at one and the same time excited at its prospect and rendered dejected through knowing that we are not yet there.

The term "heaven" is used frequently in the Pauline writings of the New Testament to refer to the Christian hope. Although it is natural to think of heaven as a future entity, Paul's thinking appears to embrace both a future reality and a spiritual sphere or realm which coexists with the material world of space and time. Thus "heaven" is referred to both as the future home of the believer (2 Corinthians 5:1–2; Philippians 3:20) and as the present dwelling-place of Jesus Christ, from which he will come in final judgment (Romans 10:6; 1 Thessalonians 1:10; 4:16).

As we shall see, one of Paul's most significant statements concerning heaven focuses on the notion of believers being "citizens of heaven" (Philippians 3:20), and in some way sharing in the life of heaven in the present. The tension between the "now" and the "not yet" is evident in Paul's statements concerning heaven, making it very difficult to sustain the simple idea of heaven as something which will not come into being until the future, or which cannot be experienced at all in the present. For Paul, the hope of heaven impacts upon life in the here and now, even though heaven, in all its fullness, remains to be consummated in the future.

Probably the most helpful way of conceiving the modest New Testament affirmations concerning heaven is to see it as a consummation of the Christian doctrine of salvation, in which the presence, penalty, and power of sin have all been finally eliminated, and the total presence of God in individuals and the community of faith has been achieved. Some such idea underlies the vision of heaven set out in the *Catechism of the Catholic Church*:

> Heaven is the ultimate end and fulfillment of the deepest human longings, the state of supreme, definitive happiness . . . this consummation will be the final realization of the unity of the human race, which God willed from creation and of which the pilgrim Church has been "in the nature of sacrament." Those who are united with Christ will form the community of the redeemed, "the holy city" of God, "the Bride, the wife of the Lamb." She will not be wounded any longer by sin, stains, self-love, that destroy or wound the earthly community.

The beatific vision, in which God opens himself in an inexhaustible way to the elect, will be the ever-flowing well-spring of happiness, peace, and mutual communion.

It should be noted that the New Testament parables of heaven are strongly communal in nature. Heaven is here portrayed as a banquet, a wedding feast, or as a city – the new Jerusalem. Eternal life is thus not a projection of an individual human existence, but is rather to be seen as sharing, with the redeemed community as a whole, in the community of a loving God.

We begin our exploration of the theology of heaven by engaging with a biblical image which is of central importance to our theme.

## An image of heaven: the New Jerusalem

Theology often involves wrestling with images, as much with ideas. We have already seen how Christian theologians struggled to do intellectual justice to immensely difficult ideas, such as the "two natures" of Jesus Christ, or the doctrine of the Trinity. Yet theologians are also called to explore images – such as God as a shepherd, or a father. As the Oxford scholar and theologian Austin Farrer (1904–68) argued, Christianity represents a "rebirth of images," both in terms of the importance assigned to images in conceiving and sustaining the Christian life and the new impetus given to the religious imagery which the church inherited from Israel. In the case of the Christian understanding of heaven, it is an image, rather than an idea, which plays a decisively important role for Christian theology – namely, the image of the "New Jerusalem."

Many Old Testament passages speak of the city of Jerusalem, which is seen both as a tangible image of the presence and providence of God within its sturdy walls, and also as a pointer to the fulfillment of messianic expectations. Jerusalem is the city of David, within which the coming messiah will dwell. The New Testament gives a new twist to this focus, not least in the remarkable reworking of the theme of the "city of God" found in the Revelation of St. John, the final book of the Christian Bible. For this biblical writer, the fulfillment of all Christian hopes and expectations centers on the new Jerusalem, the city of God within which the risen Christ reigns triumphant. This image has stimulated intense reflection on the part of Christian theologians. The image of the "New Jerusalem" has exercised a decisively important influence over Christian reflection on heaven down the centuries.

The origins of this evocative image lie primarily in the book of Revelation, the closing book of the Christian Bible. Its powerful imagery has saturated Christian hymnody and theological reflection, and perhaps nowhere so clearly as the church's reflection on how heaven is to be visualized. The consolation of heaven is here contrasted with the suffering, tragedy, and pain of life on earth. The book of Revelation – also known as "the Apocalypse" or the "Revelation of St. John" – is traditionally held to reflect the conditions of social exclusion or perhaps persecution faced by Christians in this region of the Roman empire in the later years of the reign of the emperor Domitian.

Perhaps its most enduring image – and certainly that most relevant to this final chapter – is its portrayal of the New Jerusalem:

> Then I saw a new heaven and a new earth; for the first heaven and the first earth had passed away, and the sea was no more. And I saw the holy city, the new Jerusalem, coming down out of heaven from God, prepared as a bride adorned for her husband. And I heard a loud voice from the throne saying, "See, the home of God is among mortals. He will dwell with them; they will be his peoples, and God himself will be with them; he will wipe every tear from their eyes. Death will be no more; mourning and crying and pain will be no more, for the first things have passed away." And the one who was seated on the throne said, "See, I am making all things new." (Revelation 21:1–5)

The theme of the New Jerusalem is here integrated with motifs drawn from the creation account – such as the presence of the "tree of life" (Revelation 22:2) – suggesting that heaven can be seen as the restoration of the bliss of the garden of Eden (Genesis 2), when God dwelt with humanity in harmony. The pain, sorrow, and evil of a fallen world have finally passed away, and the creation restored to its original intention.

The New Jerusalem – like its earthly counterpart – is portrayed as a walled city. Its security is beyond question. It is perched on the peak of a hill that no invading army could hope to ascend. Its walls are so thick that they could not be breached by any known siege engine, and so high that no human could hope to scale them. Its twelve gates are guarded by angels. Just as return to Eden was once prevented by a guardian angel, so the New Jerusalem is defended against invasion by supernatural forces.

It is important to note that the twelve gates of the New Jerusalem, though guarded by angels, are permanently thrown open. Whereas the classic fortified city of ancient times was designed to exclude outsiders, the architecture of the New Jerusalem seems designed to welcome them within its boundaries. The city is portrayed as perfectly cubical (21:36), perhaps signifying that it is a perfection of the square temple which the prophet Ezekiel envisaged for the rebuilt Jerusalem after the return from exile (Ezekiel 43:16; 48:20).

The careful attention paid to imagery suggests that the New Jerusalem is to be seen in terms of the fulfillment of Israel through the restoration of its twelve tribes (21:14). Most significantly of all, the New Jerusalem does not contain a temple (21:22). The cultic hierarchies of the old priestly tradition are swept to one side. All are now priests, and there is no need for a temple, in that God dwells within the city as a whole. In a remarkable transformation of images, the city has itself become a temple, in that God is now all in all.

Where the prophets of the Old Testament had yearned for the rebuilding of the temple, Revelation declares that it has become redundant. What it foreshadowed had now taken place. With the advent of the reality of God's presence, its symbol was no longer required. The dwelling-place of God is now with the people of God; it can no longer be contained within a physical structure. The New Jerusalem is thus characterized by the pervasive presence of God, and the triumphant and joyful response of those who had long awaited this experience.

This image of heaven resonates strongly with one of the leading themes of Paul's theology – that Christians are to be regarded as "citizens of heaven" (Philippians 3:19–21). Paul makes a distinction between those who "set their minds on earthly things" and those whose citizenship is "in heaven." Paul himself was a Roman citizen, who knew what privileges this brought – particularly on those occasions when he found himself in conflict with the Roman authorities.

For Paul, Christians possessed something greater: the "citizenship of heaven," which is to be understood as a present possession, not something which is yet to come. While believers have yet to enter into the full possession of what this citizenship entails, they already possess that privilege. We have no permanent citizenship in this world, in that our citizenship is in heaven (Philippians 3:20). As the author of the letter to the Hebrews puts it, "here we have no lasting city, but we are looking for the city that is to come" (Hebrews 13:14).

## The appearance of the human body in heaven

The New Testament affirms that Christians are "citizens of heaven." But what do citizens of heaven look like? If heaven is to be compared to a human city, what are its inhabitants like? The New Testament has remarkably little to say on the matter, in that it hints at such matters as a mystery, rather than disclosing them as facts. The image of a seed, used by Paul in 1 Corinthians 15, was taken by many writers to mean that there was some organic connection between the earthly and heavenly body. Resurrection could thus be conceived as the unfolding of a predetermined pattern within the human organism. Yet even this image had to be treated with caution. Where some theologians took the view that this obliged them to treat such matters with restraint, others appear to have seen themselves as liberated from the traditional constraints imposed by the biblical text, and launched into the most stratospheric of theological speculations.

One possibility would be to imagine the streets of the New Jerusalem as inhabited by disembodied souls. On this model, the human being consists of two entities – a physical body and a spiritual soul. Death leads to the liberation of the soul from its material body. This view was commonplace within the Hellenistic culture of the New Testament period. However, this idea was vigorously opposed by most early Christian theologians. The most significant minority voice in this matter belonged to Origen, a highly creative theologian with a strongly Platonist bent, who held that the resurrection body was purely spiritual. This view was contested by most Christian writers, who insisted that the phrase "the resurrection of the body" was to be understood as the permanent resurrection of both the body and the soul of the believer.

But what would these resurrected individuals look like? Many early Christian writers argued that the "citizens of heaven" would be naked, recreating the situation in paradise. This time, however, nakedness would neither give rise to shame nor sexual lust, but would simply be accepted as the natural and innocent state of humanity. Others, however, argued that the inhabitants of the New Jerusalem would be clothed in finery, reflecting their status as citizens of God's chosen city.

It was clear to many writers that the final state of deceased believers was not of material importance to their appearance in heaven. The issue emerged as theologically significant during a persecution of Christians in the city of Lyons around the years 175–77. Aware that Christians professed belief in the "resurrection of the body," their pagan oppressors burned the bodies of the Christians they had just martyred, and threw their ashes in the River Rhône. This, they believed, would prevent the resurrection of these martyrs, in that there was now no body to be raised. Christian theologians responded by arguing that God was able to restore all that the body had lost through this process of destruction.

Methodius of Olympus (died ca. 311) offered an analogy for this process of reconstitution which would prove highly influential in discussing this question. The resurrection could, he argued, be thought of as a kind of "rearrangement" of the constituent elements of humanity. It is like a statue which is melted down and reforged from the same material – yet in such a manner that any defects or damage are eliminated.

> It is as if some skilled craftsman had made a noble image, cast in gold or other material, which was beautifully proportioned in all its features. Then the craftsman suddenly notices that the image had been defaced by some envious person, who could not endure its beauty, and so decided to ruin it for the sake of the pointless pleasure of satisfying his jealousy. So the craftsman decides to recast this noble image ... Now it seems to me that God's plan was much the same as this human example. He saw that humanity, his most wonderful creation, had been corrupted by envy and treachery. Such was his love for humanity that he could not allow it to continue in this condition, remaining faulty and deficient to eternity. For this reason, God dissolved humanity once more into its original materials, so that it could be remodeled in such a way that all its defects could be eliminated and disappear. Now the melting down of a statue corresponds to the death and

dissolution of the human body, and the remolding of the material to the resurrection after death.

A similar argument is found in the *Four Books of the Sentences*, the masterpiece of the great twelfth-century theologian Peter Lombard. This book, which served as the core textbook for just about every medieval theologian, took the view that the resurrected body was basically a reconstituted humanity, from which all defects had been purged:

> Nothing of the substance of the flesh from which humanity is created will be lost; rather, the natural substance of the body will be reintegrated by the collection of all the particles that were previously dispersed. The bodies of the saints will thus rise without any defect, shining like the sun, all their deformities having being excised.

The twelfth-century Irish *Book of the Dun Cow* (Leabhar na Uidhre) – so-called because the vellum upon which it is written is supposedly taken from the hide of St. Ciaran's cow at Clonmacnoise – raises a further question concerning the nature of the resurrection body. What happens if the believer is *eaten*? The *Book of the Dun Cow* – presumably responding to genuine pastoral concerns at this point – argues that the various fragments of humanity, however scattered and variously decomposed they may be, are "recast into a more beautiful form" by the "fire of Doom." However, the work recognizes the locational importance of the precise place at which the believer dies:

> Those who have been devoured by wild animals and dispersed in various locations will arise according to the counsel of the Lord, who will gather them together and renew them . . . In this case, they will arise at the place at which they were devoured and dispersed, for this is what is reckoned to be their tomb.

A final question that has greatly vexed Christian theologians concerns the *age* of those who are resurrected. If someone dies at the age of 60, will they appear in the streets of the New Jerusalem as an old person? And if someone dies at the age of 10, will they appear as a child? This issue caused the spilling of much theological ink, especially during the Middle Ages. By the end of the thirteenth century, an emerging consensus can be discerned. As each person reaches their peak of perfection around the age of 30, they will be resurrected as they would have appeared at that time – even if they never lived to reach that age.

Peter Lombard's discussion of the matter is typical of his age: "A boy who dies immediately after being born will be resurrected in that form which he would have had if he had lived to the age of thirty." The New Jerusalem will thus be populated by men and women as they would appear at the age of thirty (the presumed age, of course, at which Christ was crucified) – but with every blemish removed.

## Heaven as an encounter with loved ones

One of the most interesting theological themes associated with heaven is that of reunion. Perhaps the most distressing aspect of death is that of *separation* – being forcibly, and it might seem irreversibly, cut off from close friends and relatives, never to see them again. Classic mourning rites and funeral ornaments point to the sense of desolation which traditionally accompanied the death of a significant other. The Hellenistic world had become accustomed to the Hades myth, which portrayed Charon as ferrying the dead across the River Styx to the underworld for the fee of one obol – a coin which was placed in the mouth of a dead person for this purpose. Once on the other side, the dead person took part in a family reunion.

This basic belief undergirds two of Cicero's more important dialogues, *On Old Age* and perhaps more importantly *Scipio's Dream*. In this latter work, Cicero portrays Scipio meeting prominent Roman citizens in paradise, who take advantage of the occasion to lecture him on political ethics. Yet the work takes on a new tone as Cicero describes Scipio's reunion with his father: "I now saw my dead father, Paulus, approaching, and I burst into tears. My father put his arms around me and kissed me, urging me not to weep."

This classic scenario of a family reunion in the world to come had a significant impact on the style and subject matter of the Christian writings of the era, even if they ultimately rested on rather different theological foundations. Cyprian of Carthage (died 258), a martyr-bishop of the third century, tried to encourage his fellow Christians in the face of suffering and death at times of persecution by holding before them a vision of heaven, in which they would see the martyrs and apostles, face to face. More than that; they would be reunited with those whom they loved and cherished.

Cyprian here conceives heaven as the "native land" of Christians, from which they have been exiled during their time on earth. The hope of return to their native land, there to be reunited with those who they knew and loved, was held out as a powerful consolation in times of trial and suffering.

> We regard paradise as our native land . . . Many of our dear ones await us there, and a dense crowd of parents, brothers, children, is longing for us, already assured of their own safety, and still longing for our salvation. What gladness there will be for them and for us when we enter their presence and share their embrace!

Cyprian himself was martyred for his faith in 258, presumably consoled by precisely the ideas with which he sought to console others.

This important motif is also found in Ambrose of Milan's funeral eulogy for the emperor Theodosius, who died in Milan in January 395. Theodosius had earlier had a serious altercation with Ambrose as a result of his decision in 390 to order the slaughter of seven thousand citizens of Thessalonica to avenge the murder of the Roman governor Butheric. Ambrose, having consulted with his fellow bishops, informed Theodosius that he must do severe public penance before being allowed again to receive the sacraments. Theodosius eventually stripped himself of every sign of royalty and publicly repented of his sin. In his funeral oration, Ambrose asked his listeners to imagine the scene in heaven, in which Theodosius embraces his wife Flaccila and his daughter Pulcheria, before being reunited with his father and his predecessor as a Christian Roman emperor, Constantine.

The same theme is found in Protestant understandings of the nature of heaven. The "classic" Protestant conception of heaven is probably most clearly stated in the Puritan author Richard Baxter (1615–91), who emphasized that the primary characteristic of heaven is a total reverential focus on God. In his *The Saints' Everlasting Rest*, Baxter argued that the worship of God was the supreme activity of the saints in heaven. Nothing could distract them from the adoration of the God who had created and redeemed them, and had finally brought them to eternal rest in the heavenly places. The contemplation of the hope of heaven was an antidote to the sorrow and distractions of this world. "Thus as Daniel, in his captivity, daily opened his window towards Jerusalem, though far out of sight, when he went to God in his devotions; so may the believing soul, in this captivity of the flesh, look towards 'Jerusalem which is above.' "

Yet during the nineteenth century, alternative ways of envisioning heaven began to emerge, especially in the aftermath of the American Civil War. This war saw unprecedented levels of casualties, and caused distress and mourning throughout the nation. A new interest in spiritualism flourished, as anguished families sought to reestablish contact with relatives who had died on the field of battle. The new genre of "consolation literature" emerged, reconceiving heaven primarily as a reencounter with loved ones. In *The Gates Ajar* (1868), Elizabeth Stuart Phelps (1844–1911) rejects the traditional idea of heaven as "harping and praying," and argues that it is about the restoration of life and relationships. Heaven is portrayed as an extended nineteenth-century family, in which little children are busy "devouring heavenly gingersnaps" and playing rosewood pianos, while the adults listen to learned discourses from glorified philosophers and the symphonies of Beethoven.

## Heaven and the worship of the church

One of the most interesting aspects of the Christian idea of heaven is the role that it plays in informing and sustaining worship. Especially within the Greek Orthodox tradition, the public worship of the church represents a drawing close to the threshold of heaven itself. Worshippers are encouraged to see themselves as peering through the portals of heaven, catching a glimpse of the worship of heavenly places. The Orthodox liturgy celebrates the notion of being caught up in the worship of heaven, and the awesome sense of mystery that is evoked by the sense of peering beyond the bounds of human vision.

To share in worship is thus to stand in a holy place (Exodus 3:5) – a place in which humanity, strictly speaking, has no right to be. Whenever the Divine Liturgy is celebrated on earth, the boundaries between heaven and earth are removed, and earthly worshippers join in the eternal Heavenly Liturgy chanted by the angels. During these moments of earthly adoration, worshippers have the opportunity of being mystically transported to the threshold of heaven. Being in a holy place and about to participate in holy things, they on the one hand become aware of their finitude and sinfulness, and on the other gain a refreshing glimpse of the glory of God.

The idea of liminality – that is, being on the threshold of the sacred, peering into the forbidden heavenly realms – is represented visually in the structure of Orthodox churches, especially the way in which the sanctuary and the altar are set apart from the people on account of a deep sense of the awesomeness of the mystery of God. In their treatises on worship, Chrysostom and other Greek patristic writers repeatedly draw attention to the liturgical importance of this sense of the sacred. Whatever else worship may be, it is an anticipation of the life and worship of heaven, something that sustains believers throughout the long pilgrimage of faith.

## Heaven and the millennium

Christians have always enjoyed speculating about origins and endings. A particularly interesting eschatological debate flared up in the nineteenth century, particularly within American Protestantism, and has continued unabated since then. In view of its intrinsic interest, we shall explore it in a little detail.

Much of the debate has centered on the notion of the "millennium," an idea that is mentioned in the book of Revelation (Revelation 20:2–5). The millennium refers to the hope of a restored earthly kingdom lasting for a period of one thousand years, separating the second coming of Christ and the subsequent establishment of a totally new cosmic order. Although some early Christian writers – such as Irenaeus of Lyons – interpreted this passage literally, a consensus soon developed that it should be understood figuratively. The reference to a period of a thousand years should not be understood as a literal prediction of the chronological duration of an earthly kingdom, but as an allegorical indication of the grandeur of the heavenly kingdom.

Since the nineteenth century, however, the notion of the millennium has made a major comeback in sections of popular Protestantism, especially in North America. One of the most distinctive features of contemporary American conservative Protestantism is its rediscovery of the idea of the millennium. Three quite distinct ways of dealing with this idea are now found in the North American Protestant constituency.

1. The *amillennial* standpoint refuses to become involved in speculation about the endtime, holding that this distracts people from the more important business of leading the Christian life, and addressing the world's problems. This approach was widespread within mainline Protestantism during the sixteenth century, with leading writers such as Martin Luther and John Calvin refusing to get involved in such pointless debates. Although their Anabaptist opponents enjoyed looking forward to a social revolution as a result of an apocalyptic divine intervention, most Protestants of the age had little interest in such things. This remained the case until the middle of the nineteenth century, when a new interest in the millennium began to emerge.

2. The *postmillennial* viewpoint was particularly influential in American Protestantism during the nineteenth century. It holds that the return of Christ will occur at the close of a long period (not necessarily lasting one thousand years) of righteousness and peace, commonly called the millennium. Leading conservative Protestant theologians, such as the Princeton academics Charles Hodge (1797–1878) and Benjamin B. Warfield (1851–1921), took the view that God was bringing about his purposes through steady human progress over evil, progressively leading to a Christianized world. Postmillennialism sees the church as playing a major role in transforming whole social structures before the Second Coming of Christ, and endeavoring to bring about a "Golden Age" of peace and prosperity with great advances in education, the arts, sciences, and medicine. During this process, the church would rise in power, influence, and integrity, the standard-bearer for the coming kingdom of God on earth. Its credibility was severely damaged by the suffering and damage of the two world wars, both of which increased the appeal of premillennialism, especially in North America.

3. The *premillennial* viewpoint holds that the figure known as "the Antichrist" will appear on earth, ushering in a seven-year period of suffering known as "the Tribulation." This great period of destruction, war, and disaster on earth will finally be ended by God defeating evil at the battle of Armageddon. After this, Christ will return to earth to rule for a period of a thousand years (the millennium), during which the forces of evil will finally be subdued and conquered.

Premillennialism offers a strongly pessimistic view of the world, believing that things are deteriorating on earth and will go on doing so until God brings history to an end. It resonates strongly with a sense of cultural alienation within many parts of conservative American Protestantism, especially its belief that anti-Christian forces are gaining the upper hand in America, as in the world in general. This degeneration of the world is seen as a sign that the end of the world is near, and thus allows this negative development to be seen as a harbinger of something positive.

Beliefs about the end times have had a major impact on American popular Protestantism, as is evident from the huge sales of novels reflecting these standpoints. Hal Lindsey's end-times book *The Late Great Planet Earth* (1970) was one of the best-selling novels of that decade. More recently, the success of the best-selling "Left Behind" novels, written by Tim LaHaye and Jerry Jenkins, has ensured that premillennial ideology retains a high profile across America.

## The beatific vision: seeing God face to face

The Christian hope is often expressed in terms of seeing the face of God directly, without the need for created intermediaries. In the Old Testament, divine favor is indicated by the face of God being turned towards an individual, just as disfavor is signaled by that face being averted. In cultic petitions of this period, a worshipper might invoke God to "lift up [God's] countenance" (2 Kings 13:4; Isaiah 1:12; Ezekiel 32:11) as a means of securing the acceptance of the sacrifices or prayers being offered. If the face of God were "hidden" or "turned away," the believer had no hope of finding divine acceptance (Deuteronomy 31:17; Ezekiel 7:22).

Yet the image of the "face of God" concerns far more than the notion of the divine pleasure and favor; it evokes the possibility of an encounter with the living God. To "see the face of God" is to have a privileged, intimate relationship with God – seeing God "as God actually is" (1 John 3:2), rather than having to know God indirectly, through images and shadows. Now we see God "as through a glass, darkly," but we shall finally see God face to face (1 Corinthians 13:12). The book of Revelation affirms that this will be the privilege of those in heaven, where the saints will finally "see God's face" (Revelation 22:4).

This hope of seeing the face of God was developed extensively in the Christian tradition. In his *Letter 92*, Augustine of Hippo wrote to Italica, a noble widow, who had some questions concerning the hope of heaven. Augustine responded by fleshing out the brief biblical statements concerning "seeing God." While we are in exile on earth, we are not "fitted" or "adapted" to beholding the full glory of God; it is only when we ourselves are raised to glory and trans- formed that we may hope to see the radiance and glory of God in all their fullness.

> We see God according to the measure by which we are adapted to him...no matter how far we may advance, we still fall short of that perfection of likeness which is fitted for seeing God, as the apostle says, "face to face." ... When you read, "Now we see through a glass darkly, but then face to face" (1 Corinthians 13:12), learn from this that we shall then see God face to face by the same means by which we now see him through a glass darkly. In both cases alike, the vision of God belongs to the inner person, whether while we walk in this pilgrimage still by faith, in which it uses the glass and the shadow, or when, in the country which is our home, we shall perceive by sight, a vision denoted by the words "face to face."

For Augustine, the vision of God possesses a unique capacity to satisfy human desire, utterly surpassing the ability of any created being or thing in this respect. Such a vision is the *summum bonum*, the supreme good, the "light by which truth is perceived, and the fountain from which all blessedness is drunk."

Augustine develops this idea further in the *City of God*, arguing that the vision of God in heaven sustains believers throughout their pil- grimage of faith:

God himself, who is the Author of virtue, shall be our reward. As there is nothing greater or better than God himself, God has promised us himself. What else can be meant by his word through the prophet, "I will be your God, and you will be my people" than "I shall be their satisfaction, I shall be all that people honorably desire – life, health, nourishment, satisfaction, glory, honor, peace, and all good things? This, too, is the right interpretation of the saying of the apostle "That God may be all in all." God shall be the end of all our desires, who will be seen without end, loved without cloy, and praised without weariness.

The nature of the vision of God enjoyed by the saints in heaven was the subject of no small debate throughout the Middle Ages. Pope John XXII (1249–1334) provoked a particularly vigorous controversy through his argument that the saints who are now "under the altar" – a phrase deriving from Revelation 6:9 – are able to find consolation through contemplation of the humanity of Christ; after the resurrection and final judgment, however, they will finally be able to enjoy the full and perfect joy of seeing God directly. His successor Benedict XII (died 1342) tried to dampen down the somewhat heated exchanges which John provoked by arguing that those who were already purified were able to enjoy the vision of God before the end of time; others, however, would have to wait until history ended before the full revelation of the glory of God. But, he insisted, it would be worth waiting for.

The Psalmist set out the longing to see God in these words (Psalm 27:4):

> ⤙ One thing I ask of the Lord,
> This is what I seek;
> That I may dwell in the house of the Lord
> All the days of my life,
> To gaze upon the beauty of the Lord.

The Christian vision of heaven affirms that what the Psalmist longed for all his life will one day be the common privilege of the entire people of God – to gaze upon the face of their Lord and Savior, as they enter into his house, to dwell in peace for ever. It is no accident that Dante's (1265–1321) *Divine Comedy* reaches its

**Figure 21**    Gustav Doré, *The New Jerusalem*, woodcut, ca. 1866.

climax when the poet finally, after his epic journeys through hell and purgatory, emerges to behold "the love that moves the sun and the other stars."

## Engaging with a text

John Donne (1571–1631) is perhaps one of the greatest spiritual poets in the English language. The poem which follows is taken from the collection of "Divine Meditations," which deal with a range of theological and spiritual issues. The poem that we will be considering personifies death, and argues that it has been overthrown through the resurrection of Christ. The poem ends with the assertion of the final defeat and death of death through the resurrection, which undergirds the Christian hope of heaven.

Death be not proud, though some have
    called thee
Mighty and dreadful, for thou art not so;
For those whom thou think'st, thou dost
    overthrow,
Die not, poor Death, nor yet canst thou
    kill me.
From rest and sleep, which but thy
    pictures be,
Much pleasure; then from thee, much more
    must flow,
And soonest our best men with thee do go,
Rest of their bones, and soul's delivery.
Thou art slave to Fate, Chance, kings, and
    desperate men,

**Figure 22** John Donne, painting by Isaac Oliver, 1615. AKG Images.

And dost with poison, war, and sickness dwell;
And poppy or charms can make us sleep as well
And better than thy stroke; why swell'st thou then?
One short sleep past, we wake eternally,
And death shall be no more; Death, thou shalt die.

Donne's religious poetry is saturated with biblical themes, images, and ideas. It is important to bear in mind that the English translation of the Bible which Donne knew best is the great version commissioned by King James I in 1604, which was published in 1611. This is generally known as the "King James Bible," after the monarch who ordered it to be produced, although in England it is still often referred to as the "Authorized Version." In what follows, we shall explore how biblical themes are incorporated into the poem.

1. Read the following verse from the King James Version of the Bible: "The last enemy that shall be destroyed is death" (1 Corinthians 15:26). How is this theme of death as an enemy incorporated into the poem? You might like to read the context in which this passage is set, and see how other images and ideas from this same source are worked into the poem. We shall consider another immediately.

2. Now go on to read the following verses from the King James Version of the Bible: "Then shall be brought to pass the saying that is written, Death is swallowed up in victory. O death, where is thy sting? O grave, where is thy victory? The sting of death is sin; and the strength of sin is the law. But thanks be to God, which giveth us the victory through our Lord Jesus Christ" (1 Corinthians 15:55–57). How is the theme of victory over death developed in the poem? In what way does Donne develop this idea? You might also like to reflect on the way in which this relates to those "theories of the atonement" which stress that Christ's death and resurrection are primarily to be understood as a victory over death, sin, and Satan.

3. Now notice how Donne develops the idea of various analogies ("pictures") for death that we know from everyday life. Chief among them is sleep; what are the others? And how do you think Donne's use of analogies for death relates to the biblical and theological use of analogies for God?

4. Consider the following quotation from Donne: "No man ever saw God and lived. And yet, I shall not live till I see God; and when I have seen him, I shall never die." What idea does he express in this statement? How does it relate to the idea of the "beatific vision" we considered earlier in this chapter? And how does it relate to the poem you have just been reading?

# Moving On

This short introduction to the basics of Christian theology has aimed to encourage and stimulate its readers, by showing that they can learn to cope with exploring some of its leading ideas, and interact with some of its seminal texts. It has also attempted to whet your appetite to know more, so that you will end this book feeling dissatisfied. This is all that a short book can hope to achieve when dealing with so rich and complex a subject as Christian theology.

It will be obvious that this very basic introduction to Christian theology has many weaknesses, most due to limitations on space. For a start, only a few theological topics have been examined. Many others need to be covered – including, for example, the doctrines of grace, human nature, and Christian understandings of the place of other religions. Questions of "theological method" have also been treated very superficially. A much more extensive discussion of, for example, the sources and norms of theology is required.

Another serious weakness is that hardly any historical contextualization has been provided. Both Martin Luther and John Calvin are introduced to readers; they are not, however, explained and examined in the light of the rise of the European Renaissance, and the origins of the Protestant Reformation. Thomas Aquinas is also introduced – but there has not been enough space to explain how the movement known as "scholastic theology" developed, and sketch its leading features. A much longer introductory text is required. This book represents a good start – but it is only a handshake to start a much longer conversation.

*Theology: The Basics*, Third Edition. Alister E. McGrath.
© 2012 Alister E. McGrath. Published 2012 by Blackwell Publishing Ltd.

So where should you go next? Completing this book will be as far as some of its readers will wish to go in their theological explorations. But others will want to go much further. Perhaps they have chosen to read this book as an experiment – to see if there is any point in taking things further. If you were able to cope with this book, you will be able to handle the more extensive and comprehensive analysis in my more substantial work *Christian Theology: An Introduction*. This shorter book was planned and written in such a way that it could lead into this much more thorough engagement with the history, ideas, and methods of Christian theology. You will find that your basic knowledge of theology will make this much more extensive encounter with this most fascinating discipline easier and more satisfying.

*Christian Theology*, now in its fourth edition, is designed to be used in a variety of contexts, including individual private study, taught courses, and group study. It has become the field-specific best-seller in the English-speaking academic and seminary communities, and has been translated into nine languages. Its three major sections provide an overview of the history of Christian theology, its sources and methods, and its fundamental ideas. If you want to know more, this is the place to go.

You may also find the accompanying volume *The Christian Theology Reader* useful. This work, now in its third edition, contains more than 360 readings, each with its own individual introduction, commentary, and study questions. Each has been tested on readers, to ensure that it can be easily understood. If you felt encouraged by the textual engagements offered in every chapter of this basic introduction, you will be able to handle and benefit from the much more extensive coverage provided by this larger work.

But some will choose to end their studies here. If so, I would like to thank you for allowing me to accompany you on your exploration of theology, and wish you well in the future. Perhaps I might quote from Karl Barth in bidding you farewell at this point, and encouraging you to see theology as something that is helpful for the individual life of faith, as well as for the life and witness of the church.

Theology is not a private subject for theologians only. Nor is it a private subject for professors. Fortunately, there have always been pastors who have understood more about theology than most professors. Nor is theology a private subject of study for pastors. Fortunately, there have repeatedly been congregation members, and often whole congregations, who have pursued theology energetically while their pastors were theological infants or barbarians. Theology is a matter for the Church.

# Brief Glossary of Theological Terms

What follows is a brief discussion of some technical terms you will have encountered in the course of reading this text, or which arise from it.

**adoptionism**
The heretical view that Jesus was "adopted" as the Son of God at some point during his ministry (usually his baptism), as opposed to the orthodox teaching that Jesus was Son of God by nature from the moment of his conception.

**Anabaptism**
A term derived from the Greek word for "re-baptizer," and used to refer to the radical wing of the sixteenth-century Reformation, based on thinkers such as Menno Simons or Balthasar Hubmaier.

**analogy of being (*analogia entis*)**
The theory, especially associated with Thomas Aquinas, that there exists a correspondence or analogy between the created order and God, as a result of the divine creatorship. The idea gives theoretical justification to the practice of drawing conclusions from the known objects and relationships of the natural order concerning God.

**analogy of faith (*analogia fidei*)**
The theory, especially associated with Karl Barth, which holds that any correspondence between the created order and God is only established on the basis of the self-revelation of God.

*Theology: The Basics*, Third Edition. Alister E. McGrath.
© 2012 Alister E. McGrath. Published 2012 by Blackwell Publishing Ltd.

**ancilla theologiae**
A Latin phrase, meaning "the handmaid of theology," which is used to refer to the practice of using philosophical or cultural ideas as a helpmate or dialogue partner for Christian theology.

**apostolic era**
The period of the Christian church, regarded as definitive by many, bounded by the resurrection of Jesus Christ (ca. AD 35) and the death of the last apostle (ca. AD 90). The ideas and practices of this period were widely regarded as being authoritative, at least in some sense or to some degree, in many church circles.

**appropriation**
A term relating to the doctrine of the Trinity, which affirms that while all three persons of the Trinity are active in all the outward actions of the Trinity, it is appropriate to think of those actions as being the particular work of one of the persons. Thus it is appropriate to think of creation as the work of the Father, or redemption as the work of the Son, despite the fact that all three persons are present and active in both these works.

**Arianism**
A major early Christological heresy, which treated Jesus Christ as the supreme of God's creatures, and denied his divine status. The Arian controversy was of major importance in the development of Christology during the fourth century.

**atonement**
An English term originally coined in 1526 by William Tyndale to translate the Latin term *reconciliatio*, which has since come to have the developed meaning of "the work of Christ" or "the benefits of Christ gained for believers by his death and resurrection."

**Barthian**
An adjective used to describe the theological outlook of the Swiss theologian Karl Barth (1886–1968), and noted chiefly for its emphasis upon the priority of revelation and its focus upon Jesus Christ. The terms "neo-Orthodoxy" and "dialectical theology" are also used in this connection.

### beatific vision
A term used, especially in Roman Catholic theology, to refer to the full vision of God, which is allowed only to the elect after death. However, some writers, including Thomas Aquinas, taught that certain favored individuals – such as Moses and Paul – were allowed this vision in the present life.

### Calvinism
An ambiguous term, used with two quite distinct meanings. First, it refers to the religious ideas of religious bodies (such as the Reformed church) and individuals (such as Theodore Beza) who were profoundly influenced by John Calvin, or by documents written by him. Second, it refers to the religious ideas of John Calvin himself. Although the first sense is by far the more common, there is a growing recognition that the term is misleading.

### Cappadocian Fathers
A term used to refer collectively to three major Greek-speaking writers of the patristic period: Basil of Caesarea, Gregory of Nazianzen, and Gregory of Nyssa, all of whom date from the late fourth century. "Cappadocia" designates an area in Asia Minor (modern-day Turkey) in which these writers were based.

### Cartesianism
The philosophical outlook especially associated with René Descartes (1596–1650), particularly in relation to its emphasis on the separation of the knower from the known, and its insistence that the existence of the individual thinking self is the proper starting point for philosophical reflection.

### catechism
A popular manual of Christian doctrine, usually in the form of question and answer, intended for religious instruction.

### Catholic
An adjective which is used both to refer to the universality of the church in space and time, and also to a particular church body

(sometimes also known as the Roman Catholic church) which lays emphasis upon this point.

## Chalcedonian definition
The formal declaration at the Council of Chalcedon that Jesus Christ was to be regarded as having two natures, one human and one divine.

## charisma, charismatic
A set of terms especially associated with the gifts of the Holy Spirit. In medieval theology, the term "charisma" is used to designate a spiritual gift, conferred upon individuals by the grace of God. Since the early twentieth century, the term "charismatic" has come to refer to styles of theology and worship which place particular emphasis upon the immediate presence and experience of the Holy Spirit.

## Christology
The section of Christian theology dealing with the identity of Jesus Christ, particularly the question of the relation of his human and divine natures.

## consubstantial
A Latin term, deriving from the Greek term *homoousios*, literally meaning "of the same substance." The term is used to affirm the full divinity of Jesus Christ, particularly in opposition to Arianism.

## creed
A formal definition or summary of the Christian faith, held in common by all Christians. The most important are those generally known as the "Apostles' Creed" and the "Nicene Creed."

## deism
A term used to refer to the views of a group of English writers, especially during the seventeenth century, the rationalism of which anticipated many of the ideas of the Enlightenment. The term is often used to refer to a view of God which recognizes the divine creatorship, yet which rejects the notion of a continuing divine involvement with the world.

**Docetism**
An early Christological heresy, which treated Jesus Christ as a purely divine being who only had the "appearance" of being human.

**Donatism**
A movement, centering upon Roman North Africa in the fourth century, which developed a view of the church and sacraments which placed a strong emphasis on the need for personal holiness on the part of church members and their ministers, and on the need for measures to enforce this where necessary.

**Ebionitism**
An early Christological heresy, which treated Jesus Christ as a purely human figure, although recognizing that he was endowed with particular charismatic gifts which distinguished him from other humans.

**ecclesiology**
The section of Christian theology dealing with the theory of the church.

**Enlightenment, the**
A term used since the nineteenth century to refer to the emphasis upon human reason and autonomy, characteristic of much of western European and North American thought during the eighteenth century.

**eschatology**
The section of Christian theology dealing with the "end things," especially the ideas of resurrection, hell, and eternal life.

**eucharist**
The term used in the present volume to refer to the sacrament variously known as "the Mass," "the Lord's Supper," and "holy communion."

**exegesis**
The science of textual interpretation, usually referring specifically to the Bible. The term "biblical exegesis" basically means "the process of interpreting the Bible." The specific techniques

employed in the exegesis of scripture are usually referred to as "hermeneutics."

## exemplarism
A particular approach to the atonement, which stresses the moral or religious example set to believers by Jesus Christ.

## five ways, the
A standard term for the five "arguments for the existence of God" associated with Thomas Aquinas.

## homoousion
A Greek term, literally meaning "of the same substance," which came to be used extensively during the fourth century to designate the mainline Christological belief that Jesus Christ was "of the same substance of God." The term was polemical, being directed against the Arian view that Christ was "of similar substance (*homoiousios*)" to God. *See also* "consubstantial."

## incarnation
A term used to refer to the assumption of human nature by God, in the person of Jesus Christ. The term "incarnationalism" is often used to refer to theological approaches which lay especial emphasis upon God becoming human.

## logos
A Greek term meaning "word," which played a crucial role in the development of patristic Christology. Jesus Christ was recognized as the "Word of God"; the question concerned the implications of this recognition, and especially the way in which the divine "logos" in Jesus Christ related to his human nature.

## modalism
A Trinitarian heresy, which treats the three persons of the Trinity as different "modes" of the Godhead. A typical modalist approach is to regard God as active as Father in creation, as Son in redemption, and as Spirit in sanctification.

**monophysitism**
The doctrine that there is only one nature in Christ, which is divine (from the Greek words *monos*, "only one," and *physis*, "nature"). This view differed from the orthodox view, upheld by the Council of Chalcedon (451), that Christ had two natures, one divine and one human.

**orthodoxy**
A term used in a number of senses, of which the following are the most important: orthodoxy in the sense of "right belief," as opposed to heresy; Orthodoxy in the sense of the forms of Christianity which are dominant in Russia and Greece; orthodoxy in the sense of a movement within Protestantism, especially in the late sixteenth and early seventeenth century, which laid emphasis upon need for doctrinal definition.

**parousia**
A Greek term, which literally means "coming" or "arrival," used to refer to the second coming of Christ. The notion of the parousia is an important aspect of Christian understandings of the "last things."

**patristic**
An adjective used to refer to the first centuries in the history of the church, following the writing of the New Testament (the "patristic period"), or thinkers writing during this period (the "patristic writers"). For many writers, the period thus designated seems to be ca. 100–451 (in other words, the period between the completion of the last of the New Testament writings and the landmark Council of Chalcedon).

**Pelagianism**
An understanding of how humans are able to merit their salvation which is diametrically opposed to that of Augustine of Hippo, placing considerable emphasis upon the role of human works and playing down the idea of divine grace.

**perichoresis**
A term relating to the doctrine of the Trinity, often also referred to by the Latin term *circumincessio*. The basic notion is that all three persons of the Trinity mutually share in the life of the others, so that none is isolated or detached from the actions of the others.

**radical Reformation**
A term used with increasing frequency to refer to the Anabaptist movement – in other words, the wing of the Reformation which went beyond what Luther and Zwingli envisaged, particularly in relation to the doctrine of the church.

**reformed**
A term used to refer to a tradition of theology which draws inspiration from the writings of John Calvin (1510–64) and his successors. The term is now generally used in preference to "Calvinist."

**schism**
A deliberate break with the unity of the church, condemned vigorously by influential writers of the early church, such as Cyprian and Augustine.

**scholasticism**
A particular approach to Christian theology, associated especially with the Middle Ages, which lays emphasis upon the rational justification and systematic presentation of Christian theology.

**soteriology**
The section of Christian theology dealing with the doctrine of salvation (Greek: *soteria*).

**transubstantiation**
The doctrine according to which the bread and the wine are transformed into the body and blood of Christ in the eucharist, while retaining their outward appearance.

**Trinity**
The distinctively Christian doctrine of God, which reflects the complexity of the Christian experience of God. The doctrine is usually summarized in maxims such as "three persons, one God."

**two natures, doctrine of**
A term generally used to refer to the doctrine of the two natures, human and divine, of Jesus Christ. Related terms include "Chalcedonian definition" and "hypostatic union."

# Details of Theologians Cited

**Abelard**   *see* Peter Abelard

**Anselm of Canterbury** (ca. 1033–1109)   Born in Italy, Anselm migrated to Normandy in 1059, entering the famous monastery of Bec, becoming its prior in 1063, and abbot in 1078. In 1093 he was appointed archbishop of Canterbury. He is chiefly noted for his strong defense of the intellectual foundations of Christianity, and is especially associated with the "ontological argument" for the existence of God.

**Aquinas**   *see* Thomas Aquinas

**Arius** (ca. 250–ca. 336)   The originator of Arianism, a form of Christology which refused to concede the full divinity of Christ. Little is known of his life, and little has survived of his writings. With the exception of a letter to Eusebius of Nicomedia, his views are known mainly through the writings of his opponents.

**Athanasius of Alexandria** (ca. 296–373)   One of the most significant defenders of orthodox Christology during the period of the Arian controversy. Elected as bishop of Alexandria in 328, he was forced to resign on account of his opposition to Arianism. Although he was widely supported in the west, his views were finally recognized after his death at the Council of Constantinople (381).

*Theology: The Basics*, Third Edition. Alister E. McGrath.
© 2012 Alister E. McGrath. Published 2012 by Blackwell Publishing Ltd.

**Augustine of Hippo** (354–430)   Widely regarded as the most influential Latin patristic writer, Augustine was converted to Christianity at the northern Italian city of Milan in the summer of 386. He returned to North Africa, and was made bishop of Hippo in 395. He was involved in two major controversies – the Donatist controversy, focusing on the church and sacraments, and the Pelagian controversy, focusing on grace and sin. He also made substantial contributions to the development of the doctrine of the Trinity, and the Christian understanding of history.

**Barth, Karl** (1886–1968)   Widely regarded as the most important Protestant theologian of the twentieth century. Barth moved away from liberal Protestantism during World War I and adopted a theological position which placed an emphasis on the priority of divine revelation. His early emphasis on the "otherness" of God in his Romans commentary (1919) was continued and modified in his monumental *Church Dogmatics*. Barth's contribution to modern Christian theology has been immense.

**Basil of Caesarea** (ca. 330–79)   Also known as "Basil the Great," this fourth-century writer was based in the region of Cappadocia, in modern Turkey. He is particularly remembered for his writings on the Trinity, especially the distinctive role of the Holy Spirit. He was elected bishop of Caesarea in 370.

**Baxter, Richard** (1615–91)   One of the most important English Puritan theologians.

**Bonhoeffer, Dietrich** (1906–45)   A German Lutheran theologian, influenced by Karl Barth, with a particular interest in ecumenical work during the 1930s. He was arrested in 1943, and hanged by the Nazis in 1945. His letters and papers from prison include significant discussions of the suffering of God, and the need for theology to relate to a "religionless society."

**Brunner, Emil** (1889–1966)   A Swiss theologian who, while being influenced by his fellow countryman Karl Barth, developed ideas on natural theology which distanced them during the later 1930s. He is particularly noted for his strongly personalist idea of revelation.

**Bucer, Martin** (1491–1551)   German reformer of the sixteenth century, noted for his contributions to biblical hermeneutics, ecclesiology, and the doctrine of the Holy Spirit.

**Bultmann, Rudolf** (1884–1976)   A German Lutheran writer, who was appointed to a chair of theology at Marburg in 1921. He is chiefly noted for his program of "demythologization" of the New Testament, and his use of existential ideas in the exposition of the twentieth-century meaning of the gospel.

**Cabasilas, Nicholas** (born ca. 1322)   Byzantine theologian who is remembered especially for his "Concerning Life in Christ," which elaborates the way in which the believer achieves union with Christ.

**Calvin, John** (1509–64)   Leading Protestant reformer, especially associated with the city of Geneva. His *Institutes of the Christian Religion* has become one of the most influential works of Protestant theology, and done much to shape the contours of reformed theology.

**Clement of Alexandria** (ca. 150–ca. 215)   A leading Alexandrian writer, with a particular concern to explore the relation between Christian thought and Greek philosophy, especially the forms of Platonism predominant at that time.

**Cyprian of Carthage** (died 258)   A Roman rhetorician of considerable skill who was converted to Christianity around 246, and elected bishop of the North African city of Carthage in 248. He was martyred in that city in 258. His writings focus particularly on the unity of the church, and the role of its bishops in maintaining orthodoxy and order.

**Cyril of Jerusalem** (ca. 315–86)   Major fourth-century theologian, noted particularly for his defense of Nicene orthodoxy. His "catechetical lectures" were of great importance in the teaching of theology.

**Descartes, René** (1596–1650)    French philosopher noted for his emphasis on the role of systematic doubt, and the importance of "perfection" in discussion of the nature of God.

**Didymus the Blind** (ca. 313–98)    Leading Alexandrian theologian of the fourth century, remembered chiefly for his biblical commentaries.

**Edwards, Jonathan** (1703–58)    Leading American theologian in the Reformed tradition, noted especially for his metaphysical defense of Christianity in the light of the increasingly influential ideas of the Enlightenment, and his positive statements of traditional Reformed doctrines.

**Gore, Charles** (1853–1932)    Major English theologian of the late nineteenth and early twentieth centuries, particularly noted for his contributions to Christology.

**Gregory of Nazianzus** (329–89)    Also known as "Gregory Nazianzen." He is particularly remembered for his "Five Theological Orations," written around 380, and a compilation of extracts from the writings of Origen, which he entitled the *Philokalia*.

**Gregory of Nyssa** (ca. 330–ca. 395)    Leading Cappadocian Father, with a special interest in the relation of Christian theology and Platonic philosophy.

**Gregory the Great** (ca. 540–604)    Also known as Gregory I. He was elected as pope in 590, and did much to establish the political power of the papacy, which reached its zenith in the Middle Ages. As a theologian, he is particularly noted for his pastoral and exegetical works.

**Hugh of St. Victor** (died 1142)    A theologian, of Flemish or German origin, who entered the Augustinian monastery of St. Victor in Paris around 1115. His most important work is *de sacramentis Christianae fidei* ("On the Sacraments of the Christian Faith"), which shows awareness of the new theological debates which were beginning to develop at this time.

**Ignatius of Antioch** (ca. 35–ca. 107)    A major early Christian martyr, noted for his letters to Christian churches in Asia Minor. Of particular interest is his vigorous defense of the reality of Christ's human nature and sufferings, in the face of those who wished to maintain that they were simply an appearance.

**Irenaeus of Lyons** (ca. 130–ca. 200)    Probably a native of Asia Minor, who was elected as bishop of the southern French city of Lyons around 178. He is chiefly noted for his major writing *adversus haereses* ("Against the heresies"), which defended the Christian faith against Gnostic misrepresentations and criticisms.

**Jenson, Robert** (born 1930)    North America's leading Lutheran theologian, noted for his major contributions to the doctrine of the Trinity.

**Julian of Norwich** (ca. 1342–ca. 1415)    Little is known of the life of this English mystic, apart from the details she herself provides in her *Sixteen Revelations of Divine Love*. For at least part of her active life, she lived a solitary life in the city of Norwich.

**Justin Martyr** (ca. 100–ca. 165)    One of the most noted of the Christian apologists of the second century, with a concern to demonstrate the moral and intellectual credibility of Christianity in a pagan world. His *First Apology* stresses the manner in which Christianity brings to fulfillment the insights of classical philosophy.

**Luther, Martin** (1483–1546)    Perhaps the greatest figure in the European Reformation, noted particularly for his doctrine of justification by faith alone, and his strongly Christocentric understanding of revelation. His "theology of the cross" aroused much interest in the late twentieth century. Luther's famous Ninety-Five Theses on indulgences (October 1517) are generally regarded as marking the beginning of the Reformation.

**Melanchthon, Philipp** (1497–1560)    A noted early Lutheran theologian, and close personal associate of Martin Luther. He was responsible for the systematization of early Lutheran theology, particularly through his *Loci Communes* (first edition published in 1521) and his "Apology for the Augsburg Confession."

**Methodius of Olympus** (died ca. 311)    A noted critic of Origen's theology, particularly the doctrines of the transmigration of souls and a purely spiritual resurrection body. His treatise on the resurrection develops the thesis of the continuity between the pre- and post-resurrection bodies.

**Moltmann, Jürgen** (b. 1926)    One of the most influential of modern German Protestant theologians, particularly noted for his writings on the "suffering of God," as well as his exploration of the doctrine of the Trinity.

**Origen** (ca. 185–ca. 254)    Leading representative of the Alexandrian school of theology, especially noted for his allegorical exposition of scripture, and his use of Platonic ideas in theology, particularly Christology.

**Paley, William** (1734–1805)    Leading English exponent of natural theology and the argument from design.

**Pascal, Blaise** (1623–62)    An influential French Roman Catholic writer, who gained a considerable reputation as a mathematician and theologian. After a religious conversion experience in 1646, he developed an approach to his faith which was strongly Christo-centric and experiential. His most famous writing is the collection known as the *Pensées*, first gathered together in 1670, some years after his death.

**Peter Abelard** (1079–1142)    French theologian, who achieved a considerable reputation as a teacher at the University of Paris. Among his many contributions to the development of medieval theology, his most noted is his emphasis upon the subjective aspects of the atonement.

**Peter Lombard** (ca. 1100–60)    A noted medieval theologian, active at the University of Paris, who was appointed bishop of Paris in 1159.

His most significant achievement was the compilation of the textbook known as the "Four Books of the Sentences," a collection of extracts from patristic writers.

**Rahner, Karl** (1904–84)    One of the most influential of modern Roman Catholic theologians, whose *Theological Investigations* pioneered the use of the essay as a tool of theological construction and exploration.

**Rufinus of Aquileia** (ca. 345–410)    Although born in Italy, this writer eventually settled in Egypt. He is best known for his exposition of the creed.

**Sayers, Dorothy L.** (1893–1957)    English novelist and dramatist, with a strong interest in Christian theology.

**Tertullian** (ca. 160–ca. 225)    A major figure in early Latin theology, who produced a series of significant controversial and apologetic writings. He is particularly noted for his ability to coin new Latin terms to translate the emerging theological vocabulary of the Greek-speaking Eastern church.

**Thomas Aquinas** (ca. 1225–74)    Probably the most famous and influential theologian of the Middle Ages. Born in Italy, he achieved his fame through his teaching and writing at the University of Paris and other northern universities. His fame rests chiefly on his *Summa Theologiae*, composed towards the end of his life and not totally finished at the time of his death. However, he also wrote many other significant works, particularly the *Summa contra Gentiles*, which represents a major statement of the rationality of the Christian faith.

**Thomas à Kempis** (ca. 1380–1471)    A leading representative of the *Devotio Moderna*, who is widely accepted to be the author of the classic work of spirituality known as the *Imitatio Christi* ("The Imitation of Christ").

**Tillich, Paul** (1886–1965)    A German Lutheran theologian who was forced to leave Germany during the Nazi period, and settled in the United States. He held teaching positions at Union Theological

Seminary, New York, Harvard Divinity School, and the University of Chicago. His most significant theological writing is the three-volumed *Systematic Theology* (1951–64).

**Turrettini, François** (1623–87)    Reformed theologian of Italian origin, who became professor of theology at the Genevan Academy in 1653. He is regarded as one of the leading representatives of Calvinist thought during this period.

**Vincent of Lérins** (died before 450)    A French theologian who settled on the island of Lérins. He is particularly noted for his emphasis on the role of tradition in guarding against innovations in the doctrine of the church, and is credited with the formulation of the so-called "Vincentian canon."

**Wesley, Charles** (1707–88)    English writer of hymns and theologian, noted for his Pietist emphases and hostility to Calvinism. Along with his brother John, he contributed to a significant revival within eighteenth-century English Christianity.

**Wesley, John** (1703–91)    English theologian, pastor, and hymn-writer, remembered especially as the founder of Methodism. Like his brother Charles, he was deeply influenced by Pietism, which had a considerable impact on his early theology. His theology found its expression in hymns and sermons, rather than works of systematic theology.

**Zinzendorf, Nicolas Ludwig von** (1700–60)    A German writer who reacted against the rationalism of the theology of his day, and emphasized the emotional and experiential aspects of Christian faith. There is a clear connection between Zinzendorf's ideas and those of Pietism. He is remembered especially as the founder of a religious community at Herrnhut.

**Zwingli, Huldrych** (1484–1531)    Also known as "Ulrich Zwingli." A leading Swiss reformer, particularly associated with the vigorous denial of the real presence of Christ at the eucharist, a view usually designated "Zwinglianism." He died in battle, as a result of his attempts to spread his reforming ideas in his native Switzerland.

# Index

*Theology: The Basics*, Third Edition. Alister E. McGrath.
© 2012 Alister E. McGrath. Published 2012 by Blackwell Publishing Ltd.